GREECE & ROME STUDIES
VOLUME IV

GREECE & ROME STUDIES

HOMER

Edited by
IAN McAUSLAN
and
PETER WALCOT

Published by
OXFORD UNIVERSITY PRESS

on behalf of
THE CLASSICAL ASSOCIATION
1998

Oxford University Press, Walton Street, Oxford OX2 6DP

Oxford   New York

Athens Auckland Bangkok Bogota Bombay Buenos Aires
Calcutta Cape Town Dar es Salaam Delhi Florence Hong Kong Istanbul
Karachi Kuala Lumpur Madras Madrid Melbourne Mexico City
Nairobi Paris Singapore Taipei Tokyo Toronto Warsaw

and associated companies in
Berlin Ibadan

Oxford is a trade mark of Oxford University Press

Published in the United States
by Oxford University Press Inc., New York

British Library Cataloguing in Publication Data
Data available

Library of Congress Cataloging in Publication Data

Homer / edited by Ian McAuslan and Peter Walcot.
—(Greece & Rome studies ; v. 4)
Includes bibliographical references (p.   ).
1. Homer—Criticism and interpretation.   2. Epic poetry, Greek—
History and criticism.   3. Odysseus (Greek mythology) in
literature.   4. Achilles (Greek mythology) in literature.   5. Trojan
War—Literature and the War.   6. Civilization, Homeric.
I. McAuslan, Ian.   II. Walcot, Peter.   III. Series.
PA4037.H7745   1998   883'.01—dc21   97-44153
ISBN 0-19-920188-9
ISBN 0-19-920187-0 (pbk)

1 3 5 7 9 10 8 6 4 2

Typeset by Regent Typesetting, London
Printed and bound on acid-free paper by
Biddles Ltd, Guildford and King's Lynn

CONTENTS

NOTES ON CONTRIBUTORS

R. B. RUTHERFORD: Tutor in Greek and Latin Literature at Christ Church, Oxford.

†J. T. HOOKER: was Reader in Greek and Latin, University College London.

O. T. P. K. DICKINSON: Senior Lecturer, Department of Classics and Ancient History, University of Durham.

G. S. KIRK: Regius Professor Emeritus of Greek, Cambridge.

M. M. WILLCOCK: Professor Emeritus of Latin, University College London.

JASPER GRIFFIN: Professor of Classical Literature, Oxford.

MARTIN HAMMOND: Headmaster, Tonbridge School.

N. POSTLETHWAITE: Head of Classics and Ancient History, University of Exeter.

OLIVER TAPLIN: Tutorial Fellow at Magdalen College, Oxford.

JOHN HALVERSON: Professor Emeritus of English and Comparative Literature, Stevenson College, University of California, Santa Cruz.

CHRIS EMLYN-JONES: Senior Lecturer in Classical Studies, Open University.

E. K. BORTHWICK: Professor Emeritus of Greek, University of Edinburgh.

R. W. SHARPLES: Professor of Greek and Latin, University College London.

G. M. SIFAKIS: Professor of Classical Greek Literature, New York University.

A. G. GEDDES: Senior Lecturer, Department of Classics, University of Adelaide.

INTRODUCTION

By R. B. RUTHERFORD

Homer is inexhaustible. The intrinsic interest of the work of a master story-teller will ensure that the *Iliad* and the *Odyssey* will continue to be read as long as we continue to turn to literature for relaxation and excitement; and as new approaches and new disciplines reinforce the traditional methods of classical scholarship, we also find ourselves asking new questions. Readers in a post-war, post-modernist, post-imperialist age naturally find themselves interested in different aspects of the Homeric poems and the world that they portray from those which preoccupied Arnold or Jebb or Wilamowitz. In the last fifty or so years anthropology, psychology, comparative religion, feminism, narratology, have all provided fresh insights and provocative ideas which have enriched or modified earlier certainties. Moreover, although the advanced study of Greek at university level has been damaged by changes in the educational climate, it is encouraging that so much interest in classical authors is still to be found among those who have not had the opportunity to study them in the original languages. The importance of good translations has never been greater, and one sign of the continuing health of Greek studies is the current boom in versions of Homer in both verse and prose.[1]

In these changed circumstances an important service is offered by the journal *Greece & Rome*, with its accompanying Surveys and the more recent series of Studies, of which this volume is the fourth. The policy of the editors has been to publish work which is scholarly and original, but also accessible to non-specialists, whether sixth-formers or teachers unfamiliar with a topic, or indeed the general reader. Hence contributors to this journal do not parade their learning in endless footnotes, nor do they generally concentrate on minutiae of interest only to experts. The articles in this volume, drawn from issues published over the last twenty-five years, differ widely in approach and subject, but all aim to advance understanding of some aspect of Homer, and to do so in a way that will be intelligible without reference to a library of other works on the subject.

It would be superfluous for me to summarize the papers in this volume and impertinent to pass judgements upon them, like an examiner dispensing marks. In any case, I have already given an account of the aspects of recent Homeric scholarship which seem to me most valuable in my *Homer*, which appears as no. 26 in the *Greece & Rome New Surveys* series (1996).[2] What I shall do here by way of introduction is consider Homer under three headings, each raising a different set of problems, and try to indicate how the papers collected here relate to these different debates. My headings—Homer as history, Homer as myth, Homer as poetry—are of course far from exhaustive (one might think for instance of the place of the poems in the study of the Greek language and dialects, or of the representation of Homeric scenes in the visual arts);[3] nevertheless, I hope that these brief remarks will provide some orientation for readers more familiar with the poems than with modern discussion of them.

History

The most straightforward reading, and perhaps the one with the oldest pedigree, is that Homer is 'history', or in some way preserves historical information. This was in general the view of the early Greeks: Homer was seen as a poetic chronicler, and it made sense to discuss the evidence of the poems in these terms, as Pindar complained that he had over-praised Odysseus and undervalued the more heroic Ajax. But even in antiquity these assumptions could be questioned, and not without reason. In the first place, the *Iliad* and the *Odyssey* can hardly be treated as history in the same way: the former at least narrates a major event, a war involving massive armies on both sides and with a clear winner, but the latter follows the fortunes of an individual warrior and his family, and many of the experiences of Odysseus belong to a world of fantasy rather than to any authentic record of a sea-voyage. Indeed, both epics contain many episodes that are impossible or wildly improbable. The miraculous pre-servation of Hector's corpse, the talking horse Xanthus, the visit of Odysseus to the Underworld, are all supernatural and impossible events; the slaying of the suitors, over a hundred in number, by Odysseus and three allies, is not a physical impossibility but is utterly unlikely outside fiction. Whatever the original audience may have thought, for the modern reader the numerous divine interventions in both poems are enough to set them apart from historical narrative.[4]

It would still be possible to say that the poems preserve a core of historical fact, although it has been altered and expanded by poetic imagination. On this basis we may still believe that a Trojan War took place, while doubting the accuracy of the poet's knowledge about the individuals involved. In the fifth century B.C., Herodotus and Thucydides recognized that Homer had selected his material to suit the epic dignity of his story, and that poetic licence excused exaggeration; yet they still assumed that the basic story was founded on fact (Hdt. 2. 116. 1, Thuc. 1. 10). The difficulty here is that even if we set aside the supernatural, it is hardly possible to distinguish fact from fiction, historical from imaginary characters, without some risk of arbitrariness. The excavations at

Mycenae, Pylos, and Troy, while they have revealed the greatness of Mycenaean civilization and have shown that at some stage a city in the Troad was violently destroyed, have not confirmed the story told in the *Iliad*; even less can be safely asserted about the origins of the *Odyssey*, much of which seems to owe more to the traditions of folklore. Recent work has also shown the unreliability of oral tradition, even when it deliberately sets out to preserve a record of historical events (and it is not at all clear that this was the aim of Homer or his forerunners). Distortion, compression, imaginative elaboration, invention to fill unwanted gaps— these, it seems, are the rule rather than the exception.[5]

If Homer echoes or reflects history at all, we may still be uncertain which part of history. How close was he to the events he believed he was commemorating? Ancient and modern estimates of the date of the Trojan War and the age of heroes varied widely; no less diverse were the attempts at dating Homer. Herodotus seems to have placed him in the ninth century B.C., but other historians, such as Theopompus, put him later, in the seventh. The special problems of the traditional character of Homer's poetry mean that it is hard to tie the works down within even quite broad limits. Current fashion places him a century or more later than many nineteenth-century authorities would have thought possible: the *Iliad*, it is commonly claimed, came into being around 700 or even later, the *Odyssey* later still, perhaps well into the seventh century. Various arguments combine to associate the great flowering of Homeric epic with the so-called 'Greek Renaissance' at the end of the Dark Age. However that may be, there is a growing tendency to downplay the Mycenaean content of the epic and to see the historical element, such as it is, as rooted in the poet's own time or the recent past. This tendency, ably represented by Dickinson's essay in this volume, sees Homer as composing poetry which describes the age of heroes in terms which would not be altogether remote from his own audience's experiences of society and warfare. Certainly there is archaism, and also epic exaggeration, to make the heroes stronger and wealthier than ordinary men; but the values and the cultural assumptions would have been immediately comprehensible.[6]

Some of the most interesting work of recent scholarship has focused on these values and on the complex interweaving of morality, religion, etiquette, and social practice in the Homeric world. Institutions such as guest-friendship, religious constraints such as supplication and pollution, have been analysed in both epics and compared with the customs of unquestionably historical societies.[7] The influential description of Homer's world as essentially a shame-culture, in which men are most influenced by the fear of losing face or the respect of their peers, has stimulated much valuable discussion: Hooker's paper in this volume is a useful counterblow in a continuing debate.[8] The argument put most firmly by Finley, that the value system we find in Homer is so coherent and consistent that it must reflect the world-view of a genuinely historical society, has considerable persuasive force, even if we may differ from him in the actual dating of the period reflected. Nevertheless, caution is still needed: even if Homer does portray the heroic age in quasi-historical terms, the epics unquestionably also contain much invention and fantasy; and our uncertainty as to the date and place in which they originated makes it difficult to bring any external evidence into play. However fascinating the mirror with which the poet shows us a distant age, we cannot move with great confidence to any large conclusions about his own society.

Whether or not Homer is a valid source for history of earlier times, we know that later Greeks used the epic as authority for political and territorial claims. The Athenians are said to have improved their own claim to the island of Salamis by modifying the relevant passage of the Catalogue of Ships, placing Salaminian Ajax amongst the Athenian forces (*Iliad* 2.557 ff.; Arist. *Rhetoric* 1375b30). Further afield, they laid claim to Sigeum on the Hellespont, again citing Homer as evidence in their case against Mytilene (Hdt. 5. 94. 2). 'Assertions about the mythical past expressed the political perceptions and aspirations of the present.'[9] In the related field of genealogy, mythical ancestors in Homer raised the prestige of the modern descendants. Even where the blood relationship was far-fetched or elusive, the influence could be strong: thus Alexander the Great in his conquests of eastern empires seems to have seen himself as a new Achilles.[10]

It is also possible to see the Homeric poems as espousing an ideology of monarchy or aristocracy under threat: in the *Iliad*, this argument works best with Thersites, the rebellious commoner, almost the only human presented by Homer in thoroughly disparaging terms.[11] But this negative reading of Thersites, as presented by Finley and others, does not do justice to the parallel between his criticisms of Agamemnon and what Achilles has put as strongly in the previous book. Postlethwaite's article in this volume puts the other side, arguing that Thersites is not a mere clown or upstart, but a spokesman for the 'unheroic' army and a means whereby Homer can allow the common man a voice. Even if this argument is overstated, the Thersites episode is too exceptional to justify a reading of the *Iliad* purely in terms of justification of aristocratic rule. The *Odyssey*, with its affectionate treatment of humbler figures such as Eumaeus, falls still less easily into this ideological pattern. We may allow that the poems present an idealized world without assuming that this presentation carries a simple propaganda message to the bard's audience. Halverson's paper in this volume even argues that one area which has almost universally been seen as 'political' in its significance, the suitors' desire to wed Penelope, has no such implications.

Whatever the case with Odysseus' household and kingdom, much recent work has suggested that the political outlook of the *Iliad*, like its morality, is more problematic, that there is room for doubt as to whether a clear-cut 'heroic code' existed, for characters or poet.[12] On this view, literary texts ask questions and pose problems about such issues as power, competition and status, loyalty and revenge, property and identity: the poet is not spelling out the answers.[13] At the very least, we must recognize that the poet only rarely passes explicit judgement or tells his audience that a character is right or wrong (though the *Odyssey* does so more frequently than the *Iliad*).[14] The characteristically dry comment of Aristotle, who emphasized the prominence Homer gives to direct speech by characters, anticipated many modern observations: 'Homer especially deserves praise as the only epic poet to realise what the epic poet should do in his own person. In his own person he should say as little as possible' (Arist. *Poet.* 24.1460a5 ff.).

Myth

If not history, perhaps Homer is better viewed as myth? After all, we learn many of the best-known myths from the *Iliad* and the *Odyssey*. But in a sense this makes the issue more obscure, for no generally accepted definition of myth has been formulated, and some connoisseurs of mythology see Greek myth as an unusual case anyway.[15] Also, although it is possible to speak of 'the myth of Achilles' and to tabulate the events of a hero's lifetime in the manner of ancient and modern handbooks, in classical literature myths are most memorably embodied in particular texts, of which the Homeric poems are two among many. If, however, we take the term myth to mean, amongst other things, a traditional tale about characters who are of at least ambiguous historical status, then the poems undoubtedly treat of mythical gods and heroes; and the common requirement that a myth should convey or imply something of importance to the society that hears it seems to be satisfied by the seriousness with which the two epics treat life and death, glory and humiliation, victory and defeat, quite apart from the retrospective political importance of the Trojan War as a panhellenic achievement.[16] But Homer cannot be equated with myth, if only because so many of the myths already existed: they are re-told by Homer as by others. The epic poets enlarge and extend an already vast repertoire of mythological detail: a broad structure is provided by the genealogies of gods and heroes, more prominent in Hesiod, Homer's near contemporary.

Homer, in the sense of the composer(s) of the *Iliad* and the *Odyssey*, certainly adapted and probably invented some of the mythical material we

find in these texts. On a trivial level, it is most implausible that the poet
found authority in his predecessors for the name of every warrior slain or
wounded on the plain of Troy. Elsewhere mythological episodes are sometimes adapted to a new context (Odysseus rather than Jason braves the
Clashing Rocks), or the poet selects or creates a version which suits the
circumstances (Phoenix's tale of Meleager is probably an example). Also,
Homeric epic and especially the *Iliad* excludes certain types of myths:
explicit eroticism and homosexuality are omitted, as are the eerier or more
terrifying aspects of the supernatural sphere (Hades and Persephone never
appear; the dreaded Furies are sinister presences off stage; Dionysus is
mentioned, but bacchic ecstasy remains only a metaphor).[17] Homer is in
fact concerned with the gods chiefly in their relationships with mankind:
contrast the early poems, such as the *Titanomachia*, which dealt with the
affairs of the gods as a separate subject. In certain cases we may be
uncertain whether he is ignorant of a particular myth or suppressing it: a
case in point is the sacrifice of Iphigenia for a fair wind at Aulis. When
Agamemnon complains of the bad advice Calchas has given him in the
past (*Iliad* 1. 106–8), it is natural for readers of Aeschylus to think of this
grim episode; but when Achilles is offered any of Agamemnon's daughters
in marriage in Book 9, they are three in number, and one is called
Iphianassa, later an alternative form of Iphigenia (9.287). Another case
where good critics have disagreed is the episode later seen as the moment-
ous origin of the war, the occasion on which Paris judged Aphrodite the
fairest of the goddesses, moved by her promise of the beautiful Helen as
his bride. Does the *Iliad* presuppose the Judgement of Paris, and is the
single passage where that fateful decision is mentioned an authentic part
of the poem? The probability seems to be that Homer did know the story,
but this major interpretative question will probably never be settled
beyond dispute.[18]

More examples could be given, in many of which the probability is that
Homer knew one of several versions; in other cases, new versions or fresh
aspects were developed by later poets, often following Homer's lead or
deliberately adjusting and reacting to his account of events. Even the *Iliad*
and the *Odyssey* do not agree in all mythical details: in the former
Hephaestus is married to a Grace, in the latter to Aphrodite. Although in
some respects the *Odyssey* may be seen as a response to the *Iliad*, in this
particular case there is little sense that a daring innovation has been introduced; rather, the poet exploits the rich potential of a far larger mythological tradition. Although Homer enjoyed progressively greater prestige,
revisionism and polemic were always possible: neither in their account of
'the myths' nor in other respects do the Homeric epics represent a canon.
To this extent Herodotus' famous pronouncement is misleading: 'Homer
and Hesiod through their poetry gave the Greeks a theogony and gave the

gods their titles; it is they who assigned to them their statuses and skills and gave an indication of their appearance' (2. 53.2). It is valid in that Homer and Hesiod did indeed have immense influence on later Greeks' conception and visual representation of the gods; but it is inadequate because much that we, like Herodotus, see first in Homer and Hesiod must predate their works, and because other early poetry, not least the Epic Cycle, had almost as much influence.

Poetry

The *Iliad* and the *Odyssey*, then, have a complex relationship to both historical events and mythical tales: they use but are distinct from both. Our third heading looks more promising: no one would deny that the epics are poetry, and critics from Longinus to Matthew Arnold have used them as 'touchstones', treating them as a standard by which other poetry can be judged. The quality of the poetry comes through in the best trans- lations, though not in all: the contribution by Geddes to this volume sets out the criteria thought necessary for any worthy rendering of the *Iliad*, and finds weaknesses in one version which has been widely praised.[19] Is it enough to say that the epics are poetic creations, to be enjoyed by their original audience and subsequent generations for their own sake? That poetry gives pleasure to listeners is a pre-eminently Greek view, and indeed enshrined in the text of Homer himself.[20]

Much could be said on the subject of Homer's poetic powers and tech- niques, but the focus of attention in this century has been principally on the nature of the poetry: how was it composed, performed, transmitted? The arguments associated above all with Milman Parry, who has been called the Darwin of Homeric studies, seem to most scholars to have established beyond doubt that Homer's epics derive from a tradition of oral poetry which developed over a number of centuries. In particular the analysis of the epic diction, with its stock epithets, formulaic phrases, and recurring lines, has established that an elaborate and highly developed system exists, which is unlikely to be the work of a single bard. If Homer's language is traditional, so too are the subjects which he describes in that language. Leaving aside the problems of historicity considered above, we may be fairly confident that Homer was not the first to tell of the return of Odysseus. Milman Parry's other major contribution was to revitalize the comparative method: by exploring the oral traditions of Yugoslavia in the 1930s, he excitingly showed how major works could be produced without literacy, and although the Yugoslav epics may not be the best analogy, much further work in this area has been done since, and the perspectives of Homeric studies healthily extended.[21] In different ways the papers by

Borthwick and Sifakis in this volume explore the insights that comparative work may bring.

Since the 1950s G. S. Kirk, whose invaluable *Songs of Homer* remains a standard work, has done much to explain and develop Parry's views: his contribution to this volume helpfully sets out some of the basic points, and there is much more from him and others in the magnificent commentary on the *Iliad* of which he is general editor (Cambridge, 1985–93), the most significant collaborative contribution to Homeric studies in many years. His essay presupposes the Parryist demonstration of the oral background, and considers some of the consequences for the critic. That Homer is himself an oral poet, as Kirk and many others hold, is another step, which not everybody is willing to take; some still prefer to see him as a literate poet drawing on a still-vital oral tradition (as Willcock explains in his paper, this view is particularly prevalent in Germany).

Oral or literate, how much does it matter to the modern literate reader who inevitably encounters these poems in a book? One answer is that it helps us understand why Homer does certain things, especially repeating lines or working with a repertoire of 'typical' scenes such as sacrifices, assembly-scenes, episodes where a guest arrives and is entertained, and so forth. These are the bard's stock-in-trade; they make composition simpler for the hard-working poet and allow the audience a moment of respite. Negatively, oral composition could perhaps explain or excuse the occasional points at which 'Homer nods'—as when, by a venial oversight, a minor warrior who has been killed reappears to fight again.

More interesting questions concern the relation between tradition and innovation. Post-Romantic readers valued originality and imagination, whereas Parry's findings, if accepted, seemed to limit Homer's achievement and attribute much of his genius to his predecessors. It is indeed true that Parry sometimes wrote as though he saw the epic as the poetic voice of a whole people, a *Volkspoesie*. Yet, as Jasper Griffin has argued, it is wrong to suppose that the formulaic diction provided such perfect tools for the oral bard that a masterpiece would inevitably emerge, whatever poet was using this diction. There is some evidence that the other early epics were different in character from the *Iliad* and the *Odyssey*: certainly later critics judged them much inferior.[22] Other approaches take it for granted that tradition plays a part, as in all literature (after all, not even Shakespeare writes purely from his native imagination), and try to identify particular areas in which Homer is probably doing things differently from his predecessors. Modern criticism is happier with the idea of a poet re-deploying familiar material, playing variations on themes, allusively referring to other poets' works or reshaping his own. There is a welcome recognition nowadays that the assumption that Homer is 'oral' does not imply that he is primitive or unsophisticated.

Various papers in this collection demonstrate different ways in which we may hope to isolate the individual within the typical: for instance, in the most important death scenes in the poem, those of Sarpedon, Patroclus, and Hector (Kirk); in the long-range planning of a significant sequence of events (Willcock, on the scenes between Hector and Poulydamas); in the subtle allusiveness of the Odyssean similes (touched on by Taplin).[23] Similes are a particularly important area, since philologists seem generally to agree that they represent a particularly late layer of the epic tradition— closest to Homer's own time? It is remarkable that similes are almost never repeated verbatim, despite the frequent recurrence of actual subject matter:[24] is this a sign that the poets of the *Iliad* and the *Odyssey* were increasingly independent of the repetitive formulaic tradition?

It is now recognized that subtle interplay between narrative and simile does occur, in Homer as in 'literary' Virgil; with this comes a deeper appreciation of the psychological insights of Homer, for similes quite frequently describe psychological states rather than physical action (e.g., *Od.* 8.521–31, 23.233–9).[25] The delicate intelligence of Homer's psychology is perhaps best conveyed by Emlyn-Jones's admirable treatment of the complex scenes between Penelope and her disguised husband in the *Odyssey*.[26] Another method which was for many years surprisingly neglected in Homeric studies is close reading, which Griffin and Hammond in a joint paper effectively apply to the opening scenes of the *Iliad*. This small-scale analysis has large implications, as both authors show the effortless skill with which Homer utilizes epithets, titles, vocatives, transitional phrases, and other devices: 'typical' scenes and 'formulaic' epithets seem to be over-simplifying labels once we begin to consider them in close relation to their contexts. Hammond's contribution lays valuable stress on the 'archetypal' qualities of Homer's characters, how the words and actions, even the gestures of individuals seem to sum up whole aspects of human experience. He also brings out the imaginative power of passages which have lost some of their force through familiarity: for instance, the scene in which the priest leaves the assembly and walks away to the lonely shore, leaving the hostility of men and turning to seek the aid of the god he serves.

Recent acknowledgement of Homer's sophistication has paid particular attention to the self-conscious references to poetry, especially in the *Odyssey*.[27] It is traditional to see Phemius and Demodocus, the bards of the *Odyssey*, as idealized images of Homer: the idea is already current in ancient criticism, and Demodocus' blindness may well be the source of the story that Homer himself was blind. The songs of Demodocus in Book 8 of the *Odyssey* may collectively allude to the *Iliad*, suggesting that the *Odyssey*, whether or not by the same poet, was conceived as a 'sequel'.[28] But there is much narration elsewhere in the *Odyssey*, notably by the hero himself, who is several times compared with a bard. Story-telling comes close to lying, and Odysseus is a past-master at both: one of Chris Emlyn-Jones's excellent essays discusses the fascinating border-area between lies and fiction as represented in the *Odyssey*. It is less easy to detect poetic self-consciousness in the *Iliad*, but Oliver Taplin's suggestive paper on Achilles' shield points to one area where this is probably important. The shield, created by a divine craftsman, is analogous to the vastness of the poem, and the scenes upon it amount to a representation of human life in microcosm.[29] On the shield we see, as in the similes, a world which is more familiar, in some ways more everyday and comfortable, than the world of the poem: the audience recognizes the activities they pursue in their normal lives, and the grandeur and horror of the heroes' sufferings are more powerfully apprehended because a window has been opened on a safer and happier world.

Homer's epics are important not only in themselves, but as a major influence on much of western literature. To remain only within the Greek tradition, posterity recognized him as the fountainhead not merely of epic (which always held to the hexameter, and often adopted the archaic Homeric dialect), but also of other genres which had roots in epic: tragedy, oratory, historiography, New Comedy, the novel. Aeschylus' Aristophanes called him 'divine'; the real Aeschylus allegedly referred to his dramas as 'fish-slices from Homer's banquet'. In time he could be cited simply as 'the poet'. The highest praise for later writers was to describe them as 'Homeric'.[30] The further adaptation of Homeric themes in other literatures would be a vast subject, though much good work has been done.[31] His influence extends beyond the purely literary realm: in the present volume Sharples shows how the problem of indecision and moral conflict as presented in Homer was re-worked and reformulated by philosophic thinkers: the constant quotation of Homer in Plato, Aristotle, and other thinkers makes clear that this was a natural way for the ancients to clarify their ideas. Homer might be the springboard or stimulus for theories he never imagined.

Any attempt to explain Homer's influence would be trite and obvious.[32] Memorable speeches, imaginative similes, spectacular adventures, all had an inescapable impact on successive generations of readers. Perhaps the comments in Hammond's article mentioned above give us the most promising lead, encouraging the reader to recognize the importance of the great archetypal situations in these poems, situations readily transferred to very different cultures: the youthful warrior who dies while his elders live on; the great sorrow of the mourners; the aged king whose kingdom totters on the brink of ruin, humbling himself before a figure who holds the power of life and death over him;[33] the parting of husband and wife for the last time, or their reunion beyond all hope; the son who seeks to live up to the high standard set by his father; the hero doomed to an early end; the loveless marriage charged with bitterness and self-reproach; the kindness and the cruelty of divinity. Even the weirder and more fantastic events of the Odyssean wanderings carry something of this emblematic, almost universal status—the clash of human wit against natural obstacles, civilization versus barbarism, in the Cyclops-episode; the encounter with the past, reliving old rivalries and alliances, in the Underworld; and, woven like a leitmotif amid the many episodes of Odysseus' wanderings, the temptation to relax, to forget, to accept an easier path, as the companions wish to do with the lotus-caters and as Odysseus might have done with Calypso.[34]

Scholars with a non-specialist interest in Homer will find enlightenment on both general and specific problems in these articles; those reading Homer for pleasure or out of curiosity will see something of the range of modern debates and the extent of disagreement even on central topics. Many of the contributions to this volume have already provoked dissent, and the arguments remain finely balanced; in other areas discussion continues, but one feels that real progress has been made. Each of these papers makes points which deserve careful consideration, and it is a pleasure to see gathered together a set of essays which acknowledge the complexities of the subject while abstaining from futile dogmatism and polemic. May the next twenty-five years of *Greece & Rome* provide as much illumination!

NOTES

1. To the anthology of versions in T. E. Higham and C. M. Bowra (edd.), *The Oxford Book of Greek Verse in English Translation* (Oxford, 1938) may now be added those compiled by G. Steiner (ed.), *Homer in English* (Harmondsworth, 1996), and by A. Poole and J. Maule (edd.), *The Oxford Book of Classical Verse in English Translation* (Oxford, 1995).

2. That survey (cited below as *Homer*) contains a much fuller though still far from exhaustive bibliography on many points discussed below, and I have not thought it necessary to document in detail matters covered there.

3. For the former, see L. R. Palmer, *The Greek Language* (London, 1980 and 1995), 83–101, and his essay 'The Language of Homer' in A. J. B. Wace and F. H. Stubbings (edd.), *A Companion to Homer* (London, 1962), 75–178; for the latter, e.g., M. R. Scherer, *The Legends of Troy in Art and Literature* (London, 1963), and other bibliography cited in my *Homer*, 27 n. 72.

4. The relation of the gods as characters in Homeric epic to the gods worshipped with sacrifice and prayer in historic cult is a long-standing problem. For the major Homeric hymns, which deal with the Olympian gods rather more directly and with fuller reference to cult sites and rituals, see the valuable paper by R. Parker, 'The *Hymn to Demeter* and the *Homeric Hymns*', *G & R* 38 (1991), 1–17.

5. M. I. Finley, 'Myth, Memory and History' in Finley, *The Use and Abuse of History* (London, 1973), ch. 1; R. Finnegan, *Oral Poetry: its Nature, Significance and Social Context* (Cambridge, 1977); R. Thomas, *Oral Tradition and Written Record in Classical Athens* (Cambridge, 1989), esp. chs. 1–3.

6. Finley, *The World of Odysseus* (originally published in 1954; 2nd edn. New York, 1978) is

the starting-point for all more recent discussions; an encyclopaedically detailed treatment of many aspects is provided by H. van Wees, *Status Warriors: War, Violence and Society in Homer and History* (Amsterdam, 1992).

7. See, e.g., Finley (n. 6), 95–103 on guest-friendship; J. Gould, 'Hiketeia', *JHS* 93 (1973), 74–103 on supplication; Parker, *Miasma. Pollution and Purification in Early Greek Religion* (Oxford, 1983) on pollution.

8. For earlier discussions see esp. E. R. Dodds, *The Greeks and the Irrational* (Berkeley and Los Angeles, 1951), 17–18, 28, 47–50, and other works cited in my *Homer*, 54–5 nn. 42, 47–8.

9. M. L. West, *The Hesiodic Catalogue of Women* (Oxford, 1985), 10, with other examples; cf. M. P. Nilsson, *Cults, Myths, Oracles and Politics in Ancient Greece* (New York, 1972).

10. R. Lane Fox, *Alexander the Great* (Harmondsworth, 1973), ch. 3; P. A. Brunt, *Arrian* i (Harvard, 1976), Appendix 4.

11. Finley (n. 6), 110–12, I. Morris, 'The Use and Abuse of Homer', *Cl. Antiq.* 5 (1986), 81–138; van Wees (n. 6), 78–89.

12. Cf. O. Taplin, *Homeric Soundings: the Shaping of the Iliad* (Oxford, 1992), 6–7, 50–1, 71–2, 166.

13. S. Goldhill, *The Poet's Voice* (Cambridge, 1991), chs. 1–2.

14. J. Griffin, 'Homeric Words and Speakers', *JHS* 106 (1986), 36–57, with modifications by I. J. F. de Jong, 'Homeric Words and Speakers: an Addendum', *JHS* 108 (1988), 188–9.

15. See G. S. Kirk, *Myth: its Meaning and Function* (Berkeley and Los Angeles, 1974); Griffin, 'Greek Myth and Hesiod', in J. Boardman, J. Griffin, O. Murray (edd.), *The Oxford History of the Classical World* (Oxford, 1986), 78–98; F. Graf, *Greek Mythology* (Johns Hopkins U. P., 1993); S. Said, *Approches de la mythologie grecque* (Paris, 1993). Penetrating discussion of various definitional problems by W. Burkert, *Structure and History in Greek Mythology* (Berkeley and Los Angeles, 1979), ch. 1.

16. On the emergence of this conception see esp. E. Hall, *Inventing the Barbarian: Greek Self-definition through Tragedy* (Oxford, 1989).

17. See Griffin, 'The Epic Cycle and the Uniqueness of Homer', *JHS* 97 (1977), 39–53.

18. *Iliad* 24.27–30. Cf. Euripides, *Andromache* 274–92, *Iphigenia at Aulis* 1283–318, and other passages gathered in the valuable study by T. C. W. Stinton, *Euripides and the Judgement of Paris* (Hellenic Society Papers, Suppl. 11, 1965), ch. 1 =Stinton, *Collected Papers on Greek Tragedy* (Oxford, 1990), 17–26; also Richardson ad loc., a characteristically judicious discussion.

19. H. A. Mason, *To Homer through Pope* (London, 1972) provides a more extended critique of Lattimore's version, with extensive comparisons; on the other side, see H. Lloyd-Jones, *New York Review of Books*, 14 Feb. 1991 =Lloyd-Jones, *Greek in a Cold Climate* (London, 1991), 1–17.

20. M. Heath, *The Poetics of Greek Tragedy* (London, 1987), 5–11.

21. A. T. Hatto (ed.), *Traditions of Heroic and Epic Poetry* i (London, 1980) and ii (London, 1989), and other works cited in Taplin (n. 12), 26 n. 24.

22. Callimachus, *Epigram* 28 Pfeiffer; Horace, *Ars Poetica* 132, 136; see also Griffin (n. 17).

23. A. J. Podlecki's 'Some Odyssean Similes', *G & R* 18 (1971), 81–90, notably anticipates more extensive treatments, e.g., by H. Foley, ' "Reverse Similes" and Sex Roles in the *Odyssey*', *Arethusa* 11 (1978), 7–26 =J. Peradotto and J. P. Sullivan (edd.), *Women in the Ancient World: the Arethusa Papers* (Albany, 1984), 59–78, and by C. Moulton, *Similes in the Homeric Poems* (*Hypomnemata* 49, 1977), chs. 4–5.

24. For a list of the very few exceptions, and some discussion, see W. C. Scott, *The Oral Nature of the Homeric Simile* (*Mnemosyne* Suppl. Vol. 58, 1974), 127–40.

25. See also *Od.* 19. 204–12 with my commentary (Cambridge, 1992).

26. Emlyn-Jones's Afterword cites more recent work on this theme; see also J. Winkler, *The Constraints of Desire* (London and New York, 1990), 129–61.

27. See further my *Homer*, 60, 78 nn. 7–13; also 55 n. 62 on the Iliadic shield, often discussed in the same context.

28. C. Macleod, 'Homer on Poetry and the Poetry of Homer', *Collected Essays* (Oxford, 1983), ch. 1.

29. See also P. R. Hardie, *Virgil's Aeneid: Cosmos and Imperium* (Oxford, 1986), ch. 8 for the shield in ancient criticism.

30. See my *Homer*, 20–2, and now A. Cameron, *Callimachus and his Critics* (Princeton, 1995), 273–7.

31. See further J. L. Myres (rev. D. Gray), *Homer and his Critics* (London, 1958); Scherer (n. 3 above); W. B. Stanford, *The Ulysses Theme* (2nd edn. Oxford, 1963); W. B. Stanford and J. V. Luce, *The Quest for Ulysses* (London, 1974); H. W. Clarke, *Homer's Readers* (Newark, London, Toronto, 1981); B. Rubens and O. Taplin, *An Odyssey round Odysseus* (London, 1989).

32. But for a richly suggestive paper on the earliest stages, see W. Burkert, 'The Making of Homer in the Sixth Century B.C.: Rhapsodes versus Stesichorus' in *Papers on The Amasis-painter and his World* (J. Paul Getty Museum, 1987), 43–62.

33. E. R. Curtius, *European Literature and the Latin Middle Ages* (Oxford, 1953), ch. 9, esp. 170–3, has interesting remarks on this and other topics, though one need not follow him in invoking the theories of Dumézil on ancient religion.

34. Cf. Rutherford, 'The Philosophy of the *Odyssey*', *JHS* 106 (1986), 146 n. 6.

HOMERIC SOCIETY: A SHAME-CULTURE?

By †J. T. HOOKER

It is widely known that in the first two chapters of his *Greeks and the Irrational* E. R. Dodds borrowed the terms 'shame-culture' and 'guilt-culture' and applied them to early Greek society. According to Dodds, the society depicted by Homer knew nothing of guilt or the sanction of guilt: what acted as a motivating force was *aidōs*, 'shame' or 'sense of shame', of which the sanction was *nemesis*, 'righteous indignation'. In other words, the warriors of the heroic caste were impelled to certain courses of action, or were restrained from others, by *aidōs*: they were ashamed of 'losing face' among their equals or inferiors, and this fear of public indignation kept before the mind of the heroes where their duty lay. As the Archaic Age advanced (Dodds contends), the sense of guilt became manifest, without however displacing entirely the assumptions of the earlier 'shame-culture'.

Nobody will quarrel with Dodds's argument so far as 'guilt-culture' is concerned. It is clear that the Homeric heroes had no concept of 'guilty feeling', while the very word later used to mean 'guilty' (*aitios*) never has this sense in Homer. What I should like to question is the case made by Dodds (and widely accepted since) that the 'sense of shame' inter-penetrates Homeric society so pervasively that we are justified in calling this society a 'shame-culture'.

The key-passage adduced by Dodds in support of his interpretation comes in Hector's soliloquy before his duel with Achilles (*Iliad* 22). As is customary in Homeric soliloquies, the hero considers one by one the options open to him: to take refuge inside the city, to go unarmed to Achilles and offer recompense, to keep on his armour and fight Achilles (lines 99–130). The first option he rejects for this compelling reason: 'Now that I have ruined the host by my blind folly, I have shame before the Trojans and Trojan women with long robes, in case someone of lower rank than I should say, "Hector, trusting in his own might, has ruined the host"' (lines 104–7). There is no doubt that both the situation and Hector's reaction to it are appropriate in a 'shame-culture'. Whether they lead irresistibly to the equation 'Homeric society = shame-culture' we may now enquire.

It is *prima facie* improbable that a 'sense of shame' should play a major role in determining the actions of the heroes. When we observe their arrogant and self-sufficient character, we may feel that their conduct is likely to arise from more positive causes. These causes are given typical expression in Homeric poetry by the terms 'status' (*timē*) and 'good reputation, glory' (*euchos* or *kleos*). When a hero is left to his own devices (that is, unless some god sends 'infatuation' upon him or fills his heart with 'battle-fury'), his actions tend to increase his status and to satisfy his longing for glory. For instance, at the end of the very speech of Hector already mentioned, he decides to fight Achilles, 'to discover upon which of them Zeus will bestow glory' (line 130).

In *Iliad* 22, then, I identify a desire for glory as the decisive factor in determining Hector's choice. His feeling of shame before his countrymen is a contributory factor only. Still, such as it is, Hector's sense of shame does hold interest for us: not, I think, because it is typical of the way that the heroes in general reason or behave but because it illuminates Hector's own character and his role in the *Iliad*.

Hector is unique among the heroes. He is explicitly contrasted with his brother Paris and implicitly with the warriors on the Achaean side. What sets him apart from the rest is, to use a modern expression, his 'sense of responsibility'. He is a family man to an extent that none of the others is: he has a care for his wife and child, beyond them for his aged father and mother, and even beyond these for the entire Trojan community. Because of this wider ambit of interests than is perceived by the other heroes, Hector in *Iliad* 22 is first of all deaf to his parents' pleas to come inside the gates, and then capable of 'feeling shame' before the community. The peculiar position of Hector, and the peculiar sense of responsibility he feels towards his community, were earlier brought out in the brilliant scene of Book 6, which brings into sharp focus the various levels of his commitment. When he is implored by Andromache to cease from fighting, afraid that he will leave her a widow and their son an orphan, he replies, 'All this is a care to me as well, yet terribly I have shame before the Trojans and Trojan women with long robes, if like a coward I lurk away from the battle' (lines 441–5). The formulation is the same as in Book 22; it is used by no one else, for no one else has the sense of duty towards the community that Hector feels. But in Book 6, just as in the later passage, the allusion to 'shame' is followed by a mention of the 'glory' (*kleos*) which Hector desires to win for Priam and himself (line 446). Only in these two passages of the *Iliad* is 'shame' before specific persons adduced as a motive for a certain course of conduct; that it is so adduced we may attribute to the character and situation of Hector, with his strongly developed sense of belonging to the Trojan community; and on both occasions the desire for glory is brought forward as another, and even more powerful, motive. (I note that at *Odyssey* 21.323–9 Eurymachus expresses the same sentiment as Hector, and in phraseology which recalls his; needless to say, however, the desire for glory does not form part of Euymachus' plans, or of his character, and indeed Penelope observes that he and his friends will not win good report among the community, line 331.)

Since the formulation 'feel shame before certain specific persons' is peculiar to Hector, it cannot be regarded as symptomatic of a whole society; and, although there are occasional references to 'public opinion' (as in Eurymachus' 'having shame before the *phatis* of men and women'), I do not think that Dodds has provided adequate evidence that public opinion has a decisive influence on the heroes' conduct. The truth is that, while *aidōs, aideomai,* and cognate words are very common in Homer, they embrace a much wider area of meaning than can be accommodated within in a single term in any modern language. The original meaning of the *aidōs*-words is not 'shame' but 'awe', especially 'religious awe'. This sense, or a somewhat weakened meaning 'respect', is found in the majority of Homeric examples; only as the result of a later, specialized development do these words come to mean 'shame'.

What I postulate as the original meaning, that of '(religious) awe', has left few traces in Homeric poetry. There are perhaps only two clear examples. In *Iliad* 15 Ares is filled with fury against the Achaeans when he hears of the death of his son Ascalaphus. True to his impetuous nature, he is eager to rush off at once and avenge Ascalaphus, contrary to the will of Zeus. Athene restrains him, saying that he has lost his *noos* and his *aidōs* (line 129). While *noos* must mean 'wits' or 'intelligence', and is closely connected with the preceding words, *aidōs* here refers to the 'awe' which the gods feel (or ought to feel) for the overmastering power of Zeus: the latter theme is still quite fresh in the listener's mind, thanks to the terrifying reminder Hera received from Zeus in lines 18–24. The sense of 'religious awe' recurs, I think, in *Iliad* 24.44, where Apollo accuses Achilles of having lost his pity, 'and he has no *aidōs*'. This *aidōs* cannot mean 'shame', partly because Achilles is the last person to display a 'sense of shame' or to have regard for the sanction of 'public opinion', partly because Apollo's words are addressed to an assembly of the gods and express a divine, not a human, view of Achilles' conduct. (If this interpretation is correct, it provides a further reason for doubting the authenticity of line 45: only on the supposition that *aidōs* means 'shame' could a case be made for accepting that verse as genuine; in the corresponding verse of Hesiod's *Works and Days* 318, *aidōs* clearly does mean 'sense of shame'.)

But in the great majority of instances, the sense of 'awe' (whose sanction is, of course, the divine displeasure) has become mere 'respect'. Both the suppliant and the guest expect, and claim, to be treated with *aidōs*. In the suppliant's case, *aidōs* is often connected with a word for 'pity' (*eleō, eleairō*); as good an example as any may be found in Hector's speech in *Iliad* 22, already discussed: 'No, let me not approach Achilles, for he will not pity me, nor show me any respect' (lines 123–4). A guest who deserves and demands respect is called *xeinos aidoios* in the *Odyssey*; and it is interesting to notice that on one occasion an adverb, *aidoiōs*, is formed to express respectful treatment in the context of guest-friendship (19.243).

We observe further that *aidōs*-terms are frequently associated either with the concept 'love' or with the concept 'fear': in *Odyssey* 8.21–2, *aidoios* is associated with both *philos* and *deinos*, so implying that the respect due to Odysseus is composed of the superficially contradictory elements of love and fear. That these are in fact the elements which go to make up the notion of 'respect' is shown by the fact that in *Iliad* 18 Thetis is called in one place 'respected and loved' (line 386) and in another 'respected and feared' (line 394). In a precisely analogous way, the noun *aidōs* may be associated with *philotēs* (*Iliad* 24.111, *Odyssey* 14.505), while the verb *aideomai* is coupled with a verb of 'fearing' in *Iliad* 24.435 and *Odyssey* 17.188.

As already stated, I regard the meaning 'shame' as representing a further development from that of 'respect'. In two passages of the *Iliad* this semantic shift seems actually to be in process. When in 4.402 Diomedes stays silent in the face of Agamemnon's rebuke and 'shows respect' for it (*aidestheis*), his reaction is prompted by a 'sense of shame', as becomes clear from his further comment to Capaneus at lines 413–14. Contrariwise, on hearing that Apollo 'was ashamed (*aideto*) to come to blows with Poseidon' (21.468–9), we can easily sense that it was his respect for the elder god which restrained him. Both these passages give evidence of a convergence of the notion of 'respect' and that of 'shame'. It is worth noting, in this connexion, that the phrase with *aideomai* in *Odyssey* 14.145–6 could in theory mean either 'I am ashamed to speak his name' or 'I speak his name with respect'. It is only the immediate context which compels us to understand the expression in the latter sense.

The *Odyssey* contains some *aidōs*-words in which the meaning 'shame' has become predominant. In Book 3, when Athene has led Telemachus to Pylos, she tells him that he need no longer feel *aidōs* (line 14): by this word she must mean the bashfulness, or sense of shame, which characterized him before the goddess came to Ithaca and endowed him with *menos*. In his reply, Telemachus' use of *aidōs* likewise refers to the bashfulness which comes over a young man in asking questions of an older (line 24). On a number of occasions, too, an *aidōs*-word is used in the negative to describe the 'shameless' suitors (e.g., *Odyssey* 20.171 and 23.37).

The development in the meaning of *aidōs* from 'religious awe' to 'shame' is closely paralleled by the history of another, much rarer, Homeric term, namely *sebas*. What I regard as its original sense is found twice in *Iliad* 6. On both occasions a man is said to have refrained from committing a certain deed; 'for he had awe of it (*sebassato*) in his heart' (lines 167 and 417). But elsewhere the meaning is 'shame'. 'Are you not ashamed (*sebesthe*)?', asks Agamemnon of the Argives (*Iliad* 4.242);

aideisthe would have meant the same thing. And when Iris says that *sebas* should come upon Achilles' heart (18.178), her meaning could have been conveyed just as well by *aidōs*.

'Shame before others', 'respect for others', 'awe before the gods': these are the meanings which may be conveyed by the *aidōs*-words in Homer. Such senses are not mutually exclusive, and I have indicated a few passages in which one seems to merge into another. But that 'religious awe' represents the earliest meaning there can be little doubt; and it is this feeling, much more than shame before one's equals or inferiors, that acts as a constant and powerful constraint upon the heroes.

ADDENDUM

The contrast between shame-culture and guilt-culture, and the range of *aidōs* in Homer, have now been discussed exhaustively by Douglas L. Cairns, *Aidōs, the Psychology and Ethics of Honour and Shame in Ancient Greek Literature* (Oxford, 1993), 27 ff. and 48 ff.   P. W.

HOMER, THE POET OF THE DARK AGE

By O. T. P. K. DICKINSON

This paper began as a lecture to an extramural weekend course on the Greek Dark Age, organized in Oxford by the Department of External Studies in December 1983.[1] It was intended to suggest that the world of the Homeric poems, insofar as it had any relationship with reality, was more likely to reflect the conditions of the Dark Age than those of Mycenaean Greece, and it was born of increasing frustration at the dominance of what I will call the 'Mycenaean' interpretation of Homer, particularly at the popular level. The BBC television series by Michael Wood, *In Search of the Trojan War* (followed by a book of the same name, published 1985 by BBC Books and by Penguin Books in 1996), did nothing to lessen this dominance—indeed, it barely suggested that such an interpretation had been seriously challenged—and the theme of the lecture has therefore lost none of its relevance. In presenting a considerably revised version here, I have not attempted to offer an exhaustively argued and documented discussion, which would require a book, and must refer the reader to more extensive treatments of the topic for fuller details.[2] Rather, I have decided to leave it as a rather provocative exposition of a case which deserves to be made. I have made some attempt to step outside the framework in which the discussion has often been conducted, which to my mind unduly favours the 'Mycenaean' interpretation, but readily acknowledge that many of my arguments have been presented in similar form by others,[3] and that some have been admitted to have force by those who in general support the 'Mycenaean' interpretation. Given the quantity of writing on the topic, it is only too likely that I have neglected some discussions, and I have given references mainly to Homeric sources and to recent archaeological finds of relevance. Finally, I should make it clear that it is not my primary purpose to discuss the historicity of the Trojan War or of the Greek heroic legends generally, though this has often been made to depend on the supposedly Mycenaean content of the Homeric poems, at least in part.

In analysing the way that Homer has often dominated reconstructions of the Mycenaean age, E. Vermeule wrote, 'We say in justification that large parts of the poems incorporate Mycenaean traditions, that the five hundred years separating the fall of Troy VIIA from the Homeric version of its fall have wrought only minor innovations, a few misunderstandings of the past and adaptations to more modern experience. We hope that the core of those great poems has not been terribly changed by successive improvisations of oral poets—surely poets will guard for us the heritage of the past.'[4] These somewhat ironical comments usefully summarize widely prevalent attitudes and assumptions that need to be questioned. In particular, those five hundred years ought to stick in the scholarly throat a good deal more than they seem to—after all, they represent an equivalent length of time to that between the battle of Marathon and the death of Augustus—but, as Finley has written, 'The human mind plays strange tricks with time perspective when the distant past is under consideration; centuries become as years and millennia as decades.'[5] Precisely because until recently little was known about the Dark Age which constitutes the bulk of the five hundred years, scholars seem to have found it easy to treat the period as an interlude in which very little happened, or changed, before the expansion of the eighth century (all cited dates are B.C.). Thus, features which are undoubtedly 'old', such as the form of many of the Greek names, are assumed to be Mycenaean at latest rather than early Dark Age or even ninth century, which would still be a century or more before an acceptable date for the poems' composition; and in discussing references to items that are old, it is often suggested that because they cannot be eighth century, they must be Mycenaean, as if Homer could not be drawing on some piece of description composed at a stage in between. In fact, there is good reason to suggest that there were very significant developments in the Dark Age and that these gave rise to many of the most characteristic features of Greek civilization.

It has to be pointed out that some assumptions still seem to be widely prevalent among specialists in Aegean prehistory and early history about 'oral tradition', which are not substantiated either by studies of oral traditions concerning known historical events or by cases where bodies of traditional material, such as genealogies, are recorded at successive periods and can be checked. It is becoming increasingly clear that it was not the business of those who 'guard . . . the heritage of the past' to give a factually accurate account of the past or even to preserve inherited traditions unchanged; it was to validate by their account of the past the social and political conditions of the present. If these changed, so too must the 'tradition'.[6] To believe that the Greeks were uniquely free from this attitude is to be guilty of the worst kind of romanticism about them, and moreover is to ignore the classical evidence, which not only shows poets freely altering and developing famous stories, but doing so on occasion with politically inspired motives, as in the transference of Agamemnon and Orestes to Sparta.[7] The very fact that divergent versions of myths, as of more recent historical traditions, could be cited by Herodotus surely indicates the absence of any disinterested love of truth, for if this operated every source should preserve the same story! The undoubted fact that immense quantities of information can be memorized and passed on orally is no guarantee that the material is historically true and untampered-with, even if this was claimed for it.

The supposition that has been used to bolster oral tradition in this case, that the formulae used in the construction of epic verse by their very nature preserved elements of a bygone world, also has to be questioned. For it has been emphasized by linguistic specialists that the Greek language changed quite considerably over the period in question; many formulae, then, cannot be of Mycenaean date, for they would not fit the hexameter metre in Mycenaean form. Even the description of a genuine Mycenaean object, the boar's tusk plated helmet, apparently contains linguistically late forms.[8] One might go further and ask whether, granting the likelihood of Mycenaean epic, its metre was the hexameter; if so, it would have been uniquely complex for a Bronze Age metre and have lasted without further change for a remarkably long time. I see no inherent reason why the remoter predecessors of the Homeric poems should not have been composed in simpler forms of verse or even in formal, repetitive story-tellers' prose interspersed with verses, like the Irish legends, and why the whole system of formulae should not have been developed, along with the hexameter, during the Dark Age, as indeed M. L. West has argued.[9] That Homeric linguistic forms are often old does not prove that they cannot be later than the Mycenaean period, for we have only the vaguest idea of the chronology of the linguistic changes in Greek, which has often been made to depend on that of supposed events such as the Ionian migration, itself not fixed.

But it would be quite misleading to suggest that the 'Mycenaean' interpretation depends purely on faith in the veracity of oral tradition or the antiquity of the hexameter. Rather, the case has generally been argued by proving to the satisfaction of the scholar concerned, that some features referred to *are* Mycenaean, which can then be used to suggest, if desired, that much or all of the poems' content *could be*. Here the temptation is not always resisted to argue, in the case of a feature that could be either Mycenaean or later, that it must be the former, even if only a few uncharacteristic Mycenaean examples are known. At worst, an item which is unique in the archaeological record, and cannot date much later than 1500, the cup found by Schliemann in Shaft Grave IV, is used to prove that the description of Nestor's cup (*Il.* 11.632–7), itself unique in Homer, is genuinely Mycenaean; since the description is by no means entirely clear, it would be better to suspend judgement entirely. But this is symptomatic of the approach often adopted, to find a Mycenaean parallel by hook or by crook. The underlying assumption, that over several hundred years the poetic tradition would sternly continue to eschew all reference to the contemporary and deal entirely in descriptions of a world that was becoming increasingly remote, not even making use of creative imagination, has never been supported by argument from analogy and has never been watertight, for it is undeniable that features of a much later age than the Mycenaean have been incorporated.

A good example is provided by the references to iron as a material in common use. Iron items were certainly known in Mycenaean times, but iron only began to be worked in Greece in the eleventh century, and was at first used for a restricted range of objects, those that could most easily be forged. Thus, grave groups of around the middle of the eleventh century contain flat iron daggers, but more complex forms, socketed spearheads and shield bosses, are still bronze. Iron spearheads hardly appear before the tenth century, other objects such as tools later still. But Achilles, in offering a lump of iron as a prize at Patroclus' funeral games, assumes that the competitors will have *continual* need of iron: the winner will not have to send someone to town to get more for five years.[10] Such a reference would be meaningless before 1100, when hardly any items were made of iron, probably even before 1000; but a later audience would appreciate that iron was something of which it was useful to have a good supply.

It is the very casualness of this reference that, to my mind, is significant. When something contemporary is referred to in a piece of elaborate description, such as the Gorgon face on Agamemnon's shield (*Il.* 11.36), which seems best related to seventh-century work, then it is reasonable to suggest that the poet has introduced a contemporary embellishment. But when he is, as it were, off his guard, and makes or has his characters make a reference that is not intended to be particularly noted, then I think we have an indication of the true milieu of the poems. There are many such references, which have convinced me that this is the Dark Age rather than anything else, but I must make two qualifications. The first is that I would concede that the last phase of the Mycenaean period, which followed the collapse of the palace societies around 1200 and extended into the eleventh century, might well have resembled the Dark Age proper and the picture of 'old Greece' so brilliantly reconstructed by Thucydides from the early poetic tradition (1.2–8), in which he stresses the constant insecurity, fear of invasion or raid, lack of trade and of capital. I would still flatly deny that it could be made to apply to the palace period even in its latest phase, the time to which the mounting of a great expedition is usually considered appropriate.[11]

My second qualification is that I would not wish to suggest that the poems present a wholly realistic picture of the Dark Age or of any phase within it. No epic is a realistic presentation of a society or age; rather, it is a fantasy, but a fantasy in which, because neither composer nor audience can imagine or sympathize with a wholly alien world, reality keeps breaking through. Its interests are specialized, more concerned with war than with trade (though there are in fact several references in Homer). Its characters move part of the time in a world of dreamlike magnificence, encountering gods and other supernatural beings, but at other times their behaviour and preoccupations will be familiar to the audience and may be slightly incongruous in their magnificent setting.

Often enough this magnificence is, in my view, quite simply that of fairy tale. The constant description of vessels and jewellery as of precious metals, especially gold, need not be a genuine reminiscence of the Mycenaean world, which by the palace period seems to have been notably sparing of precious metal though still lavish with bronze; it is conventional in epic and heroic tales of all sorts.[12] I would suggest that the elaborately described shield of Achilles, cuirass of Agamemnon, and palace of Alcinous, and the much more hazily suggested wealth of Menelaus' hall have little more relationship with reality than the robots that serve Hephaestus or the self-propelled wheeled tables that he makes for the gods, and that if they had a model it is more likely to have been the wealth of Egypt and the Near East as apprehended from imports and tales of the later Dark Age, than any clear memory of the Mycenaean past.

In point of fact, a degree of magnificence was possible even in the depths of the Dark Age, the tenth century, as is evident from the finds at Lefkandi, especially the burials in the 'Heroön'.[13] Moreover, the discovery of the 'Heroön' underlines an important general point, that to compare the Mycenaean period and the Dark Age is to compare periods well and poorly documented in the archaeological record; hence, unexpected Dark Age finds can change the terms of the discussion, and a Dark Age date cannot be denied to a reference simply because it suggests wealth or elaboration. In particular, I believe that the 'Heroön' removes any need to relate Homeric burial practice to the Mycenaean period, since it provides convincing parallels for many features of the burial rite, most elaborately described for the burials of Patroclus and Hector, which includes cremation, the storage of the ashes in a precious container, and the sacrifice of animals, perhaps humans also; the mound also referred to in these and other contexts is a later feature at the 'Heroön', involving the filling-in of a building.

Cremation, the heaping of a mound over the pyre or the grave constructed to hold the ashes-container, and the placing of a marker on the mound are referred to separately or together many times in Homer, sometimes in contexts that suggest that this is the normal burial rite, not that of heroes alone.[14] This is remarkable, since even in the Dark Age cremation was the rite of a minority of the Greek communities, while in the final Mycenaean period it was limited to a few individuals, whose ashes, generally in some form of pot, were placed alongside their inhumed relatives in tombs of the traditional rock-cut or stone-built types that do

not seem to be hinted at in Homer. Only the most intricate special
pleading has ever been able to suggest a relationship between Homeric
burial customs and Mycenaean; the problem is that they do not even seem
'normal' for the Dark Age, although there are examples of ninth- and
eighth-century cremations under mounds, and some have been found
in Asia Minor where the poems are generally thought to have been
composed. The example of the Lefkandi 'Heroön' might encourage the
supposition that elaborate cremations were thought particularly appropriate for important persons in parts of the Greek world as early as the tenth
century.

This, then, is one important area of human behaviour frequently
described or referred to in the poems which is consistently un-Mycenaean,
and whose only real parallels date after 1000. That some features of the
burial ritual have Mycenaean parallels, such as the wailing, which is shown
in precisely similar fashion on the late Mycenaean Tanagra larnakes and
on eighth-century Athenian vases,[15] is not surprising; it would be far more
strange if there were no such parallels, for the Mycenaean population was
directly ancestral to the later Greeks, and the Dark Age did not involve a
total social breakdown requiring an entirely new start. As has frequently
been pointed out, in the wider field of religion, the names of several of the
Greek gods are to be found in the Linear B tablets; it would, again, be
remarkable if this were not so. But it is not so frequently stressed that
several of the most important Olympian gods, such as Apollo, Aphrodite,
and Demeter, are absent, that the case for identifying others is question-
able, and that there are many figures in the tablets of whom there is no
trace later.[16] The gap between the evidence of the tablets and of
Mycenaean archaeology and the picture in the Homeric poems, already
very close to classical Greek religion, is very wide and not easily argued
away, even if the very occasional reference to temples and to Delphi, once
quite plainly as an oracle,[17] are discounted as definitely late features. I
would suggest that Greek religion underwent fundamental changes in the
Dark Age: practice, the forms of worship, may have remained very much
the same, but the recipients of worship very probably changed their
names, natures, and positions in the divine hierarchy.

This is an even more significant area than burial customs, but one in
which the facts are more open to dispute. In other cases the evidence is
less controversial, such as dress. Men's dress seems to change little
between the Mycenaean period and Dark Age: tunics short or long were
normal wear, with cloaks over the top in many cases. Odysseus once
describes himself as wearing a cloak pinned with an exceedingly ornate
brooch,[18] a practice for which there is no clear Mycenaean parallel, but
again this might be discounted as a piece of late elaboration. Women's
dress, however, when any detail is given, is consistently presented as being

secured with two or more pin-like fasteners—Penelope is offered a robe with a dozen such items. These are best interpreted as the fibulae of the Dark Age, as long ago argued by Lorimer.[19] Fibulae first begin to appear before 1200, but only very occasionally and as single specimens; they are more common in the twelfth century, but are only regularly found from the eleventh century onwards and begin to become elaborate, sometimes of gold, in the tenth and ninth centuries. Surely what is described as a regular feature should be taken as a reference belonging to a period when it was a regular feature, not one in which it was a rare novelty. In addition, earrings with triple pendants are twice mentioned; it seems impossible not to relate this to ninth-century earrings found at Lefkandi, and in any case the wearing of earrings was not, after the earliest phase, Mycenaean practice.[20]

Next we may consider the bronze tripods which figure so frequently as symbols of wealth, named as prizes and gifts, even listed first among the presents which Agamemnon offers to Achilles as reparation for his wounded honour. Examples of bronze tripods do occur before 1200, but they are plain unspectacular items, found alongside a wealth of other metal vessel types. It is in the Dark Age that they are likely to have been highly valued items symbolizing great wealth: two types are known, one consisting of a three-legged stand on which a separate cauldron is placed, the other of a cauldron to which handles and legs are attached. The first was originally produced in Cyprus, but was certainly being produced at Lefkandi by 900; the other, closer to the Mycenaean type, may have survived occasionally (clay imitations are known from an Athens grave of the eleventh century) and was certainly being made again by the eighth century, during which it was developed to extremely large and elaborate non-functional forms. Both types were dedicated at sanctuaries during the ninth and eighth centuries, which seem the most appropriate time for references to them as highly valued items.[21]

The field of warfare bulks large in the poems, especially the *Iliad*, and here the position is more complex. On occasion old-fashioned gear is referred to, and the concentration on the activities of heroes makes for an unreal picture of battle in any period, but much of what is described could fit a Dark Age context as well as, if not better than, a Mycenaean one. Armour is frequently described as of bronze, presumably bronze-plated, and such armour is certainly known, if rarely, from Mycenaean times, appearing even in very late contexts; by the last quarter of the eighth century it is appearing again in graves, in such well-developed forms that it is likely to have had some earlier history. But it can never have been as common as the epic makes it, and a degree of unreality in such references seems probable. Since in the ancient world bronze was the only normal form of extra protection, any attempt to provide heroes with special armour would be almost bound to involve it, unless reality is abandoned altogether, as with the references to golden armour and other extravagances. The material of weapons is also normally bronze, where it is referred to at all, and this is undoubtedly 'old', but as I have pointed out the introduction of iron was a slow process, and bronze weapons survived past it—a bronze spearhead was buried with a great Eretrian noble in the last quarter of the eighth century—so that the memory that weapons had once been of bronze alone would surely survive; such references need not, themselves, derive from the period when this was the case.

What is done with the weapons will often suit a very late Mycenaean or Dark Age context better than the world of the palaces. Spears, often carried in pairs, may be thrust with or thrown. The size of a standard Mycenaean spear seems to preclude its being thrown effectively, but small javelin-like spearheads have been found in twelfth- and eleventh-century graves, and there is at least one twelfth-century representation of a warrior carrying two spears;[22] when representations of warriors become common again, in the eighth century, this is normal. A reference to this practice might, then, be appropriate to any time between the latest Mycenaean period and the Dark Age, but hardly earlier.

Swords are used to cut and thrust with, including the notorious ξίφος ἀργυρόηλον or silver-studded sword which has been thought not only to be a genuine Mycenaean reference but to indicate the existence of *early* Mycenaean hexameter epic, since rivet-heads capped with precious metal (more often gold than silver) are commonly found on early Mycenaean weapons. But such weapons are not suitable for a cutting stroke, and it must moreover be assumed that the reference is to the rivet-cappings and not the rivets themselves; that silver rivets would not be functional would not bother a poet who speaks of golden armour and tin greaves! Since silver cappings are found on the rivets of iron swords in Cyprus, if so far only of eighth- and seventh-century date,[23] the technique clearly survived through the Dark Age or was reinvented in it, which suggests a need for caution in giving a date to this formulaic phrase.

The other equally notorious item that has been adduced as a genuine Mycenaean reference is the helmet plated with boar's tusk described in *Il.* 10. 261–5; the book is, incidentally, widely believed to be an addition to the original poem! Here it seems indubitable that a Bronze Age object is being referred to, but the item is described as special and it does not seem impossible that the description was inspired by some relic from the past like the occasional bronze weapon. The characteristic plates have been found in contexts as late as the end of the Bronze Age, and representations, which are still quite common in late Mycenaean art, could also survive: a plaque showing a warrior with such a helmet and a body-covering shield was buried at Delos in a foundation deposit that cannot have been laid down until the late eighth century.[24] But a Dark Age poet could probably not have interpreted a representation correctly (L. Morgan, pers. comm.), unless a relic, or at least plates from it, survived.

References to body-covering shields, particularly Ajax's shield 'like a tower', have also been thought specifically early Mycenaean, but as just noted representations are known in late Mycenaean art, though the twelfth-century warrior scenes show them carrying short shields. Given that no shields have survived *in corpore* from any relevant period, I do not see that it can be proved that body-covering shields were not used in the Dark Age. Some representations of the type known as the 'Dipylon' shield do suggest a long shield, though in general it and other types look short;[25] it has been argued that the 'Dipylon' shield itself is a confused memory of the Mycenaean 'figure of eight' shield and is included in eighth-century scenes to indicate that a heroic reference is intended, but this is a contentious point, and it seems just as likely that a genuine Dark Age shield type is being represented.

Ajax's shield, with its bronze facing on top of seven layers of oxhide, is in any case a practical impossibility because of the weight, and the facing is without Mycenaean parallel; thus, if a genuine Mycenaean reminiscence is involved it is, like the ξίφος ἀργυρόηλον, out of context. The common description of shields as 'bossed' is a point of some interest, for it surely refers to the prominent bronze bosses found in graves of the twelfth and eleventh centuries and again in the eighth century; such a reference, then, is at best very late Mycenaean and will not suit the body-covering type of shield. The extremely elaborate metal facing of Achilles' shield seems likely to have been inspired by Oriental-style bronze shield facings of the kind found in eighth- and seventh-century contexts in Crete;[26] there is no suggestion that Mycenaean shields were decorated in any comparable way.

Finally, the warriors frequently ride to war in chariots and dismount to fight. After years of debate it has been shown, to my mind conclusively, that this is the only way that the chariot was used in the Bronze Age Aegean or Near East, other than as a shooting platform; notions of cavalry-like charges are out of the question, though there is evidence for them later.[27] Descriptions may have been influenced by the early use of the horse to carry hoplites to battle, but this is not forced and there seems no reason why genuine reminiscences of chariot use should not be involved. For as has been pointed out, the eighth-century representations of chariots are so close to twelfth-century representations that it seems easiest to suppose that the chariot survived through the Dark Age, if likely to be obsolescent by the eighth century.[28] The poet, then, is in all probability describing the practice of the past, but not necessarily the remote, Mycenaean past.

A field in which it is much harder to feel confidence in a non-

Mycenaean interpretation is the palace, so constantly the scene of the action in the *Odyssey* that it is possible to build up a detailed if still not totally clear reconstruction. While an element of epic or 'fairy tale' elaboration may be detected in the continual references to finely smoothed stone and total omission of the basic Mycenaean and Dark Age building material, mud brick, and while Priam's palace with its sixty-two bedrooms for his sons and sons-in-law may be inspired by tales of the great palaces of Egypt and the Near East,[29] it is undeniable that what is described in the *Odyssey* is more complex than any Dark Age building so far discovered, but seems to have many features in common with Mycenaean palaces. Increasingly complex buildings of the ninth and eighth century are being discovered, which can provide parallels for such un-Mycenaean features as a side-entrance to the 'megaron', but none have so far produced evidence of a second storey and none have any distinction as architecture.[30] But there are many features of the account that cannot easily be squared with what is known of Mycenaean palaces and should not be discounted. There is no reference to the characteristic Mycenaean use of fine plaster, often decorated with painted scenes or patterns, on the floors and walls, even in the courtyard; rather, the 'megaron's' floor seems to be plain earth, and it and the yard (which in Odysseus' palace contains a dung heap) are used for the butchering, cooking, and eating of animals in a way that is scarcely possible to envisage in the central room of a Mycenaean 'megaron'-suite. Nor is there any mention of the great ceremonial hearth that dominates this room in the main Mycenaean palaces and would, with its flanking columns, make the use of the room by more than a few people extremely uncomfortable! The palace and yard are enclosed by a fence or wall with lockable outer door, and despite the supposed splendour guests seem to sleep in a makeshift manner in the anteroom to the 'megaron' or perhaps a sheltered area around the edge of the yard. One gets the impression that a veneer of elaboration, which might include Mycenaean reminiscences, is being imposed on a fairly simple kind of big farmhouse. More general references to dwellings are indistinct, and the clearest account of a town, that of the Phaeacians, with its city wall and market place containing a god's temple or shrine, is generally reckoned to be more like a Greek town than anything Bronze Age.[31]

Thus, in my view, many features of the setting, including some of the most fundamental, contain at best the occasional, not always very convincing, Mycenaean reference, and a strong Dark Age element. But even those sceptical about all else have generally been prepared to see genuine Bronze Age tradition in features of the geography, the places and peoples mentioned. It must be commented that overall the picture of the non-Greek world is unreal in a way characteristic of epic and folktale, presenting all peoples as mutually intelligible and as living in much the same way.

Yet it is undeniable that any reference to Troy as a great centre can only be Bronze Age, since the site always believed in antiquity to be that of Homer's Troy was an insignificant Greek settlement in the eighth century, though the Bronze Age remains suggest at best an important fortress, not the great walled city of Homer. But most of the allies of the Trojans will be sought for in vain in those Hittite records that appear to deal with western Anatolia; they seem rather to be the neighbours of the later Greeks of Asia Minor and the north Aegean, though under 'old-fashioned' names in some cases. Similarly, the Phoenicians or Sidonians who figure as great traders, the source of many exotic items, are surely a feature of the Dark Age, when many elaborate and precious items of Near Eastern craftsmanship did indeed find their way to Greece;[32] such items are rare in the Mycenaean world, which could produce its own fine work. So the picture of the non-Greek world is, at the least, heavily tinged with features of the recent past and present.

But the famous Catalogue of Ships in *Iliad* 2 as analysed by a series of scholars, most recently R. Hope Simpson and J. F. Lazenby,[33] has convinced many that it contains a great deal of genuine information about Mycenaean Greece, to the extent that it is sometimes argued, 'If this is largely Mycenaean, why should not a good deal more be?' But it does not convince me. It would be possible to write a whole paper on this topic alone, but I will try to confine myself to the most significant points. First, if it is to be considered a list of Mycenaean sites, some explanation for the choice of these particular sites is needed. It has long been clear that it cannot be a list of all inhabited sites of the period, since far more are now known in every region, but neither can it be a list of the more significant sites in each region, as one might perhaps expect. For many sites that have been identified, often rather shakily, as Catalogue sites seem from the scanty remains to have been totally insignificant in Mycenaean times, including sites that figure largely in the poems, like Sparta, which is consistently presented as Menelaus' capital.[34] In fact, there are sites whose presence is inexplicable by such means; there are sites which, though evidently important in Mycenaean times, seem not to be represented; and there are sites like Styra and Carystus in Euboea which have obstinately refused to produce Mycenaean remains—a point of some interest, since the sites listed for Euboea are precisely those which were significant centres in Greek times, and no others, a situation paralleled in Rhodes, where the Mycenaean evidence suggests that more sites should be listed, if anything.[35]

The whole process by which the Catalogue sites are identified by Hope Simpson and Lazenby is not beyond criticism. As Chadwick has pointed out, it involves the assembling of all indications as to where a named site was, or was thought to be, and looking for a Mycenaean site on or near that place; but since Mycenaean sites are so numerous there is bound to be one on or near most classical sites, so that the coincidence is not surprising; it would only be significant if Mycenaean sites were rare.[36] Moreover, the argument is in constant danger of being circular, for the presence of Mycenaean material, especially in quantity, has often been treated as an argument in favour of the identification, which can prove embarrassing when research reveals the existence of several possible candidates, as in the case of Dorion.[37] It hardly needs pointing out that if a site has been deserted since the prehistoric period, we have no means of knowing what its name was, and the presence of Mycenaean material is not, on its own, an argument, since it assumes what is required to be proved, that the Catalogue is a list of Mycenaean names. West has also commented, 'But a Mycenaean site can only be tied to a Homeric name with any certainty where the name survived locally, whether or not there was continued occupation; in which case it was available to a poet of any period.'[38] One might add that local pride might well lead to the attachment of a Homeric name to some ancient site, whether or not this was its real name.

But it is not my purpose to deny that the Catalogue contains any information that could derive from the Mycenaean period, rather to argue that it is so thoroughly mixed, like the artefactual references, that it cannot yield a consistent picture of any age or indicate a single major source. When Hope Simpson and Lazenby suggest that more than one Mycenaean phase is being referred to,[39] then the whole case for trying to refer the Catalogue to a single period at all seems to fall to the ground. Such a repetitive, formulaic composition could be expanded at will, and we know from the famous account in Herodotus of the dispute over Salamis between Athens and Megara that there were variant versions in the sixth century. Even leaving aside various minor irritants, like the prominence of the Boeotians, whom tradition, as reported by Thucydides, brought to Boeotia *after* the Trojan War,[40] and others already mentioned, the description of the two states in the Peloponnese that were certainly important in Mycenaean times seems totally at odds with the likely Mycenaean reality.

Analysis of the Linear B tablets of Pylos has demonstrated which are the local administrative centres of the state ruled from Pylos and provided many other place names. Apart from Pylos itself, only one other adminis-trative centre and one, perhaps two, other place names in the tablets are repeated in the nine sites named in the Catalogue, and such indications as there are seem to place the whole centre of gravity of the Pylian state, as envisaged by Homer, much further north, while in the *Odyssey* Pylos is quite clearly envisaged as on or very near the coast, like classical Pylos and unlike the Mycenaean site.[41] In no way can the two accounts be squared, not even by the desperate expedient of assuming that this is a post-palatial Mycenaean Pylos, since archaeologically such indications as there are suggest some survival in the neighbourhood of the palace, but nothing very much further north until the Olympia region. Whatever the Catalogue represents, it hardly seems to be any kind of Mycenaean Pylos.

In the north Peloponnese the picture is even more clear, because we are better informed. In the Catalogue this is divided between the kingdoms of Agamemnon, based at Mycenae, and Diomedes, based at Argos. The places named are almost entirely those which were centres of petty states at one time if not throughout the Greek historical period, few of which seem to have had much significance in Mycenaean times except as local centres of population. There seems no reason why they should be named in preference to such Mycenaean centres as Dendra, the third great fortress of the Argolid after Mycenae and Tiryns, whose ancient name was probably Midea, or Nauplia and Prosymna, both of which have notably large chamber tomb cemeteries, nor why Argos, arguably less important than any of these, should be elevated to near-equality with Mycenae. This could never correspond to reality: the Argive plain can support several little centres or one big one, but not *two* big independent states, and in any case Mycenae could never have been important without control of the Argive plain and access to the sea through it. It cannot even reflect twelfth-century conditions, when Tiryns seems the great centre of the Argolid, while Mycenae still seems substantial and Argos is not particularly prominent.

The prominence of Argos is in fact characteristic of Greek tradition as a whole, which makes Argos older than Mycenae and bases more legends upon it: the great expedition of the Seven Against Thebes was mounted from Argos, and in the *Iliad* Agamemnon is made to give a very lame explanation of why Mycenae was not involved in the expedition.[42] This is surely an attempt to reconcile two different cycles of legend, respectively treating Mycenae and Argos as the great centre of the Argolid, and one might suspect that the legendary prominence of Argos reflects the histori-cal fact that from at least the tenth century it was the great centre, and may involve the attraction to Argos of legends originally associated with other centres—thus, Adrastus, leader of the Seven Against Thebes, has a strong association with Sicyon.[43] Thus, in the Catalogue Argos is given all the Argolid except Mycenae, since the tradition of Mycenae's importance could not be wholly ignored; to compensate, Mycenae is given a stretch of territory to the north and north-west, containing a string of sites of no particular Mycenaean significance and in some cases, as in that of 'rich' Corinth, surely reflecting a much later period. Corinth is not noticeably richer than half a hundred other sites in Mycenaean times, but was one of the great Greek centres in the eighth century if not earlier.

I suspect that there are many more cases where such 'political' considerations have affected the entries (e.g., the citing of Athens alone for
Attica), if they have not given birth to them entirely. In some places an
ancient tradition may be preserved: the only time that the Ionian islands,
the territory attributed to Odysseus, were of much importance was in the
twelfth and eleventh centuries, a time when there were also flourishing
centres in Aetolia, the province of Calydon, which is famous in legend but
not impressive as a Mycenaean site. But it is probably wasted effort trying
to guess the sources of the Catalogue entries.

When in so many different areas the Mycenaean element in the poems
seems at best exiguous and is often wholly disputable, and the Dark Age
element can be suggested to be large, it seems much easier to me to
swallow hard and accept that the Homeric poems relate most frequently
to the Dark Age. Their whole milieu seems better suited to this, a milieu
in which raiding and petty warfare are commonplace, horizons are limited
and news hard to get, government is personal and its foundations somewhat uncertain, depending upon the qualities of its wielders. There is
nothing here of the organized and, for some time at least, stable societies
dominated by the Mycenaean palaces. Indeed, it is not clear to me that
Homer understands kingship at all; much of the time, his references suit
better an aristocratic society, in which the heads of noble houses wield
power in federation.[44] The anarchy that prevails in Ithaca in Odysseus'
absence is an impossibility in a proper monarchy, which would have a
regent or other officials to stand in for the king; but the whole concept of
officers of government, common enough in the Linear B texts, seems alien
to Homer. (Here, though, it may be a mistake to try to wring social and
political data from a picture developed for artistic reasons; it is artistically
necessary that Telemachus should appear helpless, without even the
support of relatives, which in any period of Greek history he might
expect.) Further, Agamemnon is not the legal overlord of the Achaeans,
merely the army commander by consent, and Achilles can only be urged
to show him respect because his power is greater and he is senior. Such a
picture might suit monarchy in decline, when the collapse of stability has
removed some of its traditional props; the notion that a king can expect
obedience as of right seems to be wholly absent.

Once the unreal trappings of heroic splendour are stripped away, the
world of the poems is small-scale. Wealth is measured largely in livestock
rather than estates, a feature which may well reflect a Dark Age preoccupation. Rulers and their families can and do manage most things for
themselves; although slaves are mentioned, Nausicaa is in charge of the
linen cupboard in her father's palace, Nestor's daughter gives Telemachus
a bath, and Menelaus' guests drive sheep for his feast to the palace themselves, while their wives send in bread![45] This is a picture of a society

dominated by rustic aristocrats, who are just farmers on a larger scale; on Achilles' shield, a 'king' watches the harvesting of his estate, while Odysseus can handle a plough and seriously challenge, while in disguise, an Ithacan noble to a ploughing match. Such things cannot have seemed totally incongruous to Homer's audience, and they are hardly the effect of the poetic tradition, which tends to glorify and is hardly interested in such mundane matters as ploughing. Even aristocrats are essentially poor; Menelaus' fabulous wealth is accumulated through receiving, in his travels, the customary gifts to men of standing, and Odysseus presents himself as doing the same thing.[46] As Finley's analysis has shown, gift-giving is a basic feature of Homeric society, and it is not the sort of feature that one would expect to be basic to the world of the Mycenaean palaces, which was also basically agricultural and rather small scale, but far more organized. Its rulers could use their resources, partly derived from systematic taxation, to finance relatively vast building projects and to support hundreds of dependents of various sorts; they had no need to indulge in cattle raids, and if they went to war it would hardly be over stolen livestock or, for that matter, women.

Homer, then, is clothing in a garb of his own day or of the recent past, which might still have seemed quite remote to his audience, traditional material whose actual age is unguessable, but which had almost certainly undergone repeated changes by his time. If the Trojan War was a historical event, it is conceived in Dark Age or purely imaginary terms. Because so often his characters and their world are realized with great vividness— more, I would say, than in any other epic—the incongruities caused by the juxtaposition of heroic splendour and down-to-earth reality cease to be noticed, and petty details of artefacts represented and discrepancies in the account of them will scarcely concern the audience. Those who take the poems as a realistic and comprehensive description of a society and an age, whether Thucydides or modern scholars, are in my view bound to be wrong; but to accept that Homer has most relevance to the Dark Age is, I submit, the only reasonable conclusion to draw from the evidence.

NOTES

1. I would like to dedicate this paper to the memory of Dorothea Gray, my first teacher in Homeric and Mycenaean archaeology. I am grateful to Mr Trevor Rowley, Director of the Department of External Studies at Oxford, for the invitation to give the lecture upon which it is based. Though I have discussed this topic with many colleagues over the years, I take full responsibility for all views expressed.

2. The most comprehensive discussion of the Homeric sources is H. L. Lorimer, *Homer and the Monuments* (London, 1950), now rather outdated but still very valuable. The most recent survey of the topic in some detail is J. V. Luce, *Homer and the Heroic Age* (London, 1975). The most accessible and comprehensive discussion of the Dark Age is A. M. Snodgrass, *The Dark Age of Greece* (Edinburgh, 1971); V. R. Desborough, *The Greek Dark Ages* (London, 1972) covers the

eleventh and tenth centuries, and J. N. Coldstream, *Geometric Greece* (London, 1977) the ninth and eighth, with greater concentration on archaeological detail.

3. The most consistent proponent of a specifically Dark Age setting for the poems has been Sir Moses Finley, principally in *The World of Odysseus* (2nd edn. London, 1977). Some important comments are made by G. S. Kirk, *CAH*[3] Vol. II:2, Ch. XXXIX(b), and Snodgrass, *JHS* 94 (1974), 114–25; see also J. Chadwick, *Diogenes* 77 (1972), 1–13.

4. *Greece in the Bronze Age* (Chicago, 1964), x.

5. Finley, op. cit., 17.

6. Some of these points were made as long ago as M. P. Nilsson, *The Mycenaean Origin of Greek Mythology* (Berkeley, 1932), 3–4, 31, 187; see also for general comments J. R. Goody (ed.), *Literacy in Traditional Societies* (Cambridge, 1968), 30–4, and for more specific comments relevant to Homer and Greek mythology Finley, op. cit., 47, 170–1, and P. Cartledge, *Sparta and Lakonia* (London, 1979), ch. 5 and Appendix 2. On the Irish material see D. Ó. Corráin, *Ireland Before the Normans* (Dublin, 1972), 74–8.

7. Stesichorus seems to have been the first to associate Agamemnon and Orestes with Sparta; Pindar (*Pythians* 11.32) has Amyclae. The motive is surely the legitimation of Spartan claims to primacy in the Peloponnese as against Argos; cf. Cartledge, op. cit., 138–9 and Hdt. 7.159.

8. J. Chadwick, *The Mycenaean World* (Cambridge, 1976), 183.

9. *CQ* 67 (1973), 179–92, especially 187–8.

10. *Il.* 23.826–35.

11. The identity of 'Homer's Troy' continues to be disputed as between the last phase of Troy VI and Troy VIIA, and the absolute dates given to the ends of these two phases continue to range quite widely. It has even been argued that Troy VIIA dates to Late Helladic IIIC, so after 1200, although the indications from recent work near Troy do not seem to support this (cf. *Archaeological Reports for 1989–90*, 94); renewed excavations at Troy itself under the direction of M. Korfmann are producing new and important evidence bearing on this. But the general tendency is to place the Trojan War, and with it 'Homer's world', somewhere in the later Mycenaean palace period, and it is the basis of this approach that I wish to question.

12. See, e.g., J. Gantz, *Early Irish Myths and Sagas* (London, 1982), *passim*; also N. K. Sandars, *The Epic of Gilgamesh* (London, 1960), 73, 83, 86, 93.

13. See M. R. Popham, L. H. Sackett, and P. G. Themelis, *Lefkandi I* (Oxford, 1980), especially 168–96 on the Toumba cemetery (on which see also *BSA* 77 [1982], 213–48), and M. R. Popham, E. Touloupa, and L. H. Sackett, *Antiquity* 56 (1982), 169–76 on the 'Heroön'.

14. Anticleia's words (*Od.* 11.218–22) imply that it is normal, as does its use for the Greek and Trojan dead in general (*Il.* 7.417–32) and for the insignificant Elpenor (*Od.* 12.11–15); in no case is there a suggestion that it is an abnormal rite forced by circumstance, as the theory that it was adopted from the Trojans during the Trojan War would require.

15. D. Kurtz and J. Boardman, *Greek Burial Customs* (London, 1971), 27; the larnakes are in fact earlier than suggested there.

16. See most recently W. Burkert, *Greek Religion* (Oxford, 1985), 43–6 on the Linear B evidence, 51–2 on the absence of Apollo and Aphrodite (and 47–53 generally on continuity into and through the Dark Age), 149 with n. 3 on doubts over Artemis, and Chadwick, op. cit., 88 on doubts over Athene. Pa-ja-wo =Paieon is a separate god from Apollo even in Homer (*Il.* 6.899–900, *Od.* 4.232), so cannot represent him.

17. Delphi as an oracle, *Od.* 8.79–81, as wealthy, surely because of dedications, *Il.* 9.904–5.

18. *Od.* 19.226–31; the closest parallels seem late eighth or seventh century.

19. Lorimer, op. cit., ch. VI, especially 378–80 on Hera's use of two fasteners to pin her dress.

20. *Il.* 14.182–3, *Od.* 18.296–7; cf. Popham, Sackett, and Themelis, op. cit., 221, Pl. 231d; *BSA* 77 (1982), Pl. 30(b) shows a related form. See R. Higgins, *Greek and Roman Jewellery* (London, 1961), 72–3 on Mycenaean earrings generally.

21. See the discussion in Coldstream, op. cit., 334–8.

22. *Archaeological Reports for 1979–80*, 29, Fig. 50: a sherd from Tiryns.

23. Lorimer, op. cit., 273; *CAH*[3] III: 1, 531.

24. Probably the latest context is a Sub-Minoan grave at Knossos (*Archaeological Reports for 1982–83*, 53); see Luce, op. cit., 103–4 for some other late contexts and representations. For the

Delos plaque see *CAH³* Plates to Vols I and II, Pl. 124(c), and on the context, Coldstream, op. cit., 215.

25. Especially A. M. Snodgrass, *Early Greek Armour and Weapons* (Edinburgh, 1964), fig. 15b; in fig. 27 and in *BSA* 67 (1972), pls. 5c, 10a, the shields look long, but the whole leg below the knee seems to be shown.

26. See Coldstream, op. cit., 287–8.

27. J. H. Crouwel, *Chariots and Other Means of Land Transport in Bronze Age Greece* (Amsterdam, 1981), ch. VI, especially 121–4; also Crouwel, *BICS* 25 (1978), 174–5.

28. Crouwel, op. cit., 72–3, also 143–4 on likely obsolescence.

29. *Il.* 6.242–50; cf. Lorimer, op. cit., 431.

30. On this general topic, see M. O. Knox, *CQ* 67 (1973), 1–21 and H. Plommer, *JHS* 97 (1977), 75–83. Unit IV–1 in its later form at Nichoria (W. A. McDonald, W. D. E. Coulson, and J. Rosser, *Excavations at Nichoria in Southwest Greece* Vol. III [Minneapolis, 1983], 33–40) has a side-entrance, also a small fenced yard; it is probably ninth century, at latest early eighth, in date.

31. *Od.* 6.9–10 and 262–7.

32. J. D. Muhly, *Berytus* 19 (1970), 17–64.

33. *The Catalogue of Ships in Homer's Iliad* (Oxford, 1970).

34. Apart from the reference in the Catalogue of Ships, it is named at *Il.* 4.52, *Od.* 1.93 and 285, 2.214, 327, and 359, 4.10, 11.460, and 13.412, frequently as the equivalent of Nestor's Pylos and/or in the company of other known towns, Mycenae, Argos, and Orchomenos. As noted by Cartledge, op. cit., 338, the name of the Menelaion site, the most important known in late Mycenaean Laconia, was most probably Therapne; its absence from the Catalogue presents yet another problem to the 'Mycenaean' interpretation, since it was occupied in both the thirteenth and twelfth centuries.

35. See A. Giovannini, *Étude Historique sur les Origines du Catalogue des Vaisseaux* (Berne, 1969), 25, 31. This neglected study has gathered a great deal of useful information on the existence in the seventh century and later, so probably earlier too, of the majority of the Catalogue sites, though the ultimate conclusion, that the Catalogue is based on the itinerary of Delphic *thearodokoi*, is hard to accept.

36. *Minos* 14 (1973), 57.

37. See, for example, Hope Simpson and Lazenby, op. cit., 19 (Hyria), 44 (Lilaia), 128 (Alope), and on Dorion 85, with which compare McDonald and Hope Simpson, *AJA* 73 (1969), 141 under Malthi (Vasiliko). Giovannini's comments on the assumptions involved in the identification of Hyria, Dorion, and also Pylos and Krisa, op. cit., 19–21, seem perfectly just.

38. West, op. cit., 191–2.

39. Op. cit., 162–9; cf. also Hope Simpson, *Mycenaean Greece* (New Jersey, 1981), 251.

40. Thuc. 1.12.3; the explanation for their presence in the Trojan War is notably lame, since what is in question is not some Boeotians but a contingent representing almost the whole of classical Boeotia.

41. Cf. Chadwick, *Minos* 14 (1973), 55–8; the references in *Od.* 3.4 and 386–7 imply a virtually coastal location.

42. *Il.* 4.376–81, the excuse being that Zeus sent bad omens.

43. Cf. *Il.* 2.572 and Hdt. 5.67.

44. E.g., *Od.* 11.184–7, where Telemachus takes it in turn to be host and guest, 'as a justice-dealing man should', the implication being that those who feast him are also justice-dealing men of comparable status; cf. *Il.* 18.503–6; also *Od.* 21.21, when Odysseus' father 'and the other elders' send him on a public errand.

45. *Od.* 4.622–3, a reference not normally cited, to my knowledge.

46. *Od.* 4.81–5, 90–1; cf. 128–9 for Menelaus, 19.283–6, 293–5 for Odysseus.

ADDENDUM

I have not kept myself fully informed on all the topics covered or alluded to in this paper, and do not wish to reconsider it in detail here. I have revised the text in places, to correct errors, clarify arguments, and reflect comments received on certain points, have changed footnote 11 to take some account of new archaeological finds, and would like to comment very briefly on recent developments in the literature.

An essentially 'Dark Age' interpretation of Homer is being offered increasingly often, as in the important studies of Morris[1] and Whitley,[2] who have argued on various grounds that the Homeric setting is largely late Dark Age. The study by E. S. Sherratt,[3] which provides useful references for the whole discussion in recent years to 1989, argues that the epic tradition was first created in the early Mycenaean period, the sixteenth and fifteenth centuries B.C., but that it was substantially re-created in the Dark Age. The recent tendency of studies which make much use of the archaeology is thus to accept the basic point that Finley argued, and which my paper was trying to establish, that the background of the Homeric poems cannot be reconciled with what we know of the world of the Mycenaean palaces. This is in contrast with the prevailing tendency until recently, which has been to stress Mycenaean connections almost to the exclusion of all else. Obviously, I welcome this development, and hope that it will eventually feed through to comment in general works and ultimately school teaching materials, children's encyclopaedias, and guide-books.

Sherratt's paper deserves some further comment, for it contains major contributions to the debate, particularly its comments on the social context of the epic tradition and its proposed explanation of the survival of apparently Mycenaean references through a process of 'layering'. It is argued that this reflects a situation in which some structural elements of the poems are far more likely to be altered fairly frequently than others, which may therefore preserve more archaic references and even vocabulary.[4] Obviously this would work best if the hypothetical early Mycenaean epic was already in something like hexameter form, and Sherratt, while not considering this to be a requirement of the theory, sees no reason why it should not have been (pers. comm.). I am straying here into areas of which I have very little specialized knowledge, but I find it very difficult to believe that the hexameter could have had a history of seven or eight hundred years before the form in which it is found in Homer, where in some respects it still seems incompletely developed (e.g., the treating of syllables as 'long' simply because they are stressed). I would like to see more detailed arguments against my suggestion that the tradition could have begun with simpler verse-forms and that the formulaic system was largely developed to fit the more complex hexameter metre,[5] so that formulaic phrases incorporating Mycenaean references could have been devised in the Dark Age, though quite possibly drawing on older models; 'layering' of a kind could still occur, since I would regard the tradition as continuous, but its medium as changing. Admittedly, this suggestion was undeveloped, and Sherratt has rightly pointed out to me (pers. comm.) that the introduction or development of the hexameter metre still needs proper explanation in a social context.

It could also be questioned whether the early Mycenaean period was quite as fluid and 'heroic' as Sherratt's argument would suggest. Society in the Aegean during this period, dominated culturally if not politically by the

Minoan civilization, seems considerably more stable and organized than in the Dark Age; but it was a period in which new powers were establishing themselves on the mainland and ultimately in the Aegean, and the processes involved could arguably have become simplified into tales of epic deeds. Certainly, explanations like Sherratt's, which try to re-create the social conditions in which the epic tradition was developed, transmitted, and changed, are surely essential steps towards an answer to the 'Homeric question'.

NOTES TO ADDENDUM

1. *Classical Antiquity* 5 (1986), 81–138; cf. I. Morris, *Burial and Ancient Society* (Cambridge, 1987), 45–7.

2. *BSA* 86 (1991), 341–65; cf. J. Whitley, *Style and Society in Dark Age Greece* (Cambridge, 1991), 34–9.

3. *Antiquity* 64 (1990), 807–24.

4. It is now being suggested that in a somewhat analogous way details were constantly being added and changed during the transmission of the most archaic-seeming Irish heroic tales; cf. R. P. Mallory on the sword in the Ulster Cycle in B. Scott (ed.), *Studies in Early Ireland* (Belfast, 1981), 99–114.

5. An analogy I have in mind, admittedly remote in time and space and involving a different social setting, is the great elaboration of language that accompanied the development of more complex metre in Old Norse skaldic poetry; cf. E. O. G. Turville-Petre, *Myth and Religion of the North* (London, 1964), 14–16.

THE SEARCH FOR THE REAL HOMER[1]

By G. S. KIRK

I am not of course going to talk about a very concrete person, a little bearded man who lived in Chios or Smyrna. Yet that there was someone called Homer, who was primarily responsible for the creation of the *Iliad* at least, I take for granted, and accordingly spare you the old jokes. They applied to an entirely different situation in scholarship from the one we have today, and the cause of the difference is the realization that the Homeric poems are in essence oral rather than written poetry.

The *Iliad* and *Odyssey* (and I shall be talking mainly about the first of these) can be seen to be oral in essence because their expression depends on a system of standard phrases and verbal formulas so elaborate, and at the same time so strictly functional, that it must be the product of a tradition developed over several generations of singers. Modern heroic poetry in Russia and Yugoslavia has demonstrated how such a tradition works, though the oral singers of those regions, now almost extinct, have never created formular systems so rich as the Homeric one. Those who are not familiar with these concepts can take it that they are well documented and broadly accepted. Apart from language and phraseology, many of the narrative components, the motifs and themes, of oral heroic poems are also formular. The singer acquires a wide range of standard incidents that can be varied in length and reference to suit the needs of a chosen situation, much as a standard phrase is selected to suit the needs of metre and immediate verbal context. Moreover for any general theme, for example a duel between two warriors, the tradition provided a variety of standard patterns: A throws a spear at B and misses, B hits A but does not pierce his armour, A kills B with a second spear-throw; or A throws at B and hits someone else, B does likewise, B throws again and misses, A throws again and kills B. The variety is not of course infinite, and in the great number of such encounters in the *Iliad* certain patterns are never used; for example it is permissible to throw a stone once, but not a second time. The range of possibilities is not arbitrary (as its recent and highly effective exponent, Bernard Fenik, tends perhaps to imply),[2] but is controlled by what is heroic and appropriate. The truly heroic weapon is the spear, with sword, stone, and arrow progressively less so; and the man who has hit but failed to kill must not be allowed to succeed with a second blow—for his first failure is an indication of weakness, or that the gods are against him.

It's a strange kind of poetry, highly conventionalized yet infinitely various in appearance.[3] It can be judged in different ways, either as it might appear to the kind of audience for which it was created—listeners, not readers—or as it appears to a modern scholar who uses a written text but tries to analyse the poem in relation to its original oral conditions. What one must not do is automatically to apply the same criteria to an oral poem as to a written one; to say, for instance, that repeated passages or phrases are *either* careless *or* designed to produce a special effect. It has become fashionable to claim that one needs a particular kind of oral poetics, a substantially new set of rules of criticism that are appropriate to the methods and intentions of the oral singer as distinct from the poet as writer. That is probably going too far   at least no one has succeeded in naming such rules at any level above the obvious; and certain critics have begun to observe that where oral poetry is deeply revealing or moving, it may often be for just such reasons as would apply to a literate poet—for instance that a profound or suggestive insight is strikingly and appropriately expressed.

An oral tradition is likely to be enormously complex, because each singer makes his own selection from it and contributes a little to it, for better or worse. Many oral singers and audiences seem to enjoy elaboration and the accumulation of detail for their own sake, and in pre-war Yugoslavia the 'good' singer was often the one who, as well as having an extensive repertory, could stretch a typical passage (mounting a war-horse, for instance) to unusual length. We see the same sort of thing in Homer. Scenes in which a hero puts on his armour occur several times in the *Iliad* and follow the same general pattern, but some of them are more detailed and longer than others—indeed it is the rule that the more important the hero, the longer such scenes become. The oral epic singer works cumulatively, adding standard phrase to standard phrase and building up a whole scene by adding theme to typical theme. Each singer has his own favourite phrases, patterns, and methods of cumulation derived from the tradition, and every version of a poem (which means the poem as it happens to come out at any particular performance, for it varies a little each time) is a mixture of traditional elements and personal omissions or choices. One consequence is that you can only completely distinguish the qualities of an individual singer if you can hear him in action time after time, and compare his versions with those of others.

This is all highly relevant to what I have called the 'real' Homer. Homer was an individual singer who came near the end of a long tradition of heroic poetry; he presumably acquired a repertory of songs from other singers and reproduced them in his own manner. Most of the language and incident of his *Iliad* is 'typical' in one way or other, and must be the gift of the tradition; Homer took over the tradition and used it, yet he certainly made his own special contribution to it. What we wish to know, therefore, if we are interested in this 'real' Homer, is roughly what this contribution was. For his reality, to us, beyond the fact that he belonged to an oral heroic tradition, amounts to his special qualities as a poet. He has no biological or biographical substance; we know his name and approximately when and where he lived, but that tells us next to nothing. It is as a poet, and purely as a poet, that Homer concerns us, and I do not care if he wore purple shirts, hated his father, or enjoyed the favours of Nausicaa. That kind of thing might tell us something about a Shelley; but Shelley, poetry and all, belongs to a tangible historical context. Homer does not; he is a shadow, or rather a voice, and the only thing we can hope to know of him, the only reality we can give him, is the unique quality of this voice. That is what we want to know—not just from meddlesome curiosity or pedantic *horror vacui*, but because his poetry can only be adequately understood when we learn how to relate its strictly creative aspect, the imagination and taste of a poetic individual, to the dense background of the inherited tradition.

One thing we can say about him without further delay: he is the singer primarily responsible for a poem of quite exceptional length. It is a fair inference that oral poems were commonly designed to be sung on a single occasion—during a single morning, afternoon, or evening. Nearly all oral heroic songs collected in modern communities accord with this expectation, and most of those that do not have been responses to some special challenge or inducement. Milman Parry and his follower A. B. Lord were justifiably impressed with the length of one song they recorded in Yugoslavia, an extraordinary version of 'The Wedding of Smailagić Meho'. This version, by Avdo Međedović, has won a certain *réclame* because it contains around 16,000 verses, little fewer than the *Iliad*. But the facts are that the verses are short, the style is redundant, and the song was only spun out to such length at the special insistence of Milman Parry.[4] Other long poems have been noted from South Russia, but again the element of experiment or bravado is often present. The conclusion that nearly all oral poems are designed to be given at a single session is not seriously damaged. It is a reasonable guess, therefore, that the Greek epic tradition on which Homer drew for the *Iliad* was primarily composed of songs of this functional length. A few somewhat longer ones might have occupied the best part of a day or filled the intervals of a protracted wedding feast; efforts used to be made to trace such larger units within the *Iliad* itself, but they were unsuccessful, and it is significant that the *Odyssey*, which gives repeated descriptions of two oral singers at work, Phemius in Ithaca and Demodocus among the Phaeacians, implies clearly enough that their songs were quite short and given on a single occasion. Obviously the *Iliad* is a highly unusual affair, and apart from the *Odyssey* itself there was probably nothing like it in the oral epic tradition. I cannot give the whole argument here; but in short it looks as though Homer invented the concept of a truly monumental epic. The circumstances in which his *Iliad* was sung remain a mystery; neither royal feast nor religious festival meets the demands; the Greeks themselves reveal nothing, at least until the time when the two great epics were recited in literate circumstances at the great festival of Athene at Athens. Yet a point I have tried to emphasize in the past is that a great singer, one who wins a prodigious reputation for his powers, can *impose* an unusual and unfunctional song on his audience, and that the ideal occasion is not in these circumstances necessary.[5]

One aspect of Homer's individuality as a poet, then, is his concept of the monumental poem. That he should have had the inspiration of massive length and the ability to fulfil it, then to impose the result on others so that it survived into the era of developed literacy, reveals something important about him. Yet it is also true that the great length and scope even of the *Iliad* are to a large extent the result of accumulation, of piling traditional theme on theme and of magnifying typical patterns of action by the multiplication of familiar details. It is theoretically conceivable that virtually everything in the *Iliad* is derived from the tradition—that Homer is primarily a superb blender and organizer of an exceptionally wide repertory. Personally, I am convinced that he did much more than that; but in any case the whole central plan of the poem and its complex characterization, much fuller than can be expected for a short heroic song, of themselves presuppose special gifts, the nature of which we could broadly catalogue. The resulting list would still, admittedly, be a bloodless and abstract affair, containing entries like 'an unusual capacity for describing characters in depth'. We need to go beyond that if we are to catch sight of the real Homer. At the very least we need to be able to identify one or two specific passages that are peculiar to him, that reveal something of his own taste and style. Even then we should be dealing with an amalgam between individual and tradition, for we cannot in any case expect to come upon him creating freely, as a literate poet might, and without drawing heavily on typical theme and language. He was still an oral poet (as the persistently formular colouring of almost every part of the *Iliad* shows), and oral poets do not work like that.

With that reservation, I begin the search for such special passages by disposing of some familiar suggestions. First, one cannot baldly say that all the best bits are by Homer because Homer was a great poet, and that the rest belongs to the tradition. Some of Homer's predecessors were good singers too, and the quality of even the apparently oldest components of the *Iliad* is quite high. Conversely, since oral poetry tends by nature to be a little uneven, Homer himself may not have been invariably successful. Of course he is likely to have been a better poet, over all, than his predecessors, quite apart from questions of scale; I am merely pointing out that if we want a reliable test of Homer's own work then we cannot apply the criterion of quality alone, even supposing it could be measured. A second common assumption, seldom systematically discussed, is that, if the tradition deals with the standard and the typical, then anything untypical or unique is likely to be by Homer. In general, of course, every singer does tend to contribute something personal and new, and no doubt Homer did so more than most. Achilles passionately rejects the embassy in the ninth book of the *Iliad*, and in his speech heroic formulas are distorted so as to cast doubt on the ethos they were designed to express; this belongs to a poet working in a developed oral tradition, but with a broader conception of life than the tradition had allowed for.[6] That may well mean Homer himself—but the passage is without real parallel, and certainly does not entail that other untypical passages are also Homeric. They may, for example, be later than Homer. A few parts of the *Iliad* were certainly subjected to rhapsodic elaboration; I do not go nearly so far in this respect as the old analysts, but the night expedition in the tenth book, for instance, which results in the killing of the Trojan spy Dolon, is full of unique details of language and circumstance. It is not for that reason by Homer; on the contrary, it is almost certainly a post-Homeric accretion. Parts of the *pre*-Homeric tradition, also, may appear as untypical, often because of an unusual subject. Odysseus' building of a raft to escape from Calypso's island results in an untypical description; but no one can say that raft-building episodes had not been sung before Homer, even though they did not happen to survive in a standardized form.

Another suggestion has been that one might look for Homer's touch in obvious joining-passages, since he quite certainly had to weld together pre-existing episodes to make his monumental poem. Even if the criterion were viable, it would only tell us about Homer as a poet of joining-passages, and that is relatively uninteresting. Yet the idea, feeble as it is in practice, may be on the correct theoretical lines in trying to distinguish Homer by his special *functions* within the *Iliad*. If we are right in holding Homer responsible for the *Iliad*'s exceptional scale, then particular concomitants of that scale are likely to reveal his own poetical choice and direction. We have, therefore, to look for passages that are inextricably connected with the monumental plot as such; passages that are unlikely to belong, as they now stand, to the much shorter songs that we suppose to have been the rule in pre-Homeric poetry. That means, I suggest, three types of passage. First, those of very large scale in themselves, that are too full, leisurely, and lacking in episode or narrative content to have occurred in a song of say 500 to 1000 verses. Second, passages of special verbal complexity, such as would not be likely to arise in the ordinary tradition and, if they had arisen, would soon have lapsed because they were incompatible with the singers' normal techniques. Third, passages that belong essentially to the crucial turning-points of the monumental poem, that are likely to form part of the conception of the large-scale plot and not of any shorter song.

Even these three criteria are pretty hair-raising. We cannot be sure that occasional longer poems in the tradition did not contain leisurely sequences, or that an unusually complex passage was not the work of one of Homer's teachers rather than himself; even the basic association of monumental conception with Homer is conjectural. But let us proceed and see what happens. I deal first with scale and complexity, but it is the third criterion, of the crucial turning-points of the monumental plot, that deserves the closest consideration.

The most obvious kind of large-scale description in either *Iliad* or *Odyssey* might seem to occur in the extended battle-narratives of the *Iliad*. Yet martial poetry was a long-standing traditional genre, and to claim all of it as specifically Homeric would be absurd. The truth is, in any case, that the battle-descriptions in the *Iliad*, with a few significant exceptions to which I shall return, are not really large in scale at all; they are composed of a succession of small-scale individual encounters cumulated one upon the other. The effect is of detailed and complex action, but the description of any particular event is cursory. What I have in mind, rather, is well represented by a scene in the *Odyssey*: the protracted passage in the fourteenth book in which the disguised Odysseus comes to the swineherd's hut, and they engage in a long conversation before turning in for the night.[7] Much of their talk turns on whether or not the stranger might be speaking the truth in his claim to have met the real Odysseus; then the stranger tells a rather boring tale about how he once got hold of a cloak by guile, which is a hint to Eumaeus that the night is cold and extra bedclothes are needed.[8] It is hard to conceive of an independent short song that would be substantially composed of this kind of conversation; there is just not enough episodic content. I conclude that it was specially designed for the monumental *Odyssey*. If so, then its composer was capable of operating at a level lower than the highest. Perhaps he was straining to match the length of the *Iliad*; is there any comparable scene in that poem, which would give a less ambiguous indication of the poet we call Homer? The deceit and seduction of Zeus by Hera takes up some 300 verses of Books 14 and 15, and is of the right degree of leisureliness and detail; but it could have existed already in the pre-Homeric tradition, since it makes an excellent independent song.[9] The reconciliation of Achilles and Agamemnon in Book 19 is more to the point, since it includes a seemingly interminable wrangle over whether Achilles should take food before re-entering the battle, whether or not it is good to fight on an empty stomach.[10] The effect (like that of the Odysseus and Eumaeus encounter) can be described not unfairly as 'rambling', and it is hard to imagine an ordinary traditional song including so little in the way of movement and climax. Post-Homeric elaboration is a possibility, but there is nothing particular to suggest it; again we are left with the impression that the monumental scheme may occasionally have encouraged Homer to develop effects that are in detail, at least, unimpressive.

Complex expression may be a more fruitful criterion; it would certainly show Homer in a better light, since two obvious instances in the *Iliad* are both quite brilliant. One is the speech of Achilles to which I have already referred, in which he questions the whole point of war in disjointed language that subtly perverts the formulas of heroic belief. The other is a scene of mass fighting in the sixteenth book. From 306 on, for almost fifty lines, the sense repeatedly spills over the natural divisions of the verse in abrupt and spasmodic statements. The effect reinforces the idea of hectic and confused fighting, and could only have been maintained by a virtuoso singer capable of re-shaping the formular language so as to achieve a spectacular variety of diaeresis and enjambement. That was not the kind of thing that ordinarily became traditional, for the simple reason that the regular techniques of oral assimilation required a steadier deployment of the whole verse as a unit of meaning. There is a good chance, then, that in the rare long sequences of this complex style we see the technical brilliance of Homer himself.

The third and most promising criterion based on monumentality involves the decisive moments of the large-scale plot. Naturally it is only if these cruces are treated with special emphasis that they can be expected to reveal any of Homer's poetical characteristics. Even then certain crucial scenes are disqualified. The theme of a warrior withdrawing from battle through injured pride is a conspicuous part of the central structure of the *Iliad*, but it was quite certainly used in pre-Homeric poetry too, and occurs in the tale of Meleager that is given in abbreviated form in the *Iliad* itself.[11] So probably was the idea of the hero abandoning his wrath because of the need to avenge a comrade. Such themes might already have been quite highly developed in the pre-Homeric tradition, and might not in their Homeric form reveal much of the special taste and style of Homer himself. A further difficulty is that the most popular (and that often means the most eventful) parts of the *Iliad* were apt to be chosen time and again for singing or recitation in the period between the end of Homer's working life and the formation of a standard written text. Therefore they were particularly exposed to elaboration, and the opening book, which describes the beginning of Achilles' wrath, contains a surprising number of apparently post-Homeric locutions. Something similar happened with the last book, too; this also, since it describes the moral climax by which Achilles gives back Hector's body for burial, might be regarded as especially Homeric. So, in a way, it doubtless was; but its unexpected concentration of Odyssean phraseology suggests that it has been quite heavily revised, either by Homer or by a close follower. Again, the theme of ransoming a prince's corpse may have been an old one, but in this case the heightened pathos and leisurely tone of much of the book suggest that considerable development, perhaps including much by Homer himself, has taken place.

That is a subjective judgement, and it is prudent to turn to the scenes that in my belief reveal most accurately and objectively the stylistic tendencies of the real Homer. They are, in particular, those that encompass the death of Patroclus in Book 16 and of Hector in Book 22, two of the four or five indispensable events of the whole extended action. They imply a common poet because they have several remarkable points of motif and language in common. The general theme of one warrior killing another is admittedly so frequent that it occurs hundreds of times, and in a wide variety of forms, within the *Iliad*; yet, if we come across two scenes in which the general theme is presented in a specially elaborate way, if those two scenes represent crucial turning-points of the large-scale plot, and if they bear marked and unusual resemblances to each other, then it is reasonable to guess that they were given special attention by the creator of the monumental poem himself. Let me repeat the argument, which is critical, in a slightly different way. If it is known that a theme might be traditional, then in most cases its use in the large-scale context cannot reveal Homeric characteristics as opposed to traditional ones. But when one of the themes of heroic poetry is used in a specially elaborate form at two of the crucial turning-points of the large-scale plot, and when in addition there are independent signs of a common style, then we can reasonably expect to find the large-scale poet at work. I should add that the death-scenes of Patroclus and Hector are of quite unusual length. Scale, therefore, is an ancillary criterion (and so, in a way, might be complexity; for the two scenes are unusually complex, not so much in expression as in emotion and underlying structure).

The deaths of Patroclus and Hector cannot be completely separated from that of Sarpedon which precedes Patroclus' death in Book 16. The Sarpedon death-scene is not a hinge of the monumental plot, and is less elaborate than the other two; but it is more elaborate than any apart from them, and it shows strong similarities at certain points to either the one or the other. It also contributes essential dramatic force to the crucial death of Patroclus by establishing him, for the first time, as a warrior of the first order. It looks very much, in fact, as though the monumental poet built up by stages to the climax of the death of Hector, with Sarpedon and then Patroclus providing more and more elaborate models. I begin, therefore, with a brief account of the Sarpedon death-scene and its special characteristics. Sarpedon is king of the Lycians and an important ally of the

Trojans; he is also a favourite child of Zeus himself. At 16. 419 ff. he deter-
mines to unmask and stop the unknown Achaean in Achilles' armour who
is doing so much damage. He leaps from his chariot, so does Patroclus;
they charge at one another like vultures on a rock. So far, standard battle-
theme.[12] But then Zeus pities them and wants to save his son; Hera
professes to be shocked at his interfering with fate, and uses three verses
of reproach that occur elsewhere only in the similar scene presaging the
death of Hector. Zeus agrees to compromise by letting Sleep and Death
carry Sarpedon's body back to his home in Lycia, an idea unique in the
Iliad but known to have been applied to Memnon in the lost epic *Aethiopis*.
Furthermore Zeus sends drops of bloody rain to honour his son who is
to die, a motif used more casually in Book 11.[13] The duel begins; it is
moderately detailed, with two attacks from each side, but typical in
essence. Patroclus hurls his spear and kills not Sarpedon but his charioteer; Sarpedon replies but hits Patroclus' trace-horse; Sarpedon throws his
second spear and misses, Patroclus throws his and wounds Sarpedon
severely. He falls like a felled tree, lies raging like a bull mauled by a lion,
both fairly typical similes; he calls on his friend Glaucus to save his corpse
and armour from the Achaeans. 'When he had thus spoken the end of
death covered him', a verse used elsewhere only of the deaths of Patroclus
and Hector[14]—indeed these are the only three death-scenes in which a
mortally-wounded victim speaks. Patroclus withdraws his spear, the lungs
come with it, and the ψυχή or soul too. The release of the life-soul is an
untypical detail that will be developed in the deaths of Patroclus and
Hector.

Two hundred verses later Patroclus, encouraged by killing Sarpedon
and by a mass of minor successes, pushes his luck too far.[15] Apollo himself
has to thrust him back from the walls of Troy, then goes in disguise to urge
Hector to attack. Patroclus dismounts and throws a stone that kills
Hector's charioteer Cebriones, much as he had just killed Sarpedon's
charioteer. This time, however, a long fight develops over Cebriones' body
and interrupts the duel of Patroclus and Hector. Patroclus jeers over the
fallen Cebriones, whose eyes have been ejected by the force of the blow
and who falls from his chariot like a sea-diver; he and Hector fight over
him like lions over a deer.[16] The theme of the fight over the corpse had
already been elaborated in the case of Sarpedon's body; here it is carried
further, and with Patroclus' corpse it will occupy a complete book. Much
of the detail of the development is typical; the armies mass with the noise
of woods crashing in a gale—there had been a similar image in the fight
over Sarpedon. But now Cebriones is described in unusual and powerfully
emotive phrases as 'lying there in a spiral of dust, huge and hugely
stretched out, his horsemanship forgotten',

ὁ δ’ ἐν στροφάλιγγι κονίης
κεῖτο μέγας μεγαλωστί, λελασμένος ἱπποσυνάων   (775 f.),

part of which is later applied to Achilles as he grovels in mourning for
Patroclus. The strong pathos is emphasized in repeated apostrophes, or
direct addresses by the poet, to Patroclus; he leaps on the Trojans and
slays thrice nine of them in an access of heroic fury; 'then for you,
Patroclus, appeared the end of your life; for Phoebus met you in the strong
rout of battle':

ἔνθ’ ἄρα τοι, Πάτροκλε, φάνη βιότοιο τελευτή·
ἤντετο γάρ τοι Φοῖβος ἐνὶ κρατερῇ ὑσμίνῃ.   (787 f.)

'Terrible', δεινός, adds the poet, of Apollo, and the god was indeed especially formidable because he was invisible, concealed in a thick mist; and
he stood behind Patroclus and smote him with the flat of his hand so that
Patroclus' eyes whirled round. Then the god stripped his dazed victim of
helmet and armour—it had belonged to Achilles, and the helmet was now
unnaturally covered with blood and dirt. As Patroclus stands there helpless and naked a young fop, Euphorbus, strikes him with a running spear-
cast; Patroclus retreats towards his comrades, but Hector catches him
with a mortal spear-thrust, like a lion finishing off a fighting boar. Then in
the heroic fashion Hector boasts over his victim, tells the expiring
Patroclus that vultures will devour him, sneers at the thought of Achilles
encouraging Patroclus to capture Troy. Fainting, Patroclus replies: it was
Zeus, Apollo, fate, Euphorbus, and only then Hector that defeated him,
and Hector himself will not live for long. Patroclus dies, and the verse
used earlier of Sarpedon is expanded by the addition of a pair describing
his soul flitting mournfully down to Hades. These verses, and the elaboration of the idea of a life-soul leaving the body, recur at the death of Hector
and nowhere else.[17] Hector replies querulously, withdraws his spear, and
sets off in pursuit of Patroclus' charioteer.

It's a marvellous description, typical in detail for most of the time yet
built up into something distinctive. Throwing a stone, killing a charioteer,
fighting over a hero's corpse, the similes as champions rush forward, the
details of the duel—these are standard motifs. Even the attack on a god
and its repulse had been used before; so, in a small way, had the idea of a
god dazing a victim—only the total stripping of the armour is virtually
unparalleled. But many of the standard elements are uniquely emphasized
—the pathos, for instance, that is expressed in the repeated apostrophes to
Patroclus and not, this time, by special signs from Zeus like bloody rain or
weighing the contestants' fates; and the whole sense of what Fenik terms
'the gigantic and supernatural'.[18]

Hector's death comes six books later. It is the inevitable result of the
killing of Patroclus, decisive for the fate of Troy and essential to the

climax of the whole poem. At the end of Book 21 Apollo had assumed the form of the Trojan Agenor (who had dared to face Achilles after a frantic soliloquy that anticipates Hector's), and so enticed Achilles away from the walls. The Trojans pour in confusion into the city, but Hector is 'tied down by destructive destiny' outside.[19] His parents beseech him from the walls; this whole prelude to the encounter includes much that seems special and not typical. Achilles charges at him like a hawk after a dove (this at least is typical) and he starts running. Zeus pities him, wishes to save him, but is deterred by Athene in much the same words as Hera had used over Sarpedon—indeed that passage is the fuller and more accurate, since *moira*, fate, on which the argument hinges, is specified only there.[20] The chase is enlivened by three unusual similes and particularized by realistic details unparalleled elsewhere: the two remarkable springs, one hot and one cold, past which they run, with Hector always seeking to get under the walls for protection, and Achilles always heading him off and telling the other Achaeans not to rob him of his victory. Zeus weighs the fates—a solemn and pathetic moment, not quite unique in the *Iliad*, but nowhere so strongly developed—and Hector's sinks. Athene promises Achilles victory, then disguises herself as Hector's brother Deiphobus and so persuades Hector to stand and fight. He proposes an agreement to respect each other's corpse, which Achilles savagely rejects; Achilles throws and misses, but Athene, in a unique action, returns his spear to him. Hector does not know this, utters a confident boast and throws in turn. His spear hits Achilles' shield but does not pierce it (always a fatal sign by the Homeric conventions); he turns for Deiphobus' spear, finds no one there, and realizes in a flash that he has been divinely deluded and is doomed. He decides to die bravely, draws his sword and rushes on Achilles like an eagle; Achilles counter-charges with spear-tip gleaming like the evening star. He pierces Hector in the throat without further delay; the poet has to explain, a little awkwardly, that the dying man is still able to speak, and in reply to Achilles' ritual boasts and the threat that dogs and vultures will devour his corpse Hector intercedes for the ransom of his body. Achilles brutally refuses, Hector at last recognizes his total implacability, prophesies his death, and himself dies in terms closely matching those used of the death of Patroclus, when Hector had been victor, not victim.[21] Achilles replies angrily, much as Hector had done in that previous scene: he will die when the gods will it. He withdraws his spear, strips the corpse, and the other Achaeans gather round and jab at it; there is no fight for the body this time, for the Trojans are penned inside the city. Finally, in a unique and presumably original description that is too short to tell us much about Homer's style, Achilles pierces Hector's ankles and drives off dragging the corpse behind him: the polar antithesis of heroic behaviour, which may be brutal but is never unseemly.

Many of the elements of this remarkable scene, which in its scale (around four hundred verses including preliminaries) is unparalleled in Homeric battle-poetry, are of course typical and derive from the pre-Homeric tradition. Little in it is strictly unique, but many of the constituent motifs are powerfully developed beyond their standard form: notably the debate about the victim's body, a matter which for Hector is of paramount concern; the careful localization and tactical realism; the collaboration with a god, in which Athene conspires with Achilles more in the manner of the *Odyssey* than of the *Iliad*; and the elaboration of Hector's contradictory feelings—the rapid succession of guilt, concern for his reputation, wishful fantasy, realism, optimism, blind panic, and finally acceptance of the facts and a heroic death. Much of this special development must have been determined by the general emphasis of the poem's climax. Hector and Achilles are isolated outside the walls not only to stress the unique significance of the occasion, but also so that the standard fight for the corpse can be omitted and Achilles can proceed to the mutilation of the body, which in turn motivates Priam's dramatic redeeming of his son's corpse in Book 24. Hector's dying exchanges are protracted even beyond their model in the death of Patroclus, to stress his sense of fate, the decisive implications of his death, and Achilles' own vulnerability; and his obsessive concern for his corpse looks forward to the scene between Priam and Achilles as well as back to the untypically humane qualities that he shared with Patroclus alone.

What do the three closely-related death-scenes suggest (beyond the matter of sheer scale) about Homer's taste and style? In structure, that he was prepared to add emphasis not only in the traditional way, by extending the typical details of the event itself, but also by developing its preliminaries and conclusion—and, of course, by heightening the element of supernatural intervention. The battle over Cebriones and the chase round the walls impose a special tone on the central act of violence, as does the subsequent dying conversation that is skilfully developed in the progress from Sarpedon to Patroclus to Hector. The tone is one of melancholy and inevitability, and it accentuates the strong pathos that is already present in the apostrophes to Patroclus, in the idea of the gods calling Patroclus and Hector to their deaths ($\theta\acute{a}\nu a\tau\acute{o}\nu\delta\epsilon$ $\kappa\acute{a}\lambda\epsilon\sigma\sigma a\nu$, a phrase used of each of them and otherwise unparalleled),[22] in the bloody rain and the weighing of fates, in Zeus' concern and pity. The pathetic quality of heroic death in battle was already part of the tradition; Homer emphasizes it at these key points and makes it more profound. His methods in this respect are unusually refined. In general I am cautious about tracing complex overtones and unemphatic cross-references over large intervals of oral poetry, but I am sure that the helmet-plumes that are sullied in the dust or gleam over Achilles' head, or the similes from racing that emphasize first Achilles' confident swiftness, then the special value of the stake which is Hector's life, are placed as they are to accentuate an underlying contrast. This careful approach to the expression of emotional nuances confirms what we might otherwise doubt, that the curious mixture of fantasy and abnormal realism that appears in each of the crucial death-scenes is no mere accident of oral cumulation. With Hector, unaccustomed topographical and tactical accuracy is immediately followed by Athene's intervention in the duel itself. In Patroclus' death the combination of the two qualities is even more striking, as the invisible and therefore mysterious Apollo dazes him with an all-too-concrete blow and strips his armour in a casual, almost mundane way. The conjunction of gods and mortals is traditional enough, but here it is intensified and made to reflect some of the ambiguities of the heroic condition, as it is too in the parts played in Hector's death by such disparate agents as Zeus, fate, Athene, Deiphobus, and Achilles.

If Homer constructed these scenes, they should also reveal something about his use of traditional language. If it were the time and place to do so, I think I could show that they display an unusually careful variation, even by Iliadic standards, of sentence-length and enjambement, and that the rhetorical mechanisms of style are uncommonly diverse without being obtrusive.[23] Less expected, perhaps, are the ways in which Homer does *not* improve on the tradition; for instance he does not attempt to sharpen or expand the generalized and rather flat formula ἂψ δ᾽ ἑτάρων εἰς ἔθνος ἐχάζετο (16. 817), 'back into the tribe of his companions he withdrew' (nine times in the *Iliad*), when he comes to describe the wounded Patroclus struggling to reach the safety of his comrades.

Occasional looseness in the combination of phrases is endemic in oral poetry, and Homer was evidently no exception. Something analogous could happen in the combination of typical episodic material too. As Hector decides to stand and face Achilles he is like a malign snake lying in wait for its victim—but suddenly and a little incongruously he is envisaged as taking off his shield, 'just so did Hector possess unquenchable might and not retreat, leaning his bright shield against a jutting tower';[24] and he breaks into a despondent soliloquy about the chances of flight or surrender. Perhaps that is a small accident of post-Homeric transmission; even so there are certain things Homer does not much mind about. For instance, realism is important in the chase round the walls, but not (and this was a traditional tendency) in the details of spear-cast and armament —Hector and Achilles have a single spear each, which means that it should really be for thrusting and not throwing, yet they both throw it with apparent insouciance.

In one respect Homer is brief, almost cursory, where the tradition would be more elaborate, and that is in the use of similes to describe the appearance of Hector and then Achilles in their final charge.[25] The climax is near, and normally an exceptionally complex simile would be chosen to mark the fact. Homer is not, of course, averse to extended similes as such, and had used a complicated lion-and-boar situation to illustrate the subduing of Patroclus by Hector. His longer images (if we judge by the three great death-scenes) are more carefully related to the actual situation than is usual elsewhere in the *Iliad*. Paradoxically they are less 'Homeric' than the typical Iliadic simile with its entrancing but not strictly relevant details strung from a single point of contact; and here, where one would expect the extreme of elaboration, Homer keeps the imagery simple, even sparse. For Hector as he rushes with drawn sword is compared briefly to a high-flying eagle swooping down through dark cloud upon sheep or crouching hare, and Achilles is distinguished (in a comparison which at first seems so standard as to be banal) by the gleam of his spear-point that resembles the evening star passing through the gloom of night. The simplicity, the vividness and pathos of these images are emphasized by the audience's awareness of the complex comparisons that Homer seems deliberately to reject. That simplicity has its own obvious force in the context; but a second hearing suggests subtler associations, for the eagle is like the hawk to which Achilles himself had been compared when Hector panicked, and the fair star of evening recalls the sinister dog-star which Achilles resembled at the beginning of the episode.[26] In both cases there is an element of contrast and reversal. Furthermore the similes have one significant detail in common; the eagle swoops through dark cloud, the evening star passes through the gloom of night, and the implication of gloom, of darkness, seems to underline the dire reality and savage consequences of Hector's destruction, which in its 'typical' aspects might have seemed almost too close to just another heroic death.

These are only some of the ways in which, if I am right about the basic criteria, the real Homer revealed himself. Much more could be said about his particular way of combining typical motifs, which is no less important than his identifiable innovations. Fenik, whose purpose is to stress the predominantly typical constitution of the battle scenes, tends to imply that our three great encounters result from the *mere* accumulation of typical details and patterns of action; for example the complexity of the Sarpedon–Patroclus fight is claimed to be 'illusory' because it is composed 'almost entirely' of familiar elements.[27] I should be inclined to reply that, once the basic elements and patterns have been assembled, the process of arrangement and further cumulation becomes a matter of genuinely artistic choice. The author of these great death-scenes is working, after all, on a quite different plane from that of the Serbian *guslar* who simply piles together everything he can think of, or even from that of the singers responsible for most of the Iliadic arming scenes. In short, Homer can best be seen, not in isolation from the tradition on which his poetical existence depended, but against its background, in scenes in which the tradition is enriched if not entirely transcended, and in a kind of counterpoint between the typical (which can also be the quintessential) and the individual, the personal. It is in that region that this complex poetical character, the 'real' Homer, is to be sought and perhaps found.

NOTES

1. An inaugural lecture given at Bristol in March, 1972, and printed here more or less as delivered.

2. *Typical Battle Scenes in the Iliad* (*Hermes* Einzelschr. 21, Wiesbaden, 1968), especially 6 f.

3. See, e.g., my *Homer and the Epic* (Cambridge, 1965), ch. I.

4. *Homer and the Epic*, 19 ff.

5. *Homer and the Epic*, 192–7.

6. *Iliad* 9. 308–429; cf. Adam Parry, 'The Language of Achilles' in G. S. Kirk (ed.), *The Language and Background of Homer* (Cambridge, 1964), 48 ff.

7. *Odyssey* 14. 115–408.

8. *Od.* 14. 457–506.

9. *Il.* 14. 153–360; 15. 4–99.

10. *Il.* 19. 154–237.

11. *Il.* 9. 527–99.

12. Fenik, op. cit., 200 f.

13. *Il.* 16. 666–83, cf. 453–7 (Sleep and Death); 459–61, cf. 11. 53–5 (bloody rain).

14. *Il.* 16. 502, cf. 855, 22. 361.

15. *Il.* 16. 698 ff.

16. *Il.* 16. 756 ff.

17. *Il.* 16. 856 f., 22. 362 f.

18. Fenik, op. cit., 216.

19. *Il.* 22. 5 f.

20. *Il.* 22. 179–81 = 16. 441–3; *moira*, 16. 434.

21. *Il.* 22. 355–66; 16. 843–61.

22. *Il.* 16.693; 22. 297.

23. The effects I have in mind are discussed in relation to the whole of *Iliad* 16 in my 'Verse-structure and Sentence-structure in Homer', *Yale Classical Studies* 20 (1966), 105–52.

24. *Il.* 22. 93–7.

25. *Il.* 22. 308–11, 317–21.

26. *Il.* 22. 139–44, 25–32.

27. Fenik, op. cit., 203.

THE SEARCH FOR THE POET HOMER*

By M. M. WILLCOCK

It is difficult to prove the unitarian view of a single author of the *Iliad*. The old-fashioned unitarian scholars of this country, who paid little attention to analytical scholarship, had no doubts. They would just assume one poet; and all the extraordinary qualities of the *Iliad* could be discussed as the achievement of Homer. But simultaneously, in Germany, even more intelligent scholars were carving up the *Iliad*, arguing from inconsistencies in the story, or linguistic oddities, that what we have is the work of two or more poets, separated in time. Against this, the unitarians suddenly seem rather simple-minded, as if they were arguing subjectively, avoiding the difficult questions, saying in effect, 'I like it, and I wish it to have been the work of a single poet, and therefore it was.' In this paper I hope to present a more reasoned argument, based on certain features of the content and structure of the poem.

Homer is elusive. But the study of the *Iliad* in the years since the war has, I believe, led us closer to an actual understanding of the way his mind worked. Apart from oral poetry discussion, which does not actually define Homer, but the methods he used, and to which we shall come later, I would instance—for our possible approach to Homer's mind—first, the work of Schadewaldt, both in his adherence to neoanalytical views,[1] and more particularly in his demonstration in *Iliasstudien*[2] of cross-connections between different parts of the *Iliad*; these show a poet who planned, who structured his tale, who had a precise conception of his characters and their actions. Secondly, there has been deeper treatment of the references to other mythology in the *Iliad*, which has shown that the poet has a method of using allusions to other myths in speeches for the purpose of persuasion or dissuasion—what are called mythological exempla, or paradeigmata; this practice seems individual, as if it reflects a particular mind.[3] And thirdly, Dieter Lohmann has shown, in a book on the speeches, *Die Komposition der Reden in der Ilias* (Berlin, 1970), that there is an extraordinary technique of speech construction, of most careful balance within a speech itself by ring composition or linear development, or (more extraordinary) of exact parallelism between a pair of speeches, so that the parts can be simply balanced or ticked off against each other. This again seems to reflect the technique of an individual poet. Lohmann's book was published in 1970, and is only now having its effect on Homeric scholarship.

I propose to offer a rather complicated argument for single authorship,

for a mind which planned and structured the whole, based on a combination of European literary attitudes and the oral composition theory which
has come to us from America. For 'oral composition' is the biggest single
advance in Homeric scholarship of this century. Nobody can, or at least
should, begin to argue about Homer until he or she has assimilated
the results of the researches of Milman Parry, Albert Lord, and their
followers. It is true that some reaction is setting in, with the occasional
book suggesting that Parry went too far—for example, Norman Austin's
strangely titled *Archery at the Dark of the Moon* (California, 1975), and the
recent book *Naming Achilles* (Oxford, 1987) by David Shive.[4] But without
the powerful arguments of the Parryists there would be nothing to react
against.

I summarize briefly. Parry and Lord have shown that there is an easily
identified system of (a) formulaic phrases and (b) subjects or topics for
poetry (what Lord calls themes), which together made up the repertoire of
the oral bard. The reason for the system was utility, in that the bard had
to perform extempore, to be able to sing the tale that his audience wanted.
An alternative might have been to memorize previously composed poems,
but that is not what happens with oral bards as we have been shown.
Instead of memorized poems, they would have in their minds the *elements*
which constitute the finished poem: on the verbal level, formulaic phrases;
on the story level, themes. The word 'themes' is of extreme breadth, in my
opinion; but for the simplest definition those who discuss these matters
instance the obvious repeated situations in the poems, such things as
arrivals and departures, armings, sending of messages, and incidents in
the fighting. Such 'themes' could be appropriately brought in to a large
number of possible stories. They would not differ very much in different
tales told by the same bard. The battle incidents, descriptions of arming,
and so on, would not differ (apart from the names of the participants)
if the fighting was at Troy, at Thebes, outside Calydon, or anywhere
else.

Oral poetry theory explains the pervasive repetitions in the *Iliad*, both of
formulas and of themes. And in the extreme statement of Parryism, it
seems as if the poet operates virtually subconsciously among his options.
I am thinking of the view put forward by Michael Nagler in his difficult
book *Spontaneity and Tradition* (California, 1974). He takes the repetitions
to be 'pre-verbal', so that the phrase or the passage is created anew each
time that it occurs. It is therefore not so much a repetition as a new
coinage, deriving however from a pre-existing conformation in the
subconscious of the poet. Lord says something like this when he argues
that both formulas and themes are 'triggered off' by the situation in the
tale. It just occurs to the bard, intuitively, that this phrase, or this piece of
description, is appropriate at this moment. As a result, it appears. And

Lord pointed out that sometimes the mechanism leads to something illogical or inconsistent finding its way into the tale. A theme, for example, may be activated by the general context, but be in fact inappropriate in the particular circumstances.[5] This very important realization provides the answer in many cases to the rational objections of the analytical scholars, on which they based their arguments for multiple authorship.

Consequently, oral theory leads in practice to a belief in the single author. Parry said that his arguments did not prove that there was one poet of the *Iliad*. But, as others have seen, they weaken or remove the arguments against that belief, and thus the simpler explanation becomes the more probable. All the same, people have been uneasy. If the theme is triggered off by the situation, and is almost automatic, without the conscious choice of the poet, and in any case has been frequently used before, there is a serious diminution in the poet's apparent creativity. Taken to the extreme, the poem virtually composes itself, if the bard has full control of his techniques. Each bard will have his own repertoire, of course, and the bard with the greater repertoire, and the greater skill in using it, will produce the better performance. But this seems far removed from the creativity, the imagination, of a Shakespeare. This was one of the reasons why Parry's work was for so long little considered in this country, not until after the war; and for even longer on the continent, maybe not there until Lesky, in Vienna, around 1960. Schadewaldt did not consider Parry's arguments; nor even did Lohmann in 1970 (the author of that brilliant book about the speeches). Only slowly, and partially, through the work of Heubeck in Germany, Dutch scholars, and the Austrian followers of Lesky, has oral theory made its impact on the continent. And even so the leading German scholars tend to believe that Parry and his followers are describing the techniques of Homer's predecessors, whereas Homer himself was not an oral bard, but a fully literate poet.

There is a clash of views. Alexander Pope was of course long before any of this discussion, but he knew the *Iliad* very well, having translated the whole, and he was a poet, and he gave it as his view that 'Homer had the greatest INVENTION of any poet whatsoever'. And that sounds right. Think of any passage in Homer and compare it, for example, with Virgil; for imaginative detail there is no comparison. But how can Homer seem to have such great invention if both his language and his subject matter were prefabricated? This is the problem in the wake of oral theory.

Continental scholarship had not of course failed to notice the repetitions. Some analysts even used them as evidence for different authorship; but Schadewaldt merely treated them as one among many features of Homeric style. There were repeated 'schemes' in the composition of Homer, such as the repeated arming scenes. Indeed, the first work on these repeated 'schemes' came from German scholarship, the monograph by W. Arend, *Die typischen Szenen bei Homer* (Berlin, 1933). This work has been mentioned by everyone, because it makes a bridge between the two camps. It was even reviewed by Milman Parry, and his review is among the collected papers published by his son Adam Parry, *The Making of Homeric Verse* (Oxford, 1971). Arend discusses the obvious repetitions (what Lord called themes, and treated as part of the technique of oral poetry) merely as an aspect of Homer's style.

Here we have the distinction which is the basis of my argument. If something happens several times in the *Iliad*, do we consider these as independent examples of a common theme arising from the repertoire of the poet, along the lines of Parry or Nagler? Or do we see the separate occurrences as interconnected, with the poet making some kind of point, by way of contrast or cumulation, from the repetitions, as might a poet in the traditional European view? This question can be asked of the formulas too. Are they totally independent instances, or is there inter- action between them? Can we have it both ways—repetition as an inherent feature of oral poetry, but a poet who uses it also for his own artistic ends?

Is there an interconnection between repeated incidents? We must start from oral poetry theory, and accept that the primary reason for thematic repetition was that this poet had this particular theme in his repertoire, and up it comes when the occasion requires it. But is there more than that? Do the successive repetitions move towards a climax, with the final occur- rence cashing in on the effect of the previous ones? Or is there contrast, whereby occurrence B gets extra power because of the previous occur- rence A? If we are persuaded that such interpretations are correct, then we may reasonably claim that we are in contact with the mind of the poet; that he is utilizing the techniques of the oral bard, repetition of formula and theme, but that he is so much in control of them that he can use repetitions themselves for his artistic purpose. Put it another way. Oral theory is American; literary scholarship is European. We are half way between. Can we produce a synthesis?

I propose to look at three sets of repeated themes in the *Iliad*. In doing so, I shall make some points about oral poetry, and some about artistic intentions.

1. *Arming*

1. Paris	3.328–38	11
2. Agamemnon	11.15–46	32
3. Patroclus	16.130–44	15
4. Achilles	19.367–91	25

3	11	16	19	
330	17	131	369	First he placed along his legs the beautiful greaves linked with
331	18	132	370	silver fastenings to hold the greaves at the ankles.
332	19	133	371	Afterwards he girt on about his chest the corselet—
334	29	135	372	Across his shoulders he slung the sword—
335	32	136	373	Shield
336	41	137	380	Helmet
338	43	139	387	Spear(s)

This first group consists of the well-known arming descriptions, discussed by Arend and frequently quoted. These are: the arming of Paris before his duel with Menelaus in Book 3, the arming of Agamemnon before his *aristeia* in 11, the arming of Patroclus in Achilles' armour before he goes out to relieve the Greeks in 16, and the arming of Achilles in his new divine armour in 19. Much can be learned about oral composition from these four. The basic lines which form the beginning of the sequence (putting on the greaves, with a description of the greaves, and then the breastplate [corselet] and then the sword) are identical in all four occurrences; thereafter there is variation in the expressions, but the continuing sequence for the other pieces of equipment—shield, helmet, one spear or two javelins—follows the same order each time. There is nothing unlikely about this. The sequence is obviously natural. You would sit down and put on your greaves first; then get your breastplate on; then, because both sword and shield were on straps over the shoulders, you would put them on before your helmet. And last you would pick up your spear or spears. But the repeated exact lines show that the poet or poets of these passages had formulaic phrases automatically associated with this 'theme'; and indeed there are other formulaic phrases (e.g., about the helmet, 'with the horsehair crest, and terribly nodded the plumes above it') which do not happen to come into all four, because of variation in one or two. Essentially, however, it is clear that a pre-existing sequence is brought out in these four examples.

Why are they of different lengths (see the numbers in the right-hand column)? Not because the basic description has been varied, but because the poet has added ornamental descriptive material to a different extent in the different cases. Paris had (interestingly) borrowed his brother Lycaon's breastplate; that is the only addition to the basic sequence in his case. Agamemnon has the most royal and distinctive ornamentation described, on his breastplate, his sword and scabbard, and his shield. Patroclus is pretty basic, but there is a long explanation at the end about how he did not take Achilles' spear, alone of all the equipment which he borrowed. And there is much imagery added to the description of Achilles' new armour: the shield shone like the moon, with a simile also likening it to a fire on a mountain-side seen from the sea; and his helmet shone like a star.

These variations illustrate a constant principle in oral poetry, that expansion denotes importance. It is essential to see that the basic description is the same in all cases, but differential length, achieved by the addition of ornamental detail, singles out some descriptions as more important than others. Thus it is not at all surprising that the two longest are those of Agamemnon, the great king, who by Book 11 needs a boost from the poet, as nothing much has gone right for him so far, and Achilles. Agamemnon is to have an *aristeia*, to show that though he may make mistakes in man-management and strategy, he at least deserves his position by his status as a warrior. Consequently, the poet gives him a big arming scene. And of course Achilles' scene comes before *his aristeia*; and the poet is pulling out all the stops, to make this the greatest conceivable. Paris and Patroclus are of less importance.

So these descriptions demonstrate oral technique. But I would not argue that there is any evident artistic intention or connection between the four descriptions. They do not interact. We do not see through a comparison of them into the individuality of the poet. Merely, there is an available sequence, and expansion is used to add effect in appropriate cases.

2. *Advice fom Polydamas*

	Extent of the exchange with Hector
1. 12.60–79	22
2. 12.210–29	41
3. 13.725–47	29
4. 18.249–83	61

Polydamas, called by Homer for metrical reasons Poulydamas, gives advice to Hector four times in the *Iliad*. He is a slightly shadowy person, but we do hear some things about him. His father is Panthoüs, a Trojan elder (on the wall with Priam in Book 3), and probably priest of Apollo;[6] and two of his brothers play a part in the fighting, one of them being Euphorbus, who has chief credit for the wounding of Patroclus at the end of 16, setting him up for Hector to despatch.[7] Polydamas was born on the same night as Hector (18.251), and is in a way his *alter ego*. He plays his part in the fighting in the long middle books, but his chief function is to give Hector cautionary advice, the reaction to which helps to characterize Hector himself.

The four occasions when Polydamas advises Hector fit into a clear pattern. Twice his advice is accepted; twice it is rejected. These alternate. So, at the beginning of Book 12, when the Trojans reach the Greek ditch, outside the wall of the camp, he gives the sensible advice not to try to cross the ditch with their chariots, but to leave them there and proceed on foot. Hector acts on it. But a little later, still in Book 12, when Hector's division has still not crossed the ditch, an omen of an eagle carrying a snake, which it is forced to drop, disturbs the troops and leads Polydamas to advise that they should abort their attack. To this Hector replies with his famous comment, 'One bird-omen is best: to fight for one's country'— εἷς οἰωνὸς ἄριστος ἀμύνεσθαι περὶ πάτρης (12.243). This is heroic, but we should not fail to understand that Hector is wrong, and Polydamas is right. It does no good in their world to scorn omens. Patriotism is not enough.

The third occasion is in Book 13, when the Trojans are through into the Greek camp, but have lost cohesion in their attack. Polydamas suggests a pause for regrouping, and for the leaders to consider their best immediate choice of action. He wants them to consider the alternatives of further attack or withdrawal. Hector accepts the advice; but when the surviving leaders assemble, they do not discuss the alternatives, but move straight into the attack. So Polydamas' advice is formally accepted, but in practice partly disregarded.

The last time that Polydamas offers advice, the situation is critical. It is in 18, when the long day's fighting has come to an end with sunset. The Trojans have done extremely well, driving the Greeks back within their camp, breaking through the wall, fighting at one stage among the ships; they are now back on the plain, but the Greeks have only with the greatest difficulty recovered Patroclus' body and got it back to Achilles. On the other hand, Achilles has appeared at the ditch; and he will without doubt be back in action tomorrow, seeking revenge. Two long speeches are given, Polydamas arguing for a return to the city, Hector for a continuation of the fight round the camp. They are in extraordinary responsion with each other, argument to argument, point to point, as is shown by Lohmann in the book I referred to.[8] The structure of each speech falls into seven parts. Polydamas says:

1. Let us go back to the city.
2. *Previously*, when Achilles was angry, I was keen to fight.
3. *But now*, I fear he will drive us back to the city in disarray.
4. Let us go back.
5. *This night*, we will be safe inside;
6. *Tomorrow morning*, we will take our positions on the walls.
7. If Achilles attacks, the worse for him!

Hector replies:

1. I disagree with you.
2. *Previously*, Priam's city was full of treasure.
3. *But now*, it has all gone.
4. I disagree.
5. *This night*, we will keep watch on the plain;
6. *Tomorrow morning*, we will fight at the ships.
7. If Achilles has really returned, I will face him, and may win.

As Homer says, the Trojans supported Hector's weaker arguments, and did not support Polydamas, who had got it right. The decision was fatal for many of them, and for Hector himself who stayed out on the plain in Book 22 to fight Achilles, partly because of what he and Polydamas had said here.

We notice the lengths of the passages. Those where Hector gives a speech in disagreement obviously take longer; and the final, most significant, occasion takes far the longest. Now in this case it does seem that we can draw conclusions about the intentions of the poet.[9] Obviously there is a theme 'Polydamas gives advice to Hector', and the poet has it available at key moments of his story, when the Trojans have to take tactical decisions. To that extent, it is part of his semi-automatic system of oral composition. But the fact that the last of the four occasions is the most significant, indeed the fatal one; that it is the longest, and thus signalled as the most important; and that it is constructed with immense care, in the way shown by Lohmann to be characteristic of the most formal speeches in the *Iliad*; all of this suggests a structural plan in the poet's mind. The earlier occasions, while in themselves being examples of a repeated theme, are also preparations for this final one. The mind that planned the *Iliad* as we have it, had the end in view while composing the earlier stages. It is clear from other examples like this, where the final climactic occurrence of a theme has been prepared by previous occasions,[10] that the poet had the most capacious mind. Separate strands in the story, significant enough at their own moments, eventually come to fruition, with enhanced depth and meaning.

3. *Soliloquies*

1. Odysseus	11.404–10	7
2. Menelaus	17.91–105	15
3. Agenor	21.553–70	18
4. Hector	22.99–130	32

The third set of thematic repetitions that I wish to consider are the soliloquies.[11] There are four. It is odd that the figure four occurs here too, as with the armings and the speeches of Polydamas. It adds perhaps to a feeling of richness without randomness in the tale; a kind of 'impletion'; soliloquies are not happening all the time, when anyone gets into difficulty; on the other hand, they occur often enough to notice. Four is about the right frequency to achieve this. They are of extreme interest— more so than the two previous sets of four, because soliloquies naturally represent personality, and the characterization of the individual heroes is so much Homer's crowning achievement.

The first is the most unexpected. It occurs in the Greek defeat of Book 11, when three of their greatest leaders are successively wounded and put out of action. The soliloquy is by the thinking man, Odysseus. He is cut off in the battle, and rationalizes in his mind the need to stand and fight, not to run. This is a little surprising, because the Odysseus we have got to know so far in the *Iliad* has not been needlessly heroic; indeed in Book 8 he made his way back to the Greek camp in spite of a shout for assistance from his colleague Diomedes (8.97). In fact, I suspect the heroic stance taken here is a kind of compensation for that earlier moment. Homer appreciates his characters, and just as Agamemnon is given an *aristeia* in 11, preceded by a magnificent arming scene, to compensate for his ineffectiveness in the early books, so Odysseus must not be left under the suspicion of being less than acceptably heroic. So he stays and fights, is wounded but kills his assailant, and is then rescued by the great Telamonian Ajax—a moment which has its own powerful resonance in the light of the later dispute between these two for the arms of the dead Achilles, which was without doubt known to Homer.[12]

Ajax was urged to rescue Odysseus by Menelaus, another of Homer's favourites, no great fighter, but one who stayed up at the front and kept a good eye on events. The next soliloquy is his. At the beginning of 17 he has killed Euphorbus, that son of Panthoüs and brother of Polydamas who had been the first human to wound Patroclus. But danger approaches in the form of Hector, anxious to avenge his fellow Trojan. Menelaus communes with himself, in exactly the opposite direction from Odysseus in 11. For he rationalizes a natural desire to leave the scene. He argues that nobody will blame him for avoiding Hector. And perhaps he will find Ajax and come back with him! These two soliloquies do show a kind of contrast, with some humour—the forceful, individualistic Odysseus and the likeable, less impressive Menelaus.

Before I come to the other two soliloquies, I should point out that the two by Odysseus and Menelaus show a close structural similarity. Each begins with alternatives, speculation about what the hero *might* do under the circumstances, and what the consequences would be. Then each pulls himself together with a key line meaning, 'But what is the point of such speculation?' and comes down firmly on what must be done. That line ἀλλὰ τίη μοι ταῦτα φίλος διελέξατο θυμός; recurs in fact in all four soliloquies, and is clearly an indicator of formulaic composition. As with the arming scenes, there is a pattern to the theme of 'soliloquy'. It occurs the four times in the *Iliad*, and associated with it, at the dividing point of the soliloquy, comes that same formulaic line. So, each time, the hero considers his situation, allows himself thoughts about alternative ways of proceeding, then pulls himself together with, 'Yet, still, why does the heart within me debate on these things?' (tr. Lattimore, as are most of the translations in this paper). And the hero turns to what must be done, and what he in fact does.

The final two examples are very close, within a hundred and fifty lines of each other, across a book division, and one may easily see that the first foreshadows the second. For the situations are the same. Two important Trojans are cut off from their friends in the mass flight to the city, and face the approach of the menacing Achilles. One is a Trojan we have heard little of during the course of the epic; but he, like Polydamas, comes from a leading family in the city; and as it happens he was the first Trojan to kill a Greek, at the very beginning of the fighting in Book 4 (4.467). It is Agenor, son of Antenor. He thinks of running, away from the city to the foot-hills of Ida, with the intention of slipping back into Troy after dark. 'Yet still, why does the heart within me debate on these things? He'd catch me anyway. I must face him and fight.' So Agenor faces Achilles, and is not killed. Apollo rescues him.

That sets up the position, in many ways, by contrast and by similarity, for Hector. And he has the longest of the four soliloquies and by far the most affecting. It is affecting because of our feelings for Hector after the Farewell scene in Book 6, and because of his heroic achievements in the middle fighting, and because it is the third speech at the beginning of Book 22, the first two being by his father and mother, appealing to him to come back to safety in the city. But Hector thinks of what Polydamas will say if he goes back (so that fourth scene of advice by Polydamas has this long-term consequence); then he thinks of trying to come to a deal with Achilles, to give Helen back and half the possessions of Troy to the Greeks. Then comes the formulaic line, 'Yet still, why does the heart within me debate on these things? You can't make deals with Achilles. You can't talk to him as girls and boys talk to each other. Better to fight and see who will win.' And of course Hector does not manage to face Achilles, but runs (which Agenor did not do), and then eventually fights, and gets no protection from Apollo.

Considering then the four soliloquies, we may say the same as with the speeches of Polydamas. There is evidently a theme of 'soliloquy' in the poetic repertoire. It is shown by the fact that each of these speeches has virtually the same structure; and in each case, at the turning point in the thoughts of the speaker, comes that formulaic line ἀλλὰ τίη μοι ταῦτα φίλος διελέξατο θυμός; So the method is 'stock'. Any poet could do it. But the use of it in the *Iliad* seems conscious and intended. The first two balance each other, as if they are setting a pattern for such speeches. Then the third, at a moment of little significance (apart from the feelings of Agenor himself), prepares for the most important, the climax, the one which it has all been leading up to, the soliloquy of Hector out on the plain under the eyes of his parents. And you notice of course that it is the longest, naturally exemplifying that basic principle of oral composition, 'expansion denotes importance'.

The search seems to have found its quarry. Homer is using oral poetry techniques, composition by theme, with in some cases associated formulaic phrases. But there is an artistic aim and purpose running concurrently with the technical method. It is all planned. Speeches of Polydamas in Books 12 and 13 prepare for Book 18; soliloquies in 11, 17, and 21 prepare for 22.

I end with a solution to a problem later in Book 22. The line ἀλλὰ τίη μοι ταῦτα φίλος διελέξατο θυμός; comes into the *Iliad* five times, not just the four we have been discussing. After Hector is dead, and the Greeks have admired and abused his body, Achilles makes a speech which has worried commentators. It runs from 22.378 to 394:

'Friends, who are leaders of the Argives and keep their counsel:
since the gods have granted me the killing of this man
who has done us much damage, such as not all the others together
have done, come, let us go in armour about the city
to see if we can find out what purpose is in the Trojans,
whether they will abandon their high city, now that this man
has fallen, or are minded to stay, though Hector lives no longer.
Yet still, why does the heart within me debate on these things?
There is a dead man who lies by the ships, unwept, unburied:
Patroklos: and I will not forget him, never so long as
I remain among the living and my knees have their spring beneath me.
And though the dead forget the dead in the house of Hades,
even there I shall remember my beloved companion.
But now, you young men of the Achaians, let us go back, singing
a victory song, to our hollow ships; and take this with us.
We have won ourselves enormous fame; we have killed the great Hector
whom the Trojans glorified as if he were a god in their city.'

What has been found difficult to understand is that he first suggests that they make a show of force about Troy, now that Hector is dead; but then changes his mind, mentions the body of Patroclus still lying unburied by the ships, and tells the Greeks to go back in triumph to their camp with Hector's body. Commentators have wondered, if that is what he intends to do, why did he first suggest that they move to Troy. We note that at the point of change of mind in this speech appears that same line which appeared at the same point in each of the soliloquies. Achilles' change of mind can be explained in psychological terms; but we can see it more simply as another example of oral composition. The speech is not a soliloquy, but it bears a resemblance to one. Achilles is thinking aloud as he addresses the troops. So he first thinks of an alternative course; then uses that stock line which indicates decision-making in a soliloquy; and comes to the actual decision. In oral poetry terms, there is no problem.

NOTES

*This paper was given at the 1989 A.G.M. of the Classical Association held at the University of Sheffield.

1. *Von Homers Welt und Werk* (4th edn. Stuttgart, 1965), 155–202.
2. 2nd edn. repr. Darmstadt, 1966.
3. See *CQ* 14 (1964), 141–54.
4. See also important distinctions made by V. di Benedetto, 'Nel laboratorio di Omero', *RFIC* 114 (1986), 257–85 and 385–410; Jasper Griffin, 'Words and Speakers in Homer', *JHS* 106 (1986), 36–57; N. J. Richardson, 'The Individuality of Homer's Language' in *Homer: Beyond Oral Poetry* (Amsterdam, 1987), 165–84.
5. *The Singer of Tales* (Harvard, 1960), 97 and the application to the *Odyssey* in ch. 3.
6. 15.521–2; cf. Virgil, *Aen.* 2.319.
7. The other is Hyperenor: 14.516, 17.24.
8. Lohmann, op. cit., 30–3, 119–20.
9. On the Polydamas speeches, see also Herbert Bannert, *Formen des Wiederholens bei Homer* (Vienna, 1988), 71–81.
10. I think for example of the theme 'three times . . ., but when for a fourth time . . .', on which see Bannert, ibid., 40–57.
11. On these, see particularly G. Petersmann, 'Die Entscheidungsmonologe in den Homerischen Epen', *Grazer Beiträge 2* (1974), 147–69.
12. These two great figures compete in the wrestling in the Games of Book 23, and Odysseus is ahead on points when the bout is stopped.

CRITICAL APPRECIATION:
HOMER, *ILIAD* 1.1–52

By JASPER GRIFFEN AND MARTIN HAMMOND

I

Μῆνιν ἄειδε, θεά, Πηληϊάδεω Ἀχιλῆος
οὐλομένην, ἣ μυρί' Ἀχαιοῖς ἄλγε' ἔθηκε,
πολλὰς δ' ἰφθίμους ψυχὰς Ἄϊδι προΐαψεν
ἡρώων, αὐτοὺς δὲ ἑλώρια τεῦχε κύνεσσιν
οἰωνοῖσί τε πᾶσι, Διὸς δ' ἐτελείετο βουλή,   5
ἐξ οὗ δὴ τὰ πρῶτα διαστήτην ἐρίσαντε
Ἀτρεΐδης τε ἄναξ ἀνδρῶν καὶ δῖος Ἀχιλλεύς.
    Τίς τ' ἄρ σφωε θεῶν ἔριδι ξυνέηκε μάχεσθαι;
Λητοῦς καὶ Διὸς υἱός· ὁ γὰρ βασιλῆϊ χολωθεὶς
νοῦσον ἀνὰ στρατὸν ὦρσε κακήν, ὀλέκοντο δὲ λαοί,   10
οὕνεκα τὸν Χρύσην ἠτίμασεν ἀρητῆρα
Ἀτρεΐδης· ὁ γὰρ ἦλθε θοὰς ἐπὶ νῆας Ἀχαιῶν
λυσόμενός τε θύγατρα φέρων τ' ἀπερείσι' ἄποινα,
στέμματ' ἔχων ἐν χερσὶν ἑκηβόλου Ἀπόλλωνος
χρυσέῳ ἀνὰ σκήπτρῳ, καὶ λίσσετο πάντας Ἀχαιούς,   15
Ἀτρεΐδα δὲ μάλιστα δύω, κοσμήτορε λαῶν·
'Ἀτρεΐδαι τε καὶ ἄλλοι ἐϋκνήμιδες Ἀχαιοί,
ὑμῖν μὲν θεοὶ δοῖεν Ὀλύμπια δώματ' ἔχοντες
ἐκπέρσαι Πριάμοιο πόλιν, εὖ δ' οἴκαδ' ἱκέσθαι·
παῖδα δ' ἐμοὶ λύσαιτε φίλην, τὰ δ' ἄποινα δέχεσθαι,   20
ἁζόμενοι Διὸς υἱὸν ἑκηβόλον Ἀπόλλωνα.'
    Ἔνθ' ἄλλοι μὲν πάντες ἐπευφήμησαν Ἀχαιοὶ
αἰδεῖσθαί θ' ἱερῆα καὶ ἀγλαὰ δέχθαι ἄποινα·
ἀλλ' οὐκ Ἀτρεΐδῃ Ἀγαμέμνονι ἥνδανε θυμῷ,
ἀλλὰ κακῶς ἀφίει, κρατερὸν δ' ἐπὶ μῦθον ἔτελλε·   25
'μή σε, γέρον, κοίλῃσιν ἐγὼ παρὰ νηυσὶ κιχείω
ἢ νῦν δηθύνοντ' ἢ ὕστερον αὖτις ἰόντα,
μή νύ τοι οὐ χραίσμῃ σκῆπτρον καὶ στέμμα θεοῖο·
τὴν δ' ἐγὼ οὐ λύσω· πρίν μιν καὶ γῆρας ἔπεισιν
ἡμετέρῳ ἐνὶ οἴκῳ, ἐν Ἄργεϊ, τηλόθι πάτρης,   30
ἱστὸν ἐποιχομένην καὶ ἐμὸν λέχος ἀντιόωσαν·
ἀλλ' ἴθι, μή μ' ἐρέθιζε, σαώτερος ὥς κε νέηαι.'
    Ὣς ἔφατ', ἔδεισεν δ' ὁ γέρων καὶ ἐπείθετο μύθῳ·
βῆ δ' ἀκέων παρὰ θῖνα πολυφλοίσβοιο θαλάσσης·
πολλὰ δ' ἔπειτ' ἀπάνευθε κιὼν ἠρᾶθ' ὁ γεραιὸς   35
Ἀπόλλωνι ἄνακτι, τὸν ἠΰκομος τέκε Λητώ·
'κλῦθί μευ, ἀργυρότοξ', ὃς Χρύσην ἀμφιβέβηκας

Κίλλαν τε ζαθέην Τενέδοιό τε ἶφι ἀνάσσεις,
Σμινθεῦ, εἴ ποτέ τοι χαρίεντ᾽ ἐπὶ νηὸν ἔρεψα,
ἢ εἰ δή ποτέ τοι κατὰ πίονα μηρί᾽ ἔκηα   40
ταύρων ἠδ᾽ αἰγῶν, τόδε μοι κρήηνον ἐέλδωρ·
τίσειαν Δαναοὶ ἐμὰ δάκρυα σοῖσι βέλεσσιν.᾽
 Ὥς ἔφατ᾽ εὐχόμενος, τοῦ δ᾽ ἔκλυε Φοῖβος Ἀπόλλων,
βῆ δὲ κατ᾽ Οὐλύμποιο καρήνων χωόμενος κῆρ,
τόξ᾽ ὤμοισιν ἔχων ἀμφηρεφέα τε φαρέτρην·   45
ἔκλαγξαν δ᾽ ἄρ᾽ ὀϊστοὶ ἐπ᾽ ὤμων χωομένοιο,
αὐτοῦ κινηθέντος· ὁ δ᾽ ἤϊε νυκτὶ ἐοικώς.
ἕζετ᾽ ἔπειτ᾽ ἀπάνευθε νεῶν, μετὰ δ᾽ ἰὸν ἕηκε·
δεινὴ δὲ κλαγγὴ γένετ᾽ ἀργυρέοιο βιοῖο·
οὐρῆας μὲν πρῶτον ἐπώχετο καὶ κύνας ἀργούς,   50
αὐτὰρ ἔπειτ᾽ αὐτοῖσι βέλος ἐχεπευκὲς ἐφιεὶς
βάλλ᾽· αἰεὶ δὲ πυραὶ νεκύων καίοντο θαμειαί.

Sing, goddess, of the anger of Achilles, son of Peleus, the accursed anger which brought uncounted anguish on the Achaeans and hurled down to Hades many mighty souls of heroes, making their bodies the prey to dogs and the birds' feasting: and this was the working of Zeus' will. Sing from the time of the first quarrel which divided Atreus' son, the lord of men, and godlike Achilles.

Which of the gods was it who set these two to their fighting? It was the son of Zeus and Leto. In anger at the king he raised a vile plague throughout the army, and the people were dying, because the son of Atreus had dishonoured Chryses, his priest. Chryses had come to the fast ships of the Achaeans to gain release for his daughter, bringing with him unlimited ransom, and holding in his hands the sacred woollen bands of Apollo the far-shooter, wreathed on a golden staff. He began to entreat the whole body of the Achaeans, but especially the two sons of Atreus, the marshals of the army. 'Sons of Atreus, and you other well-greaved Achaeans, may the gods who live on Olympus grant you the sacking of Priam's city and a safe return to your homes. But release my dear child to me, and accept this ransom, in reverence for the son of Zeus, Apollo the far-shooter.'

Then all other Achaeans shouted their agreement, to respect the priest's claim and take the splendid ransom. But this was not the pleasure of Agamemnon's heart, the son of Atreus. He sent him shamefully on his way, with harsh words of command: 'Old man, let me never find you by our hollow ships, either dallying here now or coming back again in future—or you will have no protection from your god's staff and sacred bands. As for the girl, I shall not release her. Before that, old age will come upon her in our house, in Argos, far from her own country, where she will work at the loom and serve my bed. No, away with you: do not provoke me, if you want to return in safety.'

So he spoke, and the old man was afraid and did as he was ordered. He went in silence along the shore of the sounding sea. And then when he had gone a far way off, the old man prayed long to lord Apollo, the child of lovely-haired Leto: 'Hear me, lord of the silver bow, protector of Chryse and holy Cilla, and mighty lord of Tenedos, Smintheus. If ever I have built a shrine that is pleasing to you, if ever I have burnt for you fat-wrapped thigh-bones of bulls and goats, grant this my prayer: may the Danaans pay for my tears with your arrows.'

So he spoke in prayer, and Phoebus Apollo heard him. Down he came from the peaks of Olympus with anger in his heart, the bow on his shoulders, and the enclosing quiver. The arrows clattered on the shoulders of Apollo in his anger, as the god himself rushed down: and his coming was like night. He settled then at a distance from the ships, and let fly an arrow: and there came a fearful twang from the silver bow. First he attacked the mules and the quick-running dogs: but then he sent his sharp arrows at the men themselves, and kept shooting them down. And constantly there burned, close-packed, the pyres of the dead.   (tr. Hammond)

II

A long epic poem poses special problems to anyone who sets out to select a short passage and subject it to criticism. It is bound up with the nature of the epic that it does not consist of parts which can without loss be treated separately, but on the contrary flows on in one unbroken stream; 'and then . . .' is always in our ears. It is partly for this reason that Christopher Logue's Homeric poems, now published as *War Music*,[1] are so un-Homeric in feeling; for Homer does not break up his narrative with passages in italics, similes indented to show that they are poetical set-pieces, asterisks followed by a fresh start, or such vivid bits of variety as printing the name APOLLO in huge letters, across the whole of two pages, at the moment when he strikes Patroclus. The distinctive experience of Homer is that of variety within a great smoothness and an unfaltering continuity, and the high points in the epics are distinguished from the rest, not by being like virtuoso arias emerging out of plain recitative, but as possessing the same nature as the rest—only in a more compact, more intense, and more suggestive way.

A poem as long as the *Iliad*, if it was to be a unity and not a mere train of events, needed a good deal of introduction. In one sense we can see that all of the first six books are introductory. In 1 we meet Achilles and Agamemnon, and also see the divine world in its relation with the actions of men. In 2 Zeus intervenes; Agamemnon is shown up, by contrast with Odysseus, as a weak and deluded king who heads for defeat; and the two sides in the war are fully listed. In 3 we see the contrasting pairs, Paris and Menelaus on the one hand, and Paris and Hector on the other; and the position in Troy is clarified by Priam and Helen. In 4 the gods decide, within the poem, the doom of Troy, and Pandarus re-enacts the original offence of Paris. In 5 the real fighting begins; and the triumphs of Diomedes, and his rebuff by Apollo, spell out the limitations of human and divine power which define the world of the poem. And in 6 Hector's encounters with the women of Troy show the contrast between the sphere of men and that of women; we see Paris linger in the feminine world, despised by his wife, and Hector deserve the love of his by withstanding her appeal. Hector, finally, is shown to us as a human warrior, fighting because he must, to defend his wife and child, in contrast with the solitary and half divine warrior Achilles. I think that in the *Iliad* which we possess this introductory function is really present, and that it was intended by the poet to be felt as part of his grand design throughout the first quarter of the poem.

That then, is one sort of introduction to the *Iliad*. It is, however, obvious that it also has an introduction of another sort; in fact, more than one. The first seven lines form a clearly defined proem, which has a structure (Achilles' anger—deadly consequences and the plan of Zeus—angry quarrel of Agamemnon and Achilles), and which states the subject matter of the epic.[2] Secondly, the narrative from line 8 to 52 is developed in a way, and above all at a speed, which marks it off as preliminary; the compression of the speeches and the swift changes of place—Chryses in the Achaean camp, Chryses alone by the loud-roaring sea, Apollo on Olympus, Apollo coming down like the night—produce a rapidity highly unusual in Homer,[3] from which we emerge into a more typically Homeric pace when the quarrel begins between Achilles and Agamemnon. But, thirdly, that quarrel scene itself, which for vividness and richness in character can stand beside (say) the quarrel of Brutus and Cassius in *Julius Caesar* iv. 3, is succeeded (1.305 ff.) by a narration of the same events, given by Achilles to his mother. That narrative is strikingly calmer and less exciting; it is as if the injured hero spoke with the detachment we might have expected from the poet's own narrative, while it is the poet's narrative which possesses the fire and drama. In particular, it omits the direct speech of 17–21, 26–32, and 37–42. It is, I think, reasonable to say that this ordering of the material is not the result of chance: the poet gets us into the *Iliad* with an artful display of his liveliest and most emotional manner. The 'epic objectivity' of 365 ff. shows us another possibility, in that the poem could have opened with that sort of treatment of events instead; but it is immediately obvious that it would have been far less compelling. It is appropriate to compare the first book of Herodotus, most Homeric of historians,[4] which opens with piquant legends of the abduction of women (not failing to point out that 'they would not be abducted if they didn't want to be'), with the spicy tale of Candaules and his wife, with Arion on the dolphin, and with splendid stories about Croesus, before getting on to systematic history—let alone to such dry fare as the geography of Scythia. The calm narrative, like that of the uneventful trip made by Odysseus to return Chryseis to her father (430–87), is in place in the linking passage between the stormy excitement of the opening and the high point among the gods on Olympus at the end of the book; the pace of the opening is not to be kept up throughout the epic, and this judicious contrast makes that clear.

These preliminary remarks help us to see that the first 52 lines of *Iliad* 1 have not to be taken simply as 'the' proem to the *Iliad*. The opening of the great poem is complex and worked out on a large scale. Turning now to the detailed exposition, we observe at once that the poem does not begin with a straightforward and obviously impressive opening like that of the Cyclic *Ilias Parva* (fr. 1 Allen):

> Ἴλιον ἀείδω καὶ Δαρδανίην εὔπωλον
> ἧς πέρι πολλὰ πάθον Δαναοὶ θεράποντες Ἄρηος,

'Of Ilium I sing and the land of Dardania rich in horses, for which they suffered greatly, the Danaans, servants of Ares.' That explicitness gives place to a manner which does not need to tell us where we are—no mention of Troy or a Trojan until the skilfully oblique one of line 19, 'May the gods grant that you sack the city of Priam'—and which singles out from the Trojan War one incident, that of the wrath of Achilles. That is an incident which was not, in any obvious sense, decisive; we are not promised an '*Iliou Persis*', or a song like the one with which Demodocus made Odysseus weep, 'the Wooden Horse which Epeius made with Athene's help, and how Odysseus brought it on to the acropolis by deceit' (*Od.* 8.492–5). We are not promised the beginning of the story of Troy, nor its end. What we are promised is a grim tale: the superhuman wrath of a hero (μῆνις, it has been pointed out, is used in the Homeric poems only of the anger of the gods—and of that of Achilles)[5] and its horrible consequences. The Achaeans suffered 'countless pains', as the *Odyssey* hastens to tell us (1.4) that Odysseus suffered 'many pains', ἄλγεα, and the *Ilias Parva* that the Danaans 'suffered greatly'. Epics were not cheerful affairs: even the national triumph over Troy was far from being a matter of simple exultation, nor will it be told in a chauvinistic spirit like that, for instance, of *Henry V*. Those who listened to the *Iliad* did so in the knowledge that the entertainment would be a tragic one. And that is immediately underlined by the poet: not only were fine men slain, their corpses were the prey of carrion beasts and birds. The lines each juxtapose the sublime and the ghastly:

> Many noble souls / / were sent to Hades,
> Souls of heroes; / / and the men were made the prey of dogs,
> and a feast for birds; / / the will of Zeus was done. (3–5)

The style clamps the extremes together: great heroes and the will of

Zeus; death and dishonoured corpses. That conveys, in short and pregnant form, the central point in the whole Homeric view of the world and of men. Man can be great and god-like, ἴφθιμος, ἥρως, the object of the care of Zeus; but equally he is vulnerable, mortal, a creature whose death Zeus can contemplate without intolerable distress.[6] It is noteworthy that while the theme of the defilement of the corpse appears many times in the *Iliad*, we never actually see the carrion beasts at work. The idea, not the reality, is what the poet needs—great heroes can be brought so low that even that appalling fate may not be spared them; and that, too, can be part of the will of Heaven. Διὸς δ' ἐτελείετο βουλή ('and this was the working of Zeus' will') was unpacked by lesser poets into more or less elaborate stories ('the Earth was over-crowded, and so Zeus . . .'). The *Iliad* prefers to leave it mysterious. Everything that happened was Zeus' will: on the level of the obvious, because he is so powerful that he could have prevented it; and again, because he actually planned the events of the poem, with Thetis (1.500 ff.); and on another level, because what Zeus wills combines the good and the bad, the glorious and the terrible—the tragic insight which Achilles shares with Priam (24.525 ff.). As heroism and the heroic epic need the attention of gods to glorify human action, so the *Iliad* needs the inextricable combination of greatness and fragility which such gods ensure. So: it all began when they quarrelled, the son of Atreus, king of men, and god-like Achilles. That line, rich and formulaic, brings together and juxtaposes immediately the two protagonists, one defined by his status, the other by his nature;[7] the quarrel between them, the great king and the great man, will for that very reason be insoluble. And it ends with the name Achilles, so rounding off the period which began with the mention of his anger (1–7). He embraces it all.

Now the poet takes a breath. They quarrelled: why did they quarrel? Or, which in the epic comes to the same thing, what god made them do it? Events must have causes on the level of the divine, or they are not worthy of the epic. The question is in the manner of the choral lyric,[8] and its answer is 'Apollo'. When we get to Book 19 we shall hear Agamemnon himself give a different answer (19.86): 'It was Zeus and Fate and the Fury that walks in darkness—they put Atē into my mind.' Achilles accepts this analysis (19.270). The poet who said three lines earlier that 'the will of Zeus was fulfilled' would clearly not disagree; but Apollo, too, had a hand, and it is at the point where he intervened that the story is to begin. Lines 9–11 give the content of the following lines with the greatest possible compression: the offence of the king, the anger of the god. The poem could have continued with line 53, omitting 12–52, the poet narrating (without dramatic dialogue) 'It was Apollo: he was angry with the king because he did not respect Chryses his priest, and he sent pestilence among the army, so that the men began to die. Nine days did the arrows of the god rain down . . .' That is a style which is not unknown to Homer. A close parallel is provided by Phoenix' narration of the story about Meleager, 9.533 ff.: 'For Artemis of the golden throne had brought a plague upon them, in wrath that Oeneus offered her no harvest first-fruits; all the other gods had their feast of hecatombs, and to the daughter of Zeus alone he gave no offering . . . So the Archer-goddess was angry and sent against him a great wild boar, which wrought great havoc on his land; many a tall tree he laid low, roots and apple blossom and all. But Meleager slew the boar . . .' Such a comparison shows how simply the plague could have been told.[9] We should then have lost two things: the appearance of Chryses, and the description of Apollo in action.

The scene with Chryses[10] enables the poet to make his story more dramatic and to exploit the effective contrast between the arrogant king and the humble old man. It also gives us our first taste of one of the poem's great motifs: the bereaved and pathetic father. The fathers whose sons are killed in battle, on whose unhappiness the poem loves to dwell, are akin to the fuller development of the motif in old Chryses (1), old Phoenix, a surrogate father (9), and old Priam, who in the climactic scene of the series (24.504 ff.) reminds Achilles of his own father Peleus, also old and alone, whose son will not come back to him. In this first appearance of the theme its development is swift and compressed; the artistic unity of the poem demands that the scenes shall grow in length and weight, and in addition this is the one time the bereaved father is, in the end, to turn out happily. His anguish, though intense, is to be short, and that fits well with the urgent style and hurrying pace of the opening of the *Iliad*.

It was all because Agamemnon slighted the priest Chryses, and to him the poet now turns. He is presented as a pathetic figure ('he has been made pathetic in every way, with his age, his loss of his daughter, his coming among his enemies, and his bringing of gifts', observes a scholiast on 1.13). No doubt a realistic representation of the scene would give Chryses attendants to carry the 'countless ransom', but we see him as alone, no word hinting at the presence of anyone with him; for the poet, he is isolated among his enemies. In the more leisurely style of Achilles' narration, 365 ff., we are given the background in full for the first time. But while he is pathetic he also has the hint of something else, of power. He brings the rich ransom, but he also carries the symbols of his priestly office, 'the garlands of Apollo the Far-shooter'[11] (14), the arrows which we shall soon see in action. He delivers his appeal in the midst of the Achaean army—the speed of the narrative is too quick to allow the deployment of the motif of 'summoning an assembly' (short form, 1.54–7; long form, 2.85 ff.). In five lines he makes his appeal, which begins with a prayer to the gods (18) and ends with the name of Apollo (21). In between come two lines similar in rhythm, both dividing with a heavy stop after three and a half feet, and ending in words which rhyme. It is an utterance whose form resembles that of a spell; and the name of the god closes the speech with a clinching spondeiazon. We observe that there are only three lines with such a termination in the opening of Book 1: twice the closing word is the name of Apollo, and once the title of his priest (14, 21; 11). We must wait until line 74 for a verse in which that rhythm appears in another connection, and by then attention is no longer focussed on Apollo. I see in all this the deliberate artistry of the poet, as I do also in the cruel line 30, when the king says to Chryses: 'I will not let her go; no, she shall grow old ἡμετέρῳ ἐνὶ οἴκῳ, ἐν Ἄργεϊ, τηλόθι πάτρης (in my house, in Argos, far from her home).' The rhythm, hammering home the point, has the effect of making the line a taunt: 'In my house—yes, in Argos—a *long* way away.' 'Gradually building up the effect of distance he causes pain to the old man', observes the ancient commentator, correctly.[12] I see it again in the rhythm of line 42, the old man's prayer: τείσειαν Δαναοὶ | ἐμὰ δάκρυα | σοῖσι βέλεσσιν ('May the Danaans pay for my tears with your arrows'), which puts the enemy, the speaker, and the god into three separate compartments, between each of which we seem to hear the passionate old man make a pause for emphasis.

The mention of Apollo in line 21 is not explicitly a threat. It is phrased more delicately than that, but it is still effective. The Argive army is impressed, both by the man's sacral position and also, very characteristically, by the rich ransom he brings; their urging that the king should αἰδεῖσθαί θ' ἱερῆα καὶ ἀγλαὰ δέχθαι ἄποινα ('respect the priest's claim and take the splendid ransom') brings out this double motivation. A Greek saw no incongruity between what we would regard as interested and disinterested motives, as we can see when Telemachus speaks of the reasons why he must kill the suitors (*Od.* 2.130ff.) or Orestes of the pressures which drive him to kill his mother (Aeschylus, *Cho.* 298ff.).[13]

The priest's petition finds favour with the army, among whom we are doubtless meant to include the other chieftains. I observe in passing that the prudent Odysseus did respect the wife and daughter of another priest of Apollo, when he came across him in his wanderings; and the grateful father gave him the wine with which he overcame the Cyclops (*Od.* 9.197–201). It is Agamemnon alone who refuses, and his harsh speech of rejection underlines the purely personal and arbitrary nature of his decision. ἐγώ . . . ἐγώ . . . ἡμετέρῳ ἐνὶ οἴκῳ . . . ἐμὸν λέχος . . . μή μ' ἐρέθιζε . . . ('I . . . I . . . in our house . . . my bed . . . do not provoke me'): in seven lines five expressions of triumphant egotism. The address to Chryses as γέρον, 'old man', has point. Usually its tone is respectful, the chief representatives of the class of old men in the *Iliad* being the venerable figures of Nestor and Priam. Indeed, Matthew Arnold thought that the line which Achilles speaks to Priam: καὶ σέ, γέρον, τὸ πρὶν μὲν ἀκούομεν ὄλβιον εἶναι ('Of you too, old man, we hear that once you were happy', 24.543)—'for mingled pathos and dignity is perhaps without a rival even in Homer'.[14] But in this place, on the lips of Agamemnon, it conveys only the king's sense that Chryses is old and feeble, unable to defend himself against violence. 'Old age, which is respected by others, he casts at him like a reproach', is the perceptive comment of the scholiast on line 26. 'Your staff (σκῆπτρον) will not defend you, if I catch you here again', says Agamemnon, and we remember that not only priests but also kings are σκηπτοῦχοι ('staff-bearing'). Agamemnon himself has a kingly sceptre, which comes to him from Zeus by way of his ancestors (2.101 ff.). When he makes his disastrous speech to the Achaeans in Book 2, after which they try to bolt for home, it is elaborately described, and the king leans on it to speak; but Zeus who gave the sceptre has sent a false dream to undermine his leadership and plans his humiliation at the hands of Achilles. The bluster of Agamemnon in Book 1 is seen altogether in an ironic light, as we know that he is heading for defeat; his scorn of the sceptre of Chryses is part of that irony, since events will show us the discredit of his own. As he stands helplessly watching the Achaeans rushing for the ships, Odysseus has to take the sceptre away from him (2.186) and play the part of a real king.

But for the moment Agamemnon thinks things are going well: the old man, intimidated, goes off alone. So Agamemnon will soon seem to have prevailed over Achilles (he, too, finds that a σκῆπτρον is disregarded by the king, 1.234–46). Achilles goes off alone to the sea-shore and calls on a goddess; and she starts the divine plot against Agamemnon which will form the poem. We are given as it were a compact version of that when old Chryses goes off alone by the sea and calls on a god, again setting a plot in motion behind the king's back. Line 34 has often been praised for its beauty, the opening monosyllable and the silence of the old man contrasting with the long words and constant roar of the sea at the close, so that we see a long beach and the single small figure on it. An old man, γέρων and γεραιός (33, 35), he arouses our sympathy.

His prayer to his god speaks first of his silver bow, the bow which will soon be in action (49). As the first seven lines of the poem opened and closed with Achilles, so this prayer is framed between Apollo's title of Archer and his arrows. The god bestrides Chryse, he rules Tenedos by might, he is lord of the mice which bring the plague, he is an archer: the six-line prayer is packed with indications of his formidable nature. At its end Chryses disappears from view. Somehow he made his way back to Chryse, but we are not interested in that. It is perhaps worth making the point, because some people have been seduced by Erich Auerbach's famous essay 'Odysseus' Scar'[15] into believing that Homer always makes everything explicit, that 'nothing may remain hidden or unexpressed' (5) and that every step of the action is always spelled out. In fact, the narrative of the first book of the *Iliad* is in many respects unlike the account of 'the Homeric style' given in that fascinating chapter.

Apollo hears the prayer. Nine lines describe his response. In those lines certain ideas are repeated, without repetition of the identical verbal form: the god moved (βῆ, κινηθέντος, ἤιε), he was angry (χωόμενος κῆρ, χωομένοιο, νυκτὶ ἐοικώς); on his shoulders (ὤμοισιν, ἐπ' ὤμων) he carried his weapons (τόξα, φαρέτρην, ὀϊστοί, ἰόν, βιοῖο, βέλος); their sound was fearful (ἔκλαγξαν, κλαγγή). This sort of repetition, which is characterized by variety and is clearly not to be explained by any mechanical iteration of formulae, is of course a device of emphasis. We find similar passages, for instance, at *Il.* 1.505–10, 2.394–7, 13.795–801, *Od.* 19.204–8.[16] The accumulation of words of similar sense, which do not add much in terms of content, allows the poet to linger on an important scene.

The first book of the *Iliad* is remarkable for containing no long developed similes of the characteristically Homeric type. There are only three of the shortest type of comparison: at line 104 Agamemnon's eyes 'are like flashing fire'; at 359 Thetis comes up out of the sea 'like a mist'; and here Apollo comes 'like night'. The absence of long comparisons is surely connected with the speed of events in this most rapid of Homeric books: we have not the time to gaze at things and actions, and to see them in all their aspects. But when, in that urgent style, we read that the god 'came like the night', then that half-line is pregnant with significance. I should compare with it, for instance, such a weighty and memorable half-line[17] as 1.530, when Zeus nods his head in token of promise to Thetis, μέγαν δ' ἐλέλιξεν Ὄλυμπον ('and he made mighty Olympus tremble'). Again, when Athene suddenly appears to Achilles to check his impulse to kill Agamemnon, at once he knew Pallas Athene: δεινὼ δέ οἱ ὄσσε φάανθεν ('and terrible was the shining of her eyes'). Again, when Agamemnon woke after his false dream, 'the divine voice was shed about him' (2.41); when Achilles pursued Hector, 'all the gods looked on' (22.166); when the scales of Zeus condemned Hector to death, 'then Phoebus Apollo left him' (22.213).[18] Such utterances are among the very grandest of Homeric devices, and it would be a crude judgement which should suppose that only the negative motive, the desire to avoid lingering, made the poet satisfied here—satisfied with a rhythm in which some of the epic's finest effects are achieved, and with a comparison whose lack of detail makes it all the more suggestive. The passage ends with the effect of the divine archery: the pyres blazing to burn the dead.[19]

These fifty-two lines, as we said at the beginning, move swiftly. Seven lines introduce the poem in broad terms, outlining its subject matter but not giving a summary of the plot. Neither Patroclus nor Hector is named, nor are we told how long the Achaeans have been at Troy, or how close we shall come to the fall of the city. Only the darkness and tragedy of it all are foreshadowed. A short passage of compressed narrative leads to the confrontation of Chryses and Agamemnon, vivid and pathetic, and achieved with the greatest rapidity and economy. After facing the mass of his enemies, the father goes off alone to call on his god, and the god responds in a way impressive enough to be worthy of him. The first book of the *Aeneid* devotes 33 lines to introduction, before at line 34 we join Aeneas; the action of *Paradise Lost* opens at the fiftieth line of the first book; the action of the *Iliad* begins at line 12 (ὁ γὰρ ἦλθε). It is the triumph of the Homeric style that introduction is so short and at the same time so massive.

JASPER GRIFFIN

III

What do we expect of the opening of a poem of some 15,000 lines, or of any artistic enterprise of unusual scale and scope? I suppose a natural expectation is for prefatory matter of some extent and conscious gravity, an introductory section which, by its appeal to the listener's awareness of proportion, warns of considerable substance to follow: and this opening passage is likely to be grand, sonorous, tone-setting, leisurely in movement, designed, among other things, to allow a particular set of anticipations to form and settle in the listener's mind—something like the opening of *Paradise Lost*, or of the St. Matthew Passion.

When we turn to the opening of the *Iliad*, the longest and the most monumental (and consciously so) poem in Greek literature, we find something astonishingly different. The immediate impression is of speed and narrative energy: qualities which quicken (in both senses) the whole length of the poem (to this extent the opening is 'tone-setting'). The invocation is condensed into the minimum two words—an imperative and a vocative (lengthier appeals for divine guidance are made elsewhere in the poem, notably at 2.484–93). And this minimal invocation is pushed from prominence and penned in by the terse but weighty statement of theme: anger and consequence, μῆνιν . . . οὐλομένην ('anger . . . accursed'), each emphasized by position, frame a line and a quarter of polysyllabic gravity, followed by the easier movement of the relative clause which details the consequence. The introductory passage—brisk, economical, and dense—is confined to a mere seven lines: the limits of this section are marked by the two namings of Achilles, a characteristic Homeric 'frame' (Πηληϊάδεω Ἀχιλῆος . . . δῖος Ἀχιλλεύς, 'Achilles, son of Peleus . . . godlike Achilles'), which also serves to identify for the listener the character at the centre of the *Iliad*'s interest.

The next section, the first scene in the *Iliad*'s action, is also enclosed within a frame (plague-death in the Greek army, 10~52): the first example of a familiar narrative structure, in which an initial statement of event or circumstance is followed by an account of its causes, leading in direct historical sequence to a restatement of the event or circumstance (a particularly clear small-scale example of this ABA structure is in 9.529–49: there was a battle between the Curetes and the Aetolians—Artemis caused it, by sending the Calydonian boar and creating dissension over the spoils—so there was a battle between the Curetes and the Aetolians). This section moves extremely fast. After the briefest of introductory gestures (the question in line 8, addressed not to the Muse—we are done with invocation—but to the poet himself: a device used not infrequently to mark the beginning of a new section, e.g., 16.692f.), we are plunged straight into the immediacy of action. Rapid narrative is under way by line 12, and by the end of this short scene we have witnessed supplication and its rejection, prayer for vengeance, the descent of a god, and plague ravaging the Greek army. The passage is handled in a narrative style of great vigour and subtlety, which within a very small compass can invest the rapid surface events with emotion and significance, turning action and character into archetypes. Already there have been established several of the elements which determine the *Iliad*'s viewpoint and direct its shape: and it is clear that a deliberate relation is created between the very beginning of the *Iliad* and the very end. The *Iliad* opens with no elaborate scene-setting, no story-so-far retrospect (Books 2 to 4 function partly as a sort of reprise of the beginning of the war, either directly—as in the account of Calchas' prophecy at Aulis in 2.300ff.—or more often indirectly, in the 'anachronistic' presentation of events more suitable to the first than the tenth year of the war). Speed, energy, and directness characterize the narrative from the very start: the *Iliad* is a poem of action and con-sequence.

The opening statement of theme (lines 1–7) advertises a programme with terse economy. This is to be a large tale, full of deaths and disasters (*innumerable* troubles, *many* the mighty souls sent down to Hades). Achilles will be the main centre of interest (1, 7). The disasters will arise directly from his anger—as indeed they do: all the major events of the *Iliad* spring in unbroken sequence from the quarrel, including those final events which, though lying outside the *Iliad*, are yet its focus—the death of Achilles and the fall of Troy. The anger is οὐλομένη 'accursed' (LSJ explain οὐλόμενος as 'one of or to whom the word ὄλοιτο (or ὄλοιο) may be used'), and its grim consequences rebound to afflict Achilles himself, so that he is moved to curse strife and anger (saying ἀπόλοιτο of them, 18.107) when he comes to realize their destructive power. All this destruction will be seen as part of the divine governance of the world (5). The first step will be a quarrel between Agamemnon and Achilles, each asserting a claim, on different grounds, to be ἄριστος Ἀχαιῶν or 'best of the Achaeans' (Agamemnon is ἄναξ ἀνδρῶν or 'the lord of men', Achilles is δῖος or 'god-like').

From one point of view, then, we are promised an exciting story of drama and incident. But this does not exhaust the expectations aroused by the opening lines, or account for their tone. They speak of pitiable doings. The story will be one of pain, discord, destruction, desecration—of a world gone awry, in which fine men die before their time and their bodies lie unburied, torn by dogs and carrion birds. The theme of a perverted world—all running contrary to that which is rightful, δίκη—is given powerful and immediate expression in the following scene. We see the brutal rejection of the strongest appeals to a proper sense of αἰδώς or 'respect' (supplication, the call for respect for the gods), formally made by a figure of inherent dignity and pathos, whose moral case combines the claims of father, suppliant, and priest; the callous abuse of the old; unnatural death by disease. That the poet intends to create an atmosphere of wrongness and disorder is put beyond doubt by the close relation he has set between the opening scene and the great final scene of the *Iliad*, in which Priam visits Achilles to beg for the body of Hector (a vast frame which unites the action of the *Iliad*). Once more an old man, a father, and a suppliant appeals to a proud, unstable, violent man for the return of his child. There has intervened all the suffering and death of the *Iliad*, all partly determined by that first act of rejection. With suffering has come, reluctantly, fellow-suffering and understanding, acceptance in place of rejection. What was disordered is set to rights, and δίκη or 'rightness' is reestablished. Μῆνις ('anger') turns to ἔλεος ('pity') and αἰδώς ('respect'); pain and destruction are set in a universal context, as part of the human condition under divine governance; desecration, abhorrent to men and gods, gives way to proper ritual; and the *Iliad* ends with a dwelling description of that which is denied at the beginning, the honorific burial of a hero, duly lamented by family and people. This general movement, from disorder to order, is seen again, more sharply, in the *Oresteia*.

The *Iliad* is a stage for men to die on. It begins with the promise of death, and ends with lamentation for the dead. Mortals suffer and die against a vast and largely unpitying divine background. The human world is not intelligible without the divine: the divine will or whim so completely interfuses human action (and is understood to do so by the actors) that all significant events are doubly determined. The mind of Zeus is always more powerful that that of men (16.688): though human events can be 'explained' in theological terms, there is nothing ultimately explicable or responsible in the mind of Zeus. The gods dominate human life and death in the *Iliad*, and they are set at the head of the poem. The prospective account of the disastrous effects of Achilles' anger is accompanied by the opaque and chilling statement that 'Zeus' will was being accomplished'. No explanation is given, nor could be given: the statement is self-sufficient. The meaning of Διὸς βουλή, 'the will of Zeus', should not be confined to Zeus' initial promise to Thetis. The consequences of Achilles' anger extend far beyond its renunciation: and all that happens in the *Iliad* is within the mind and will of Zeus (cf. Zeus' prophecy in 15.61–8; Achilles in 19.270–4; and *Od.* 8.81 f., πήματος ἀρχὴ | Τρωσί τε καὶ Δαναοῖσι Διὸς μεγάλου διὰ βουλάς, 'the beginning of disaster for both Trojans and Danaans through the will of great Zeus'). Zeus' will, inscrutable, inexplicable, inevitable, necessarily lies at the source of all events: this cardinal and comfortless fact is set at the forefront of the *Iliad*.

The gods determine events, Zeus by his will, the other gods by direct intervention. They are quick to anger (χολωθείς, 9; χωόμενος, 44; χωομένοιο, 46), and terrible. The gods will be presented in various aspects in the *Iliad*, but the dominant aspect is that of fearful power, cutting effortlessly through the frail tissue of human action. The poet, concerned to establish in this first scene types of action and character which will run through the entire poem and set its tone, has made sure that the first appearance and intervention of a god is early, instant, frightening, violent, and decisive. The question (line 8) which begins the scene and introduces Apollo's intervention carries two implications which determine from the start our understanding of the gods' role in human affairs: that it was necessarily a god who instigated the quarrel (the question is 'Which god?', not 'Who?' or 'What?'), and that what Apollo intended as punishment for Agamemnon was the quarrel, not simply the conditions which, as a matter of contingent fact, led up to the quarrel. When the intervention comes, it is instant, heralded simply by the statement 'Apollo heard', a wordless response to the words of prayer: sinister silence of action answers the silencing of the priest. The person of the god is obscured behind his action and its effects: the poet's eye and ear are on the arrows as Apollo descends, takes position, and shoots (τόξα . . . ἔκλαγξαν ὀϊστοί . . . ἰόν . . . κλαγγὴ βιοῖο . . . βέλος, 'the bow . . . the arrows clattered . . . an arrow . . . twang of the bow . . . arrows'). Apollo settles at a distance from the ships (ἀπάνευθε νεῶν, 48). The atmosphere of his visitation is impersonal, distant, deadly. He is ἑκηβόλος, 'the far-shooter', an epithet which has moved from neutral statement (14) to veiled threat (21), and now realization in action (compare the way in which other 'fixed' epithets invade the narrative of the poem: κορυθαίολος or 'of the glinting helmet' Hector and the effect of the helmet on his own son, πόδας ὠκύς or 'swift-footed' Achilles and the fatal pursuit of Hector). The effect of horror—the incursion of the supernatural—is controlled by a double crescendo, and an ambiguity between the physical and the metaphysical. The victims in ascending order are mules, quick dogs (who even so cannot avoid the arrows), and the men themselves. There is a progression from the single sighting shot (held for a moment in isolation with its accompanying fearful twang) to the constant barrage implied in the sinister imperfect βάλλε ('kept shooting'), retained for grim emphasis to the end of the sentence and the beginning of a line, and followed not by death, but by that which presupposes the inevitability of death, a hellish landscape thick with the smoke of burning funeral pyres. The gods will dominate the *Iliad*, and the first irruption of the divine gives the measure of this terrible power—as menacing, irresistible, and elemental as the onset of night (47).

Framed between the statement of divine intervention and its description is the human action which provoked that intervention. The *Iliad* deals in archetypes, and the poet has created this first scene out of elements which have central thematic importance in the poem as a whole, and will recur constantly in various combinations and contexts until they come together again in the great concluding scene between Achilles and Priam. Chryses is the type of the old man, the innocent whose life is ruined by the war, through loss of son or daughter: a figure of dignity and pathos, for which the *Iliad* has a particular sympathy. His daughter represents that other class of pathetic innocents, Τρώων ἄλοχοι καὶ νήπια τέκνα ('the Trojan wives and their little children'), whose fate is so brutally described by Agamemnon in 29–31. The young men die, the old men, the women, and children suffer and grieve. Chryses and Chryseis contain in outline what will be fully developed in Priam and Andromache. Agamemnon has his own distinct character in the poem: but he stands also as the type of the proud, obstinate, θυμός-ridden king, quick to feel provocation, his emotions and reactions at the mercy of a θυμός ('spirit') he fails to control (θυμὸς δὲ μέγας ἐστὶ διοτρεφέων βασιλήων, 'kings ordained by god have a spirit that runs high', 2.196: compare Nestor to Agamemnon in 9.109 ff., Peleus' advice to Achilles reported in 9.255 f., Phoenix to Achilles in 9.496, Achilles to Agamemnon in 19.66 [=18.113]). And there are thematic elements in the situation: the attempt of non-combatants to win consideration from the fighting men, the appeal to αἰδώς and its rejection (so Apollo says of Achilles in 24.44 f., ἔλεον μὲν ἀπώλεσεν, οὐδέ οἱ αἰδὼς γίγνεται, 'he has murdered pity, and there is no shame in him').

The scene is presented in three sections, and its movement comes from three short passages of direct speech of carefully contrasted tone (Chryses to the Atreidae, Agamemnon to Chryses, Chryses to Apollo). Each speech is preceded by four lines of narrative which determine the moral and emotional atmosphere. The divisions and transitions are pointed with characteristic precision (ἔνθα . . . ὣς ἔφατο . . . ὣς ἔφατο, 'then . . . so he spoke . . . so he spoke'). An apparently defenceless old man is rudely spurned by an apparently powerful king. As the scene develops Chryses' apparent weakness is revealed as real strength, and Agamemnon's temporal power (swelling in the weighty designation Ἀτρεΐδη Ἀγαμέμνονι, 'Agamemnon, the son of Atreus') is reduced to insignificance under the onrush of divine retribution. Subtle use is made of names and titles. Chryses' vocatives, Ἀτρεΐδαι τε καὶ ἄλλοι ἐϋκνήμιδες Ἀχαιοί ('Sons of Atreus and you other well-greaved Achaeans'), are formal, deferential, an appeal to benevolence. In clear contrast is Agamemnon's refusal to acknowledge Chryses' name, and the substitution of the contemptuous γέρον or 'old man' (compare Achilles' respectful and sympathetic use of the vocative to Priam in 24.543: καὶ σέ, γέρον, τὸ πρὶν μὲν ἀκούομεν ὄλβιον εἶναι, 'and you too, old man, we hear that you had fortune once'). The pomp of Ἀτρεΐδη Ἀγαμέμνονι (24) is countered in advance by the implied threat of the priest's Διὸς υἱὸν ἑκηβόλον Ἀπόλλωνα ('the son of Zeus, Apollo the far-shooter', 21), which sets divine son and divine father against the human pedigree: and the full majesty of Apollo is asserted by the narrative in the complete line Ἀπόλλωνι ἄνακτι, τὸν ἠΰκομος τέκε Λητώ ('lord Apollo, the child of lovely-haired Leto', 36). When Chryses prays to Apollo, the chosen epithets ἀργυρότοξε ('lord of the silver bow') and Σμινθεῦ ('Smintheus') define the nature of the desired intervention (plague-dealing arrows).

The lines which introduce Chryses' appeal give him a sympathetic motive (λυσόμενος θύγατρα, 'to gain release for his daughter'—no detail or explanation is given), make clear the he can add the sanction of a god to the claims of a father, and establish that he is willingly fulfilling both the moral and the material ritual of supplication. His appeal, addressed to the entire Greek army, is modest and deferential, prefacing with benedictions his own request, which is given a moral, material, and theological base (παῖδα φίλην . . . ἄποινα . . . Ἀπόλλωνα, 'my dear child . . . ransom . . . Apollo'). His double prayer for the Greeks' success contains an irony (εὖ δ' οἴκαδ' ἱκέσθαι, 'and a safe return to your homes') which is mirrored in Priam's parallel double prayer for Achilles in 24.556f., that he should have enjoyment of the ransom and return to his own native land: the first and the last of a long series of partially-granted prayers in the Iliad. The acclamation of the Greeks confirms the narrative implication that Chryses is entitled to consideration and has satisfied convention (both αἰδώς, 'respect', and straightforward calculus of value demand that his appeal should be granted—the ransom is ἀπερείσια, ἀγλαά, 'unlimited, splendid': compare Achilles' protestation to the dead Patroclus in 24.594, οὔ μοι ἀεικέα δῶκεν ἄποινα, 'it was no unworthy ransom he gave me'), and serves to weight the moral scales against Agamemnon, whose rejection of the appeal is counter to popular opinion, a matter of autocratic θυμός, and explicitly condemned by the poet with the word κακῶς ('shamefully'). Agamemnon's words to Chryses (a κρατερὸς μῦθος, 'harsh words') are cruelly dismissive of all his claims, as old man, priest, and father (all categories of particular concern to the poet of the *Iliad*). Chryses' mission, one of inherent pathos and justice recognized by all others, is contemptuously described as 'hanging about the Greek ships'. The protection of his god is questioned in terms which can be used by the poet in comment on the ineluctable death of favourites (e.g., 5.53 of Scamandrius: χραισμεῖν, 'protect', is a *vox propria* in this context), but are employed in human threat at the certain peril of the speaker. 'Her I will not release', a sentence of brisk finality, continues the contemptuous anonymity of Agamemnon's opening: and he follows with a cruel account of the conditions of captivity, a crescendo of deprivations and indignities designed to cause maximum pain to the father (a taunting use of a motif put to pathetic effect in Hector's predictions for Andromache in 6.456 ff.—Hector cannot mention what Agamemnon boorishly insists upon, the serving of the master's bed).

It is the speech of a bully, and the old man is cowed (pathetic use of ὁ γέρων, 'the old man', in 33, a line which reappears, significantly, in the parallel scene between Priam and Achilles, 24.571, giving Priam's reaction to Achilles' μηκέτι νῦν μ' ἐρέθιζε, γέρον, 'Do not now provoke me more, old man': Achilles, like Agamemnon, is easily provoked, and his control of his θυμός is precarious). Rejected by men, the priest turns to his god, walking far along the sea-shore before uttering his prayer. In these four lines (33–6) the poet creates atmosphere with a marvellously sure touch. The distancing in space and time separates the world of men from the divine world to which the priest has privileged access, and allows fear to turn into confidence as the transition is made, and weak old man comes into contact with divine power in all its extent (Ἀπόλλωνι ἄνακτι, τὸν ἠΰκομος τέκε Λητώ, 'lord Apollo the child of lovely-haired Leto'). Chryses' silence (ἀκέων) does double duty. The old man is silenced (the standard reaction to a κρατερὸς μῦθος): but the silence of the priest is sinister, that of a man who knows what he will do, and whose speech when it issues will have much more drastic effect than Agamemnon's. The solitude of the sea-shore answers to his emotional state (as it does to that of Achilles in 1.350 and to Odysseus in *Od.* 5.156 ff.—in all three cases a contribution to the mood is made by the epithets for the power or vastness of the sea): but it is also a proper setting, because remote and elemental, for communion with a god (so Achilles and Thetis in 1.350 ff.; and, memorably, Pelops, οἶος ἐν ὄρφνᾳ, 'alone in the darkness', and Poseidon in Pindar, *O.* 1.71 ff.). The prayer is solemn, formally constructed, precise: its confidence is eloquent of the special relation between ἀρητήρ ('priest') and his god (μευ . . . τοι . . . τοι . . . μοι . . . ἐμά . . . σοῖσι, 'me . . . you . . . you . . . me . . . my . . . your', 37–42): the unusually tight structure of the one-line request (42) sets an immediate and emphatic relation between offenders and victim, offence and retribution. Apollo's reaction is instant, cued by the final word 'arrows': and the directness of response is crisply conveyed by the language, as τοῦ δ᾽ ἔκλυε, ('heard him') answers κλῦθί μευ ('hear me'), and Apollo's wordless descent to the Greek ships mirrors the priest's silent departure (βῆ δέ . . . βῆ δέ, 'he went . . . down he came'). The next utterance is that of the silver bow.

MARTIN HAMMOND

NOTES

1. C. Logue, *War Music*, (London, 1981). I say they are 'un-Homeric in feeling'; but they are well worth reading, all the same.

2. There is an interesting article on the first seven lines, at times perhaps rather overambitious, by J. M. Redfield in *CP* 74 (1979), 95–110; and since I wrote this piece Mark W. Edwards has published an important paper on 'Convention and Individuality in *Iliad* 1' in *HSCP* 84 (1980), 1–28.

3. 'Homer nowhere better justifies Horace's *semper ad eventum festinat* than in his proems and the few verses of additional exposition which follow them': S. E. Bassett, 'The Proems of the *Iliad* and *Odyssey*', *AJP* 44 (1923), 339. See also E. Bethe, *Homer* I (1914), 23–7.

4. Ὁμηρικώτατος: cf. [Longinus], *On the Sublime* 13.3.

5. H. Frisk, 'Μῆνις, zur Geschichte eines Begriffes', *Eranos* 44 (1946), 28–40; C. Watkins, *Bull. Soc. Ling. de Paris* 72 (1977), 187–209.

6. These are ideas which I develop in *Homer on Life and Death* (Oxford, 1980), especially chapters 3 and 6.

7. Adam Parry in *HSCP* 76 (1972), 2.

8. E.g., Pindar, *Pyth.* 4.70, of the Argonauts: τίς γὰρ ἀρχὰ δέξατο ναυτιλίας; τίς δὲ κίνδυνος . . .;, 'What was the beginning of their voyage, and what danger . . .?', Sophocles, *Trach.* 504, Bacchylides 19.15, Pindar, *Ol.* 10.60, etc.

9. When Plato criticized the opening of the *Iliad* as too dramatic, showing how it should have been told as pure narrative (*Resp.* 393), he might have pointed to this passage. Similar passages: *Il.* 6.175ff., Proetus and Bellerophon; *Od.* 15.225ff., the story of Melampus. This latter, it is worth saying, is narrated by the poet himself, not by one of the characters; that is not the reason for this style.

10. Cf. J. T. Kakridis, *Homer Revisited* (Lund, 1971), 125–37.

11. That is not the modern view of the etymology of ἑκηβόλος, but it is clear that already in the *Iliad* it was believed: cf. 1.48: ἕζετ᾽ ἔπειτ᾽ ἀπάνευθε νεῶν, μετὰ δ᾽ ἰὸν ἕηκε, 'he settled then at a distance from the ships, and let fly an arrow.'

12. The technique is like that of 1.185, Agamemnon to Achilles: I will take Briseis from you, αὐτὸς ἰὼν κλισίηνδε, τὸ σὸν γέρας, ὄφρ᾽ ἐῢ εἰδῇς | ὅσσον φέρτερός εἰμι σέθεν . . ., 'going myself to your hut, your prize, that you may well know how much better I am than you.' That passage in turn recalls the words of God to Abraham: 'Take now thy son, thine only son Isaac, whom thou lovest. . . .'

13. πολλοὶ γὰρ εἰς ἕν συμπίτνουσιν ἵμεροι, | θεοῦ τ᾽ ἐφετμαὶ καὶ πατρὸς πένθος μέγα, | καὶ πρὸς πιέζει χρημάτων ἀχηνία. . . ., 'for many motives coincide, the commands of heaven, great grief for my father, loss of my patrimony . . .'

14. M. Arnold, *On Translating Homer*.

15. The first chapter of his book *Mimesis* (Princeton, 1952). It is reprinted in *Homer: a Collection of Critical Essays*, edited by G. Steiner and R. Fagles (Englewood Cliffs, N.J., 1962).

16. Cf. J. D. Denniston, *Greek Prose Style*² (Oxford, 1960), 80, and P. E. Easterling, 'Repetitions in Sophocles', *Hermes* 101 (1973), 14–34.

17. 'Half-lines in Homer' is a less obvious title than 'Half-lines in Virgil', but it might make an interesting study.

18. See *Homer on Life and Death* (n. 6), 26–7, 158–9. *Il.* 1.5 Διὸς δ᾽ ἐτελείετο βουλή is in the same elevated style.

19. Mark Edwards (n. 2) well contrasts the full and explicit narration of the same events at 1.382–4.

THERSITES IN THE *ILIAD*

By N. POSTLETHWAITE

The character of Thersites, as presented by Homer in *Iliad* 2, has received an almost universally bad press,[1] typical of which are the comments of F. A. Paley: 'one of the turbulent and insolent malcontents in an army, who use their best efforts to misrepresent the authorities and to incite sedition in others.'[2] Paley's view is typical both in the unsympathetic view it presents of Thersites and in its tendency to see him as representative of a whole genre of subversive and recalcitrant soldiery. My concern in this paper is to examine Thersites within the context of the *Iliad* alone, without any regard for his treatment by subsequent authors, and to attempt to explain his portrayal solely in terms of the dramatic situation at the beginning of the *Iliad*. My contention will be that the episode of Thersites is an important element in Homer's introductory purpose of presenting the backcloth against which the poem's theme, the *mēnis* is acted out.

A brief survey reveals that, in general, recent scholarship has been no more sympathetic to Thersites than Paley. He is dismissed by Beye as 'rude boorish Thersites . . . a menial, a nonentity among dynastic aristocrats, has no other dimension to his being than his physical appearance'[3] and by Mueller as 'the aristocrat's image of a perfect plebeian, an ugly loudmouth and coward';[4] to Redfield he is 'dishonourable',[5] to Silk he is an 'upstart';[6] and all stress his background, or rather his lack of it: 'the only common man who takes any part in the *Iliad*',[7] 'a noisy man of the people who is not supported by the people'.[8] In general then he is seen as a loud-mouthed common soldier who has made himself unpopular both with the leadership and with his fellow-soldiers by his verbal attacks upon the leaders, and who in *Iliad* 2 oversteps the mark completely by criticizing the commander-in-chief Agamemnon and in consequence receives at Odysseus' hands a punishment which is both deserved and heartily condoned by the other Achaeans. Furthermore we are assured by some scholars of the emotions which Homer himself felt towards Thersites and which he intended to arouse in his audience by means of this portrayal: 'Only those whom he despises, Thersites and poor Dolon, are below standard, and they are so created intentionally',[9] 'the unfavourable preliminary report of Thersites' appearance and demeanour show us that the attitude we are expected to adopt towards him is one of dislike and contempt.'[10]

Finally we may note that the figure of Thersites has been interpreted as representing nothing less than a shift in the early history of Greece. Kirk[11] claims that 'the anarchical behaviour of Thersites' belongs to the end of the Mycenaean age and to the succeeding Dark Age. Rankin's historical interpretation goes even further:

He is a sophisticated cold-blooded politician, and his demagogic cynicism is represented in a most advanced and artistic fashion. This aspect of Thersites is probably drawn from life, the political life of the eighth century B.C. In historical terms the Thersites of the *Iliad* may well represent first of all an old layer of almost forgotten conflict between different groups at the close of the Mycenaean period, and secondly those elements of political disturbance which began to show themselves at about the time the Homeric poems were put in their final form, or perhaps somewhat before it[12]

and later:

In the context of Archaic history he is a proto-democratic agitator, a kind of rude Hesiod. On this level he reflects not the flux of the late Mycenaean Age, but the period of social strife and insecurity which is characterised by the discontent and resentment that we find in the *Works and Days*[13]

and finally:

As far as can be seen, 'Homer's' prime contribution was in tailoring this figure to provide a hostile image of those who protested against the rigid aristocratic dominance of the Archaic Age, and he thereby created a person who points forward to other radicals and dissenters in subsequent times . . . Ostensibly— for the real motives of 'Homer' elude our grasp—the *Iliad* provides us with an image of ineffectual revolt which gives a view of Archaic social life opposed to that which we see in Hesiod.[14]

This historical interpretation is in reality no more demonstrable than the rather facile view of J. P. Mahaffy[15] which Rankin quotes: 'we may be sure the real Thersites, from whom the poet drew his picture, was a very different and far more serious power in debate than the misshapen buffoon in the *Iliad*.' The simple fact is that there is no evidence which could remotely support an historical interpretation, since we can have no idea from which, if any, historical era Homer gleaned his Thersites, or which, if any, society's political debate he intended the character to reflect. The only reality we have is the text: the characters, like the society they inhabit, were generated by the narrative related in the text. The figure of Thersites, it may be shown, was just such a character, whose manner of presentation was generated by the dramatic context in which he was placed: the appreciation of this fact will add greatly to our understanding of the backcloth to the wrath of Achilles.

It has been suggested that it is indeed strange that a figure so un-heroic as Thersites should be given any role at all to play in the Achaean assembly:[16] in fact however no objection to his doing so is presented in the text. On the contrary, all the criticism which is levelled at Thersites is concerned with *what* he says rather than with the propriety of so lowly a character speaking at all. It is precisely this which Homer emphasizes when first he introduces him:

> . . . Thersites of the endless speech . . .
> who knew within his head many words, but disorderly;
> vain, and without decency, to quarrel with the princes
> with any word he thought might be amusing to the Argives.
>
> $(2.212–15)^{17}$

His fault is that he is ἀμετροεπής ('of the endless speech') and he speaks μάψ ('in vain'). Homer places the emphasis upon his lack of order: he knows many things but they are ἄκοσμα ('disorderly'), and his rebuking of the kings is likewise οὐ κατὰ κόσμον ('without decency'). His motive in all he says is to get a laugh at the expense of others. His insolence lies not in the fact that he speaks, for he has done so a number of times previously (2.221) and has remained healthy enough to do so again; his insolence lies rather in what he says and against whom he says it. He says things that are not acceptable to the kings or to his fellow-soldiers either, things which are not in keeping—and this surely is the meaning of ἄκοσμα and οὐ κατὰ κόσμον—with established practice. In short, he rocks the boat, and neither leaders nor led thank him for doing so.

It is to emphasize his distance from the established order that Homer endows Thersites with by far the most extraordinary description in the entire poem:

> This was the ugliest man who came beneath Ilion. He was
> bandy-legged and went lame of one foot, with shoulders
> stooped and drawn together over his chest, and above this
> his skull went up to a point with the wool grown sparsely upon it.
>
> (2.216–19)

It would be difficult to imagine a figure more physically remote from the heroes he abuses. It may well be the case that Homer intended to portray Thersites as a figure of ridicule, or even to suggest failings of character through his ugliness;[18] we can however be certain only of our observations, namely, that Thersites is everything a hero is not.

The same point must be made in respect of another feature of Thersites, the absence of any mention of his parentage. Pedigree of course was a vital ingredient of heroic status: we need only cite the instance of Glaucus' recitation of his ancestry with its extraordinary amount of detail (6.145–211). It may well be the case that Homer deliberately omitted Thersites' ancestry, and we may choose to speculate upon his possible motives for doing so; alternatively it has been argued that Homer did not inherit Thersites' ancestry through the oral tradition, and that information about him given by later authors was a fiction invented to fill the gaps which

Homer left.[19] Neither alternative may be proved, and again we may be certain only of what we may observe: that the absence of pedigree, just like his ugliness, serves to set Thersites quite apart from the heroes against whom he rails.

Although we can never know whether it was Homer who introduced Thersites' ugliness and lack of ancestry into the oral tradition or whether these were characteristics which he inherited, we can be reasonably sure that the decision to include him, and his unheroic characteristics, into the *Iliad* was Homer's own and we may speculate upon his motives for doing so. As was discussed earlier, the tendency has been to see in Thersites Homer's illustration of a certain universal type, or even of a trend in the early history of Greece. In the remainder of this paper I wish to demonstrate that there are excellent dramatic reasons for introducing Thersites where he does, for describing him in the way he does, and for putting into his mouth the words he does. The reason for the introduction of Thersites is to be found in the close, and obviously deliberate, parallels which are drawn between him and Achilles.

At first sight this is likely to appear an extraordinary proposition since, as has been argued above, Thersites is everything which the heroes—and Achilles is the most heroic of all—are not. However the effect of the quarrel of Achilles and Agamemnon in *Iliad* 1 has been to isolate Achilles from heroic society, culminating in his withdrawal of himself and his forces from the fray and his threat to return home to Phthia. It is in his isolation from the heroes after the quarrel that Achilles may be seen to be paralleled by Thersites, a parallelism which is clearly indicated by the similarities between Thersites' speech to Agamemnon and the speeches of Achilles and Agamemnon during the quarrel. In most cases these similarities are thematic, but in some they are verbally explicit. For example, in his first introduction Thersites is described as knowing

> . . . within his head many words, but disorderly;
> vain, and without decency, to quarrel with the princes.
> (2.213–14)

As we saw above, the principal objection to Thersites is his rocking of the boat, his constant urge to 'quarrel with the princes', ἐριζέμεναι βασιλεῦσιν. Likewise during the quarrel in *Iliad* 1, when Nestor tried to bring peace by showing the justice of both sides and by trying to persuade each side of the justice of the other, his advice to Achilles was:

> Nor, son of Peleus, think to match your strength with the king.
> (1.277)

The inconsistency in Lattimore's translation should not mask the identity of phrasing: Thersites' attitude towards, and manner of speaking to, the kings reflects completely that which Nestor observes of Achilles—they both like to ἐριζέμεναι βασιλῆι.

The consequence of this constant quarrelling with the kings is that Thersites is hated by them all generally, but

> Beyond all others, Achilles hated him, and Odysseus,
>
> (2.220)

a line echoing the words of Agamemnon to Achilles during their quarrel:

> To me you are the most hateful of all the kings,
>
> (1.176)

a sentiment which Agamemnon explains in the following line:

> Forever quarrelling is dear to your heart, and wars and battles.

Agamemnon's hatred of Achilles, the result of the latter's continual love of strife, parallels the leaders' hatred of Thersites because of his continual striving with them. Thersites and Achilles are thus associated as characters who speak against the established order of heroic society, a proposition supported by one further verbal echo in Homer's introduction of Thersites:

> These two he was forever abusing, but now at brilliant
> Agamemnon he clashed the shrill noise of his abuse.
>
> (2.222-3)

The 'shrill noise of his abuse', ὀξέα ὀνείδεα, is paralleled by Agamemnon's view of Achilles' words:

> yet they [the gods] have not given him the right to speak abusively.
>
> (1.291)

Again Homer associates the way in which Thersites addresses Agamemnon with Achilles' manner in *Iliad* 1.

If we turn from the manner of address to the content, we find likewise that the speech of Thersites rehearses the same ideas as Achilles put forward during the quarrel. Although there are no verbal parallels, the initial line of Thersites' speech

> Son of Atreus, what thing further do you want, or find fault with
>
> (2.224)

clearly echoes Achilles' opening line to Agamemnon

> Son of Atreus, most lordly, greediest for gain of all men.
>
> (1.122)

Both men emphasize the rapaciousness of the commander-in-chief, most recently illustrated by his removal to his own tent of Achilles' girl, Briseis.

In both cases the immediate reference is to Briseis' removal, but in both cases there seems also to be a wider reference to Agamemnon's characteristic, which is made explicit when Thersites proceeds to speak of Agamemnon's priority at the distribution of spoils:

> . . . [women] whom we Achaeans
> give to you first of all whenever we capture some stronghold.
> (2.227–8)

This recalls the central point of Achilles' argument that, by virtue of his position as commander-in-chief, Agamemnon receives the lion's share at the distribution, but during the fighting does nothing to warrant that share:

> . . . but when time comes to distribute the booty
> yours is far the greater reward,
> (1.166–7)
> never . . . do I have a prize that is equal to your prize.
> (1.163)

These words highlight the anomaly of Achilles' position, that, although he is the greatest warrior, he does not receive priority in the allocation of spoils—and thus the greatest *timē*—but instead is subject to an obviously inferior warrior. It is this anomaly which lies behind his quarrel with Agamemnon: the incident of the girl is the excuse for the quarrel, the spark which ignites his frustration. In view of the central importance of Achilles' words above to an understanding of the quarrel and of Achilles' behaviour—and therefore to an understanding of the poem as a whole—it seems an inevitable conclusion that Thersites' words are intended as a comment upon, as support for, the case which Achilles made. Willcock[20] suggests that Thersites' speech is a parody of Achilles', and is therefore presumably to be viewed as part of the general air of buffoonery which is supposed to surround him. It seems more likely however that Homer is here conveying the idea of general Achaean support for Achilles' stance, an idea which is in part supported by Thersites' succeeding insult:

> Is it some young woman to lie with in love?
> (2.232)

A woman, given by his men as a token of his *timē*, is seen by Agamemnon rather as an almost pornographic object—an effect heightened by the purpose clause.[21] It is with Achilles, not the commander-in-chief, that true heroic values reside, is the implication of Thersites' words.

Thersites next brings in the complaint that he, and the other Achaeans, are doing most of the fighting, thereby of course highlighting the minor contribution of Agamemnon himself:

one [son of the Trojans] that I, or some other Achaean, capture and bring in.
(2.231)

The wording of this may well be intended to provoke mirth: 'or some
other Achaean', added almost as an afterthought, throws the emphasis of
the line back to the 'I', and heightens the air of pomposity. The idea of this
misshapen individual providing Agamemnon with prisoners for ransom is
more than a little ludicrous, as well as introducing an air of boastfulness.
It may well be that Thersites intends to provoke merriment by his words:
what we can be sure of is that his words are again echoing those of Achilles
during the quarrel. For Achilles' case was two-fold: that Agamemnon
receives the lion's share of the spoil, as was noted above, and that he,
Achilles, does the lion's share of the fighting:

> Always the greater part of the painful fighting is the work of my hands.
> (1.165–6)

Once again, though the wording is different, the sentiment is the same:
Thersites echoes Achilles' complaint that Agamemnon is content to sit
back and allow others to do the fighting and to accumulate the spoil for
him. If we are correct in identifying the hierarchical dispute as lying at the
heart of the quarrel in *Iliad* 1, then we may again see here evidence that
the speech of Thersites is rehearsing the main elements of that dispute,
with an obvious acknowledgement of the correctness of Achilles' stance.

Thersites now urges his fellow-soldiers to pack up and return home
(2.236). It has been suggested that Thersites' proposal of retreat, intended
as a punishment of Agamemnon, is anomalous since it follows almost
immediately upon Agamemnon's own proposal of a return home.[22] In fact
however the spirit of Thersites' proposal is very different from that of
Agamemnon's: Agamemnon's motivation is an involved topic which
requires separate examination, but it does seem clear that his aim was not
to cause the army to flee to the ships—which of course was the actual
result—but rather to give them the opportunity to demonstrate their
loyalty by refusing to accept his proposal that they return home. The
proposal of Thersites, on the other hand, we may be sure is meant very
seriously, since the army has just demonstrated its feelings by scattering
eagerly to the ships. Why then did Homer include this theme of a
proposed withdrawal so soon after Agamemnon's 'testing' of the army? A
likely answer is that once again he was deliberately paralleling the speech
of Achilles in that of Thersites, since the culmination of Achilles' outburst
was:

> Now I am returning to Phthia, since it is much better
> to go home again with my curved ships.
> (1.169–70)

In effect Thersites declares that Achilles' response to Agamemnon's behaviour—both in general in his role as leader, and in particular in his words and actions during the quarrel—is justified: and, on this occasion at least, we may be sure that he speaks for all the ordinary soldiers when he proposes a return home.

The parallels with Achilles' speech are still not complete. Thersites' proposal that they return home will, he says, teach Agamemnon a lesson, to value those who have worked so hard on his behalf:

> . . . leave this man here
> by himself in Troy to mull his prizes of honour
> that he may find out whether or not we others are helping him.
> (2.236–8)

Again Thersites highlights those same defects in Agamemnon—his inactivity, his greed, and his reliance upon others coupled with his disregard for them. It was in just the same way that Achilles rationalized his decision to return home:

> . . . I am minded no longer
> to stay here dishonoured and pile up your wealth and luxury
> (1.170–1)

with the final word ἀφύξειν, literally meaning 'to draw water', conjuring an image of Achilles, as slave at the well, drawing water for Agamemnon, as master.

Thersites ends with a statement which apparently contradicts the spirit which Achilles displayed throughout the quarrel:

> But there is no gall in Achilles' heart, and he is forgiving.
> (2.241)

At best this appears an ironical representation of Achilles' attitude, at worst an outright misrepresentation. However, it will be recalled that, when in his rage Achilles drew his sword to kill Agamemnon but then relented and sheathed it once more, he did so in direct response to the advice of Athene, who appeared to him alone (1.188–222). Only Achilles (and Athene) was aware of the real reason for his action; to the other Achaeans it must have appeared an act either of cowardice or of forgiveness. It would appear that Thersites, and possibly the other Achaeans also, saw it as the latter. The fact that he was mistaken in doing so is immaterial: the important point is that he shows himself in tune with the actions of, and in sympathy with the feelings of, Achilles. Lest there be any doubt lingering in his audience's mind about the parallels which Homer has drawn between Thersites and Achilles, he chooses to end the speech of Thersites with a line

> Otherwise, son of Atreus, this were your last outrage
> (2.242)

quoted *verbatim* from Achilles' speech at the very climax of the quarrel (1.232).

Although the parallels in Thersites' speech are mainly with Achilles' words in the quarrel, it is possible to identify also two passages which allude to Agamemnon's words, although both are directly relevant to Achilles' case. Firstly Thersites makes a direct accusation, though the details are veiled, that Agamemnon is responsible for the Achaeans' present plight:

> It is not right for
> you, their leader, to lead in sorrow the sons of the Achaeans.
> (2.233–4)

It is possible that Thersites is here referring to the ravages of the plague, which the seer Calchas made clear was the sole responsibility of Agamemnon in a speech which triggered the quarrel in Book 1, or it may be that Thersites' words are of more general application, that it is Agamemnon's greed which has caused the Achaeans to be stuck at Troy for ten years. In either case his words are in marked contrast to Agamemnon's own view of his role, expressed during the quarrel:

> I myself desire that my people be safe, not perish
> (1.117)

and again place him firmly on Achilles' side in the quarrel.

A second connection with Agamemnon's speech may be found in Thersites' words:

> He has taken his prize by force and keeps her,
> (2.240)

which contains a clear verbal echo of Agamemnon's threat to Achilles:

> . . . but I shall take the fair-cheeked Briseis
> your prize, I myself going to your shelter.
> (1.184–5)

The preceding line makes clear Thersites' disapproval of Agamemnon's behaviour:

> And now he has dishonoured Achilles, a man much better than he is.
> (2.239–40)

There is in this however much more than disapproval of Agamemnon's actions, since here too the words of Thersites are echoing the quarrel: in fact this is the most important passage of all for our understanding of the role of Thersites.

The quarrel of Achilles and Agamemnon, it was argued earlier, resulted from the anomalous position of Achilles who, despite his warrior prowess, was beneath Agamemnon in the Achaean hierarchy. Agamemnon himself rehearsed the hierarchical conflict in his threat to take Briseis from Achilles:

> . . . that you may learn well
> how much greater I am than you,
>   (1.185–6)

words which caused Achilles to draw his sword against him. Also, in response to the peace-making efforts of Nestor, Agamemnon condemned the fault of Achilles in attempting to assert his superiority:

> Yet here is a man who wishes to be above all others,
> who wishes to hold power over all, and to be lord of
> all, and give them their orders, yet I think one will not obey him.
>   (1.287–9)

Finally Nestor made the 'heroic' attitude to the conflict explicit:

> Even
> though you [Achilles] are the stronger man, and the mother who bore
>   you was immortal,
> yet is this man [Agamemnon] greater who is lord over more than you rule.
>   (1.280–1)

Here then is the anomaly under which Achilles labours: he is καρτερός, the stronger, the greater warrior, but Agamemnon is φέρτερος, the greater leader, because he commands more men. It is against this background that we should view Thersites' statement that Agamemnon 'has dishonoured Achilles, a man much better than he is'.

The accepted picture of Thersites is of a loud-mouthed buffoon, a trouble-maker and rabble-rouser who addresses Agamemnon in a speech which is a coarse parody of that of Achilles during the quarrel. The analysis of his speech above has attempted to present a very different picture: the speech contains the same arguments as Achilles employed and includes a number of clear verbal echoes; it urges the same conclusion as Achilles had urged, namely, a return to their homeland; and it concludes with a value judgement upon the issue which lay at the heart of the quarrel, the relative status within the Achaean hierarchy of Agamemnon and Achilles. Thersites was introduced as the ugliest and of the meanest birth of all the Achaean soldiery, as the most unheroic Achaean at Troy, in short, as the very antithesis of Achilles. If we may accept that Thersites' speech was not a coarse parody of Achilles', but was intended rather as a rehearsal of, and comment upon, the main theme of the poem, the quarrel and consequent *mēnis*, we may tentatively suggest that, having presented the 'heroic' attitude through the words of Nestor, Homer is now presenting the 'unheroic' attitude, the view of the ordinary soldiers at the other end of the heroic spectrum of the quarrel between their superiors and, above all, of the behaviour of their commander-in-chief, Agamemnon. According to this interpretation, the speech of Thersites would constitute an important element in Homer's presentation of the backcloth to the *mēnis*, namely, the psychology of the Achaean army, apart from the heroes, at Troy.

Does the evidence then suggest that Thersites' words do indeed represent Achaean popular opinion? The accepted view is that they certainly do not, for example, Rankin's 'a noisy man of the people who is not supported by the people'. In part this view is suggested by the soldiers' reaction to Thersites' punishment for his insolence, struck across his shoulders by Odysseus wielding the great sceptre:

Sorry though the men were they laughed over him happily,
and thus they would speak to each other, each looking at the man next him:
'Come now: Odysseus has done excellent things by thousands,
bringing forward good counsels and ordering armed encounters;
but now this is far the best thing he has ever accomplished
among the Argives, to keep this thrower of words, this braggart
out of assembly. Never again will his proud heart stir him
up, to wrangle with the princes in words of revilement.'

(2.270–7)

Yet does the soldiers' laughter at the weeping and humiliated Thersites suggest any more than their pleasure at witnessing, at last, the punishment of a braggart, coupled perhaps with the relief that it is happening to somebody other than themselves? It would of course be perfectly possible for them to approve the beating of Thersites, for all his rocking of the boat in the past, whilst at the same time agreeing with the sentiments recently expressed by him: in fact there is nothing in the words which they are pictured exchanging which necessarily implies criticism of his behaviour on this specific occasion. Indeed if this explanation is not correct, it is difficult to see what Homer means by the opening words of the passage οἱ δὲ καὶ ἀχνύμενοί περ ('sorry though the men were'). Since the sorrow they feel, it is made clear, is not for Thersites' plight, it must presumably be for their own: they feel sorrow, that is, because they have been prevented from returning home, and because Agamemnon's suggestion that they do so has proved to be a deception (2.190–3). Thersites has in fact voiced the disappointment and frustration felt by them all.

One other passage may be cited as illustrating the general feelings of the army, namely, the introduction of Thersites which was considered earlier:

Beyond all others Achilles hated him, and Odysseus.
These two he was forever abusing, but now at brilliant

Agamemnon he clashed the shrill noise of his abuse. The Achaeans
were furiously angry with him, their minds resentful.
But he, crying the words aloud, scolded Agamemnon.

(2.220–4)

The problem in this passage is the identity of τῷ ('him'), in 222. Majority
opinion believes it is Thersites, for example, Kirk:[23]

The army resents his criticism, overlooking (as it seems) the king's unpre-
dictable behaviour and puzzling advice. That is the case if τῷ in 222 refers to
Thersites rather than to Agamemnon himself, as it grammatically could do
and as Leaf (for example) thought to be the case. But the language of 223,
where the army is 'horribly enraged and resentful' against this person, surely
points to Thersites. That they must have been confused by Agamemnon and
doubtful of his intentions and reactions is beyond argument, but the violence
of the language is excessive for what they might have felt for their commanding general, whereas it would have been entirely justified in relation to someone already described as Thersites has been.

On the other hand Leaf astutely observed:

Thersites is at the moment the accepted spokesman of the mob, who are
indignant with Agamemnon for his treatment of Achilles; and it is by a subtle
piece of psychology that they are made ashamed of themselves and brought to
hear reason by seeing their representative exhibited in an absurd and humiliat-
ing light, and their own sentiments caricatured till they dare not acknowledge
them.[24]

Much depends upon the sense conveyed by the adversative αὐτὰρ ('but')
in 224: on the one hand the sense may be 'The Achaeans were furiously
angry with him [Thersites], their minds resentful. But he [ignoring their
anger and resentment against himself], crying the words aloud, scolded
Agamemnon'; or on the other hand the sense may be 'The Achaeans were
furiously angry with him [Agamemnon], their minds resentful. But he
[Thersites, putting into words the anger and resentment which the others
felt in their minds but did not dare speak], crying the words aloud,
scolded Agamemnon.'

We are surely justified in dismissing Kirk's argument that 'the violence
of the language is excessive for what they might have felt for their commanding general': in view of the fact that they have endured over nine
years of warfare with, as far as they are aware, perhaps as long still to go,
and have just been offered by their commanding general the chance to
return home, only to have it snatched away with the words 'he was just
testing you', it would be wrong to underestimate the strength of feeling
amongst the Achaeans. However the most important clue lies in the word
order: despite the limitations imposed by oral theory and patterns of
localization, it seems inescapable that an intentional contrast is being

drawn by the endings of 223–4, θυμῷ . . . μύθῳ. This then will confirm the second interpretation given above: the Achaeans feel the anger in their *hearts*, but Thersites actually expresses it in his *words*. In this case the object of the anger, of both Thersites and of the Achaean army in general, is Agamemnon.

The conclusions to be drawn from the foregoing are: that the speech of Thersites is not a mere parody of Achilles' quarrel with Agamemnon, but rather is a careful review of, and comment upon, that quarrel; that the speech reflects the attitude of the ordinary non-heroic Achaeans to the quarrel in condemning Agamemnon's treatment of Achilles; and that the speech is therefore a most important part of Homer's portrayal of the background to the Wrath of Achilles. The speech represents the demoralization of the ordinary soldiers after the withdrawal of Achilles and his Myrmidons and illustrates their lack of confidence in Agamemnon as commander. This lack of confidence is to be set alongside the continual self-doubt felt by Agamemnon and expressed most recently in his need to test his troops earlier in Book 2. The speech of Thersites therefore introduces the morale of the Achaean army and helps to highlight the psychology of the commander, whilst at the same time providing a value judgement upon the central theme of the poem, the quarrel and *mēnis*.

NOTES

1. A full discussion is to be found in H. D. Rankin, *SO* 47 (1972), 36–60.
2. *The Iliad of Homer* 1–12 (London, 1879), on 2.212.
3. C. R. Beye, *The Iliad, the Odyssey, and the Epic Tradition* (London, 1968), 86.
4. M. Mueller, *The Iliad* (London, 1984), 6.
5. J. Redfield, *Nature and Culture in the Iliad* (Chicago, 1975), 161.
6. M. Silk, *The Iliad* (Cambridge, 1987), 83.
7. M. M. Willcock, *A Companion to the Iliad* (Chicago, 1976), 20.
8. Rankin, op. cit., 38.
9. C. M. Bowra, *Tradition and Design in the Iliad* (Oxford, 1930), 213–14.
10. Rankin, op. cit., 43.
11. G. S. Kirk, *The Songs of Homer* (Cambridge, 1962), 22.
12. Op. cit., 51.
13. Op. cit., 53.
14. Op. cit., 59.
15. J. P. Mahaffy, *Social Life in Greece* (London, 1890), 13.
16. Rankin, op. cit., 39.
17. English translations are from *The Iliad of Homer*, tr. R. Lattimore (Chicago, 1961).
18. For discussion of these and other suggestions, see Rankin, op. cit., 42.
19. Full discussion in Rankin, op. cit., 44–9.
20. Willcock, *A Commentary on Homer's Iliad* (London, 1970), 51.
21. Cf. Kirk, *The Iliad: a Commentary* (Cambridge, 1985), 141. For discussion of the different attitudes to women of Agamemnon and Achilles see F. E. Brenk, *Eranos* 84 (1986), 81–2.
22. Cf. Kirk, op. cit., 140–1.
23. Kirk, op. cit., 140.
24. W. Leaf and M. A. Bayfield, *The Iliad of Homer* (London, 1965), 306–7.

THE SHIELD OF ACHILLES WITHIN THE *ILIAD*

By OLIVER TAPLIN

I

Why is the shield of Achilles, instrument of war in a poem of war, covered with scenes of delightful peace, of agriculture, festival, song, and dance? I shall try to approach an answer to this question by looking at the scenes on the shield in relation to the rest of Homer, I mean the *Iliad* and *Odyssey*.[1]

The 130-line set-piece comes as the calm before the storm at a turning point in the epic. The long central day of battle, which dawned with the first line of Book 11, has just ended (18.239–41). Achilles has without a second thought determined to return to the battlefield even though he knows his death is bound to follow (18.78–126, esp. 95–8). Hector has made the no less lethal decision to stay outside the city and fight, though he on the contrary does not realize that it seals his fate (18.243–314).[2]

This is the shield that Achilles will carry through the massacre of Books 20 and 21 and which will avert Hector's last throw (22.290–1; cf. 313–14). It is the defiant front presented to the foe by the most terrible killer in the *Iliad*. What would the audience have expected the poet to put on the shield of such a warrior? Consider first the shield which Agamemnon takes up before his gruesome *aristeia*:[3]

> And he took up the man-enclosing elaborate stark shield,
> a thing of splendour. There were ten circles of bronze upon it,
> and set about it were twenty knobs of tin, pale-shining,
> and in the very centre another knob of dark cobalt.
> And circled in the midst of all was the blank-eyed face of the Gorgon
> with her stare of horror, and Fear was inscribed on it, and Terror.
>
> (11.32–7)

The demons are designed to inspire terror in the enemy. Compare also the aegis of Zeus donned by Athene (5.736–42: Panic, Strife, and their crew surround the Gorgon's head), and the baldrick which Odysseus sees on the ghost of Heracles at *Od.* 11.609 ff., covered with beasts and carnage. 'May he who artfully designed them . . . never again do any designing', comments Odysseus. Looking outside Homer (and leaving aside the shield of Aeneas in *Aeneid* 8), the ready comparison is the description in lines 141–317 of the fragment of epic narrative usually known as 'The Shield of Heracles' and associated (undeservedly) with the name of

Hesiod.[4] This too is a shield made by Hephaestus for a great fighter, and it is moreover obviously under the influence of the shield in the *Iliad*. Yet it is dominated by terror and slaughter. Here is a typical extract: 'By them stood Darkness of Death, mournful and fearful, pale, shrivelled, shrunk with hunger, swollen kneed. Long nails tipped her hands, and she dribbled at the nose, and from her cheeks blood dripped down to the ground. She stood leering hideously, and much dust sodden with tears lay upon her shoulders' ([Hes.] *Aspis* 264–70, tr. Evelyn-White).

So the joys of civilization and fertility on our shield are peculiar. Why all this and not the usual horrors? The question is reinforced by the representations of Achilles' shield in later visual art, which do not try to reproduce Homer's scenes but simply show the Gorgon and other standard devices.[5] More tellingly, Euripides actually protests against the Iliadic shield. The chorus of his *Electra* (442–86) make it clear that they are singing of the celebrated shield (κλεινᾶς, 455); but it is designed to terrify the Trojans (456–7). In the centre it has the sun and constellations, as in Homer, but they are there to panic Hector (468–9), and round the edge skims Perseus with the Gorgon's head (458 ff., a motif from the 'Shield of Heracles'). A more recent poet, reacting like Euripides to a brutal and all-consuming war, has also reforged the Homeric shield to suit its fell recipient. W. H. Auden's fine poem 'The Shield of Achilles' begins[6]

> She looked over his shoulder
>   For vines and olive trees,
> Marble well-governed cities
>   And ships upon untamed seas,
> But there on the shining metal
>   His hands had put instead
> An artificial wilderness
> And a sky like lead.

Three times Thetis looks to see the scenes which she expects because she knows them—or rather we know them—from Homer, and each time she is presented with a scene from a world of militaristic and totalitarian inhumanity. At the end even the child is corrupted and knows no better:

> A ragged urchin, aimless and alone,
>   Loitered about that vacancy, a bird
> Flew up to safety from his well-aimed stone:
>   That girls are raped, that two boys knife a third,
>   Were axioms to him, who'd never heard
> Of any world where promises were kept,
> Or one could weep because another wept.

> The thin-lipped armourer,
>   Hephaestos, hobbled away,
> Thetis of the shining breasts
>   Cried out in dismay
> At what the god had wrought
>   To please her son, the strong
> Iron-hearted man-slaying Achilles
>   Who would not live long.[7]

It appears that Auden sees Achilles as the prototype of the Aryan superman and makes his shield prefigure accordingly. In the same way Euripides presents the events of his *Electra* as the aftermath of the inhumanity of Agamemnon and his chiefs of staff.

Why, then, does Homer fill his shield with scenes which he repeatedly insists are beautiful and with people who delight in their innocent activities? My question does not seem to have concerned English-speaking critics in our times: at least, I cannot find it raised in any of the standard books on Homer, by which I mean the ten or so books by Lord, Bowra, Page, Finley, and Kirk.[8] I can, however, offer three explanations which would be in keeping with the attitudes to be found in these books. One would be that the shield is based on some actual artefact, perhaps some heirloom fossilized by the oral tradition (this is the standard explanation of, for instance, the boar's-tusk helmet at 10.257 ff.). This must be mistaken.[9] Nothing really like this shield has ever been found nor ever will be, no more than the exemplars of Hephaestus' automata at 18.417 ff. That is the whole point: the shield—like those golden gynaikoids—is a wonder of divine craftsmanship unlike anything known in our age. The decoration of the shield is derived from poetic invention not from history.

Next it might be answered that the shield affords relief from the protracted battle narratives. It is orthodox to claim this as a function of Homeric similes (though most similes are in fact placed to intensify rather than relieve). It is true that the shield takes us far from the Trojan War, but that is hardly enough to explain its detail. After all, the rest of Books 18 and 19 are relief from battle scenes.[10] We are still left with the question, why this particular sort of relief?

Thirdly the explanation which is, I suspect, most in keeping with the dominant school of what might be called 'primitive oral poetics', namely that the oral poet has simply wandered on from one thing to another as the improvisatory Muse has taken him. Once he had decided to elaborate the shield at appropriate length for its maker and recipient he has added and added inorganically. The reason why I think this would be the orthodox account is that the standard view of the elaborated similes is that after starting off from a point of comparison they develop paratactically at the poet's pleasure. 'The poet follows his fancy and develops the picture without much care for his reason for using it.'[11] According to this view the poet would have settled on the subject-matter of the shield, not because it was relevant—or come to that irrelevant—to the *Iliad* as a whole, but because that is what happened to come into his mind as he went along. I can only ask anyone who reckons this is obviously the right answer to bear with me while I look at an alternative. But I am more likely to make headway with someone who finds it hard to believe that a poet who worked in that way could have so consistently commanded the attention, indeed adulation, of our civilization.

II

My starting-point is that the shield is not the only place in Homer where we encounter peace and prosperity and people delighting in their lives. I shall survey the shield scene by scene relating each to similar pictures elsewhere, and looking for similarities of tone and feeling as well as of subject-matter. There will be three main sources. First, the settled societies of the *Odyssey*; that is, Nestor's Pylos and Menelaus' Sparta, visited by Telemachus in Books 3 and 4 and showing him, and us, a proper re-established *oikos* to contrast with Ithaca and Mycenae; and even more the Phaeacia of Alcinous which serves for Odysseus as the transition and model between the remote disordered worlds of his wanderings and his disrupted home. Indeed the description of the palace of Alcinous at *Od.* 7.81 ff., especially the gardens (112–33), is the set-piece closest of all to the shield of Achilles. Secondly there is the peacetime world of many of the similes, especially in the *Iliad*. And lastly Troy, at least Troy were it not for the war, as it was in the days of peace before the Achaeans came.

When these three elements are put together we arrive at an easy hedonistic existence spent in feasting with the pastimes of conversation, song and dance, making love—in fact a life such as the gods lead. This is the life that humans aspire to, even if they only achieve it in brief snatches. ('We live in unhappiness, but the gods themselves have no sorrows', *Il.* 24.526.) Witness Menelaus' odd homily on satiety at *Il.* 13.620–39: he contrasts war with life's pleasures, 'sleep and love-making, the sweetness of song and the stately dancing' (636–7, ὕπνου καὶ φιλότητος | μολπῆς τε γλυκερῆς καὶ ἀμύμονος ὀρχηθμοῖο). Thus when at last Odysseus' house is cleared of the suitors there are celebrations:

> First they went and washed, and put their tunics upon them,
> and the women arrayed themselves in their finery, while the inspired
> singer took up his hollowed lyre and stirred within them
> the impulse for the sweetness of song and the stately dancing.

Now the great house resounded aloud to the thud of their footsteps,
as the men celebrated there, and the fair girdled women.
                                                    (*Od.* 23.141–7)

But the Homeric good life is most memorably summed up by Alcinous'
couplet on the pursuits of the blessed Phaeacians (*Od.* 8.248–9):

> Always the feast is dear to us, and the lyre and dances
> and changes of clothing and hot baths and beds.
> (αἰεὶ δ' ἡμῖν δαίς τε φίλη κίθαρίς τε χοροί τε
> εἵματά τ' ἐξημοιβὰ λοετρά τε θερμὰ καὶ εὐναί)

The precise plan of the shield is not made so clear by the poem that it
is beyond doubt; and we should bear in mind Lessing's point that we are
told of the making of the shield not given a map of the finished product.[12]
It is not even clear that the shield is to be envisaged as decorated with five
concentric circles. Moreover it is not likely that our text is exactly as it left
Homer; some lines have probably been added and possibly others have
been omitted (see further below). The divisions and arrangement which I
shall adopt are widely accepted and make, I think, a coherent whole; but
they are not essential to my argument.

I *The first (inmost) circle* (483–9): *the earth, heavens, and sea.*[13]
    After the first all-inclusive line it is only the heavens which are given any
detail. It is enough for now to remark that the sun, moon, and constellations are the cosmic constants and the markers of the passage of time,
reflected in Homer by recurrent formulae whatever the human vicissitudes
they may accompany.

II *The second circle: city life.* The two cities are clearly set out as a pair—see
490–1, 509. Each in turn provides two scenes:

(a) *The city at peace*, (i) 491–6: *marriage celebrations*
Of all the pleasant occasions of civil life, especially in a highly kin-
conscious world, a wedding might be singled out as the most unifying and
optimistic. It is also a time for everyone to indulge in the 'good life'.
Compare with the shield the wedding celebrations for Hermione which
greet Telemachus on his arrival at Sparta:

> So these neighbours and townsmen of glorious Menelaus
> were at their feasting all about the great house with the high roof,
> and taking their ease, and among them stepped an inspired singer
> playing his lyre, while among the dancers two acrobats
> led the measure of song and dance revolving among them.
>   (*Od.* 4.15–19; see further p. 104 below)

And at such times thoughts turn in due course to bed. We have in fact
most of the delights enumerated by Alcinous.

The accomplishments of singing and dancing, which are of course useless and even despised in time of war,[14] epitomize the pleasures of peace.
The Phaeacians are, as appropriate, especially good at dancing (see
Od.8.250–65). The wives at their doors represent 'home' no less tellingly.
The marital home is what the Achaeans have had to leave behind. 'Nine
years have gone by, and the timbers of our ships have rotted away and the
cables are broken, and far away our wives and our young children are
sitting within our halls and wait for us' (*Il*.2.134–7). And the meeting of
Hector and Andromache in Troy suggests poignantly what might be if it
were not disrupted by war.[15]

(ii) 497–508: *the law case*
There has been much discussion of the precise legal problem and proce-
dure here.[16] What matters for present purposes is that we have the stable
justice of a civilized city. δίκη (508) is used here in a sense similar to that
in the famous 'Hesiodic' simile at 16.384ff. Here is no vendetta or the
perilous exile which Homer and his audience associated with a murderer
in the age of heroes. We have, rather, arbitrators, speeches on both sides,
and considered judgements.

The sceptre (505) is the symbol of a well-ordered hierarchy (though
within the *Iliad* it has been somewhat mishandled in the first two books).
Note also the well-shaped or polished stones that the elders sit on (ἐπὶ
ξεστοῖσι λίθοις, 504). This is the epithet used to describe the masonry of
the marvellous palace of Priam (6.242ff.), and even of the palace of Zeus
(20.11); but compare above all the council-stones of well-ordered Pylos
where Nestor sits and Neleus sat before him. 'Nestor went outside and
took his seat upon the polished stones which were there in place for him
in front of the towering doorway, white stones, with a shine on them that
glistened' (*Od*. 3.406–8; cf. also Phaeacia at *Od*.8.6ff.).

(b) *The city at war*, (i) 509–19: *the siege*
We do not have to seek far for parallels to this scene. Here—somewhat
altered, for we are dealing with a subtle poet not a crude emblematist—
here we have the *Iliad* and its belligerent deities.[17] On the shield there are
two besieging armies (their relation to each other is obscure), but like the
Achaeans they are not agreed among themselves. The besieged are
making a foray, not to drive the invaders back and burn their ships, but to
make an ambush for provisions. Yet we are unmistakably put in mind of
Troy by the old men, women, and children on the walls (rather than
in their doorways or in the agora as in the city at peace). Closest of all
probably are Hector's instructions at 8.518–22:

> Let the boys who are in their first youth and the grey-browed elders
> take stations on the god-founded bastions that circle the city;
> and as for the women, have our wives each one in her own house,

kindle a great fire; let there be a watch kept steadily
lest a sudden attack get into the town when the fighters have left it.

But we think also of Helen with Priam and the chattering elders on the walls above the Scaean gates (3.146 ff.), and of Priam watching and pleading with his son (21.526 ff., 22.25 ff.). We remember that Hector did not find Andromache and the child at home, but on the Great Tower (6.386 ff.); and that is where she rushes maenad-like when she hears of Hector's death (22.462; cf. 447). The city on the shield stands for every threatened homeland: within the *Iliad* Troy is such a city.

(ii) 520–34: *the ambush of the herd*

This violent devastation of the pastoral world takes us away from Troy itself to the countryside of the Troad and the neighbouring cities, which, as we are often reminded, the Achaeans, and above all Achilles, have been looting for nine years. Compare the seven brothers of Andromache, sons of Eetion king of Thebe: 'Achilles slaughtered all of them as they were tending their white sheep and their lumbering oxen' (6.423–4). He was kinder to Isus and Antiphus, sons of Priam: 'Achilles had caught these two at the knees of Ida and bound them in pliant willows as they watched by their sheep, and released them for ransom' (11.105–6).[18] The pathos of the ruthless warrior cutting down the innocent pastoral world is quintessentially Homeric, and is wonderfully conveyed here by the two herdsmen. One moment they are going along with the flock 'playing happily on pipes, and they took no thought of treachery' (526), the next they lie killed.[19]

(iii) 535–40: *the ensuing mêlée*

Here we have the kind of scene which might have been expected on a shield, monstrous ghouls fighting over the dying and the dead. And, indeed, four of the six lines (535–8) also occur on the *Shield of Heracles* (156–9). This primitive conception of battle is not typical of the *Iliad*. On this and other good grounds Solmsen has condemned lines 535–40 as an interpolation (or 'plus verses') derived from the *Shield of Heracles*.[20] We can see exactly the same phenomenon a little later, though this time the plus-verses never became canonical. In *P. Berol.* 9774 (first century B.C.) after line 608 at the end of the shield are four more verses describing a harbour full of fishes: the lines are almost the same as *Shield of Heracles*, 207–13.[21]

III *The third circle: rural life.*

There follows a series of scenes of people going about agricultural tasks. Seeing that the first three clearly represent spring, summer, and autumn, I take it that 573 ff. show winter.[22]

(a) 541–9: *spring*

Note the emphasis on the fertility of the soil: it is a dark, deep tilth, and enough for many ploughmen. For pictures of ploughing in similes see

10.351 ff., 13.703 ff. (also *Od.* 13.31 ff.). The cup of wine at the end of each furlong is a civilized touch. Hecuba offered wine to Hector in Book 6 (258 ff.); but bloody war is not the time for such ceremony and relief (6.264–8).

(b) 550–6: *summer*
We also find reapers in a striking simile:

> And the men, like two lines of reapers who, facing each other,
> drive their course all down the field of wheat or barley
> for a man blessed in substance, and the cut swathes drop showering,
> so Trojans and Achaeans driving in against one another
> cut men down . . .
>
> (11.67–9)

On the shield the children helping, their arms full of golden swathes, is the kind of touch for which Homer used to be justly famous. The harvest is hot, hungry work, and for the scene to be complete there has to be a good meal of meat being prepared, beneath, of course, thick leafy shade—ὑπὸ δρυΐ (558).[23]

But the most telling figure of all in this vignette is the lord with his sceptre standing by, silently joyful. This is his *temenos* (550), an especially desirable estate granted to him, the kind of privilege which any great *basileus* might hope to return to after the war, the kind which Achilles might have had if he had chosen long life instead of glorious death.[24] This is the life which Odysseus is striving to win back to in the *Odyssey*, and he gives a memorable account of it:

> As of some king, a fine man and god-fearing,
> who, ruling as lord over many powerful people,
> upholds the way of good government, and the black earth yields him
> barley and wheat, his trees are heavy with fruit, his sheepflocks
> continue to bear young, the sea gives him fish, because of
> his good leadership, and his people prosper under him.
>
> (*Od.* 19.109–14)

The prosperity and good government go hand in hand (see further p. 108 below).

(c) 561–7: *autumn*
The grape harvest with its heavy fruit and promise of next year's wine inspires song and dance (on which see above). The pickers are 'young girls and young men, in all their light-hearted innocence' (παρθενικαὶ (δὲ) καὶ ἠίθεοι ἀταλὰ φρονέοντες, 567). Elsewhere in the *Iliad* only the infant Astyanax is graced with this quality (ἀταλάφρονα, 6.400). But these boys and girls on the shield are older, and there is another passage where that age of ingenuous first love is most poignantly evoked: as his death approaches Hector realizes that it is no good trying to talk gently to

Achilles 'talking love like a young man and a young girl, in the way a young man and a young maiden talk love together' (22.127–8). The phrase conjures up a world of youth and delight which could not be further from the confrontation of Achilles and Hector.[25]

(d) 573–89: *winter*

The cattle are kept in the midden-yard (κόπρου, 575) during the winter nights; but as the herdsmen set off for the water meadows we seem to be entering another pastoral idyll. The lions break in on this as though to prevent the world of the shield from being too perfect. We are, of course, in the realm of the similes still, in fact we are bound to be reminded by this of the similes. In the peacetime agricultural world man's worst enemy is the lion, not other men.

(I must confess that I am not clear how the last three lines, 587–9, fit in. The scene is different from all the others, not only because much briefer, but also because it contains no human figures. Yet it is clearly marked off from the scene of the winter herding and the lions. The lines may be interpolated: see Leaf ad loc.)

IV *The fourth circle* (590–606): *the dance.*

It appears that the dance goes all the way round without subdivision. Although they sometimes move in lines (602) the emphasis is put on the circular dance by the one simile within the *ekphrasis*, the potter testing his wheel. The length and unity of this scene make it appear the climax of the whole shield.[26] As in the scene of the vintage we see ἠΐθεοι καὶ παρθένοι ('young men and young girls', 593); but in several respects this section forms a 'ring' with the wedding scene at the beginning. As before there is singing and dancing, and again the onlookers delight in the festive spectacle. There are in addition a pair of tumblers, and, if we are prepared to import a line from the otherwise identical formulae at *Od.* 4.17–19 (quoted on p. 100 above), we would have a poet, the one and only ἀοιδός to appear in the *Iliad*. We might feel that the shield would not be complete without him.[27]

Homer dwells on the clothing and appearance of the young men and women:

> These wore, the maidens long light robes, but the men wore tunics
> of finespun work and shining softly, touched with olive oil.
> (τῶν δ᾽ αἱ μὲν λεπτὰς ὀθόνας ἔχον, οἱ δὲ χιτῶνας
> εἵατ᾽ ἐϋννήτους, ἧκα στίλβοντες ἐλαίῳ)
> And the girls wore fair garlands on their heads, while the young men
> carried golden knives that hung from sword-belts of silver.   (595–8)

Fine clothing is, one might say, the hallmark of a prosperous civilized society in Homer, and its making and care the distinction of its women.

Alcinous singled out changes of clothing as a delight of the Phaeacians, and fine weaving is stressed in the utopian picture of his palace (*Od.* 7.105–11). And it is, of course, in order to wash the clothing of Alcinous' household that Nausicaa goes to the shore (*Od.* 6.13–112). Her unmarried brothers, for instance, are always wanting newly laundered clothes when they go dancing (64–5).

In the *Iliad* this kind of raiment comes almost exclusively from two places—Troy and Olympus. When Diomedes wounds Aphrodite his spear rips 'through the immortal robe that the very Graces had woven for her carefully' (5.338; cf. 5.315, and the veil of Artemis at 21.507). Athene, more used to battle, takes off her 'elaborate robe which she herself had wrought with her hands' patience' (5.735 = 8.386). And of course when Hera prepares herself to seduce Zeus she has an especially seductive toilette (14.169 ff., esp. 171–81).

Turning to Troy, the fine quality of Helen's dress in Book 3 is re-iterated,[28] and when Aphrodite fetches her to Paris she says:

> He is in his chamber now, in the bed with its circled pattern,
> shining in his raiment and beauty (κάλλεΐ τε στίλβων καὶ εἵμασιν).
> You would not think he came from fighting a man,
> but was going rather to a dance or rested from dancing lately.
>
> (391–4)

In Book 6 Hecuba goes to the palace treasure-chamber to find a robe to dedicate to Athene:

> There lay the elaborately wrought robes, the work of Sidonian
> women, whom Alexandros himself, the god-like, had brought home
> from the land of Sidon, crossing the wide sea, on that journey
> when he brought back also gloriously descended Helen.
> Hecuba lifted out one and took it as a gift to Athena,
> that which was the loveliest in design and the largest,
> and shone like a star. It lay beneath the others.
>
> (6.289–95)

That offering fails, of course, and its inevitable failure is woven into its guilty history. But it is that same treasure-chamber which Priam goes to in Book 24 to fetch the ransom for Achilles:

> He lifted back the fair covering of his clothes-chest
> and from inside took out twelve robes surpassingly lovely
> and twelve mantles to be worn single, as many blankets,
> as many great white cloaks, also the same number of tunics (χιτῶνας).
>
> (24.228–31)

This supplication succeeds, and Achilles carefully leaves for wrapping the corpse of Hector 'two great cloaks and a fine-spun tunic' (δύο φάρε᾽

ἐΰννητόν τε χιτῶνα, 580; cf. 588). The fine clothing of Troy, and above all of the household of Priam, is dispersed as ransom or used for wrapping corpses—and what is left is due to be looted or burned.

So the washing-troughs in Book 22 are no gratuitous detail (let alone a quaint record of real-life hydrography). Three times Hector is pursued by Achilles round the walls of Troy, past the springs of Scamander, the river of Troy:

> Beside these in this place, and close to them, are the washing-hollows
> of stone, and magnificent, where the wives of the Trojans and their lovely
> daughters washed the clothes to shining, in the old days
> when there was peace, before the coming of the sons of the Achaeans.
>
> (22.153–6)

So Hector's heroism and his death are closely associated with the place that epitomizes the former prosperity and delight of Troy, Troy which once Hector falls is doomed to burn. The motif is continued in Andromache's lament at the end of the book. She mourns Hector's corpse

> . . . naked, though in your house there is clothing laid up
> that is fine-textured (λεπτά) and pleasant, wrought by the hands of women.
> But all of these I will burn up in the fire's blazing,
> no use to you, since you will never be laid away in them.
>
> (22.510–13)[29]

But she is wrong. Achilles himself has the corpse of Hector wrapped in the fine raiment of Troy (24.588–90). And at the very end of the epic the ashes of Hector are buried in a casket 'wrapped about with soft robes of purple' (24.796).

The dance on the shield of Achilles shows, then, how fine raiment *should* be put to use, how it was used at Troy in the old days before the Achaeans came: the rest of the *Iliad* shows the uses they have to put it to in wartime.

V *The fifth (outmost) circle* (606–7): *Ocean*.

> He made on it the great strength of the Ocean River
> which ran around the uttermost rim of the shield's strong structure.

The inmost circle showed the heavens which are above the earth, the outmost the stream of Ocean which runs round the earth. The shield presents, that is, a kind of microcosm or epitome of the world. I hope by now that this is clear: it would, I believe, have been clear to the original audience from the first line (483):

> On it he made the earth, and sky, and sea . . .
> (ἐν μὲν γαῖαν ἔτευξ', ἐν δ' οὐρανόν, ἐν δὲ θάλασσαν)

III

The shield is a microcosm. This elementary observation is a common-place, indeed the starting-point, for critics like Schadewaldt and Reinhardt; but it is not to be found in the standard handbooks read in England, only in some less orthodox works of the kind that students are often warned off.[30] The shield is a microcosm; but that does not mean it includes in miniature every single thing to be found in the world—that would be impossible, and is not in any case the way that poetry and art work. They select and emphasize in order to impart meaning. The shield omits, for instance, poverty and misery; it omits trade and seafaring; it does not figure religion or cult, and it does not figure mythology or named heroes and places. The omissions might prove instructive, but I wish to concentrate on what is there.

I hope I have shown that on the whole the scenes are those of prosperous settled societies at peace, representing the Homeric picture of the good life. But the shield is a microcosm, not a utopia, and death and destruction are also there, though in inverse proportion to the rest of the *Iliad*. Rural life is invaded by the lions, and one of the two cities is surrounded by armies and carnage. I argued (pp. 101–2 above) that the city and its besiegers are meant to put us in mind of Troy and the Achaeans, in fact of the rest of the *Iliad*. What I now wish to suggest is that the city on the shield puts the *Iliad* itself into perspective; it puts war and prowess into perspective within the world as a whole. On the shield the *Iliad* takes up, so to speak, one half of one of the five circles. It is as though Homer has allowed us temporarily to stand back from the poem and see it in its place—like a 'detail' from the reproduction of a painting—within a larger landscape, a landscape which is usually blotted from sight by the all-consuming narrative in the foreground. This interpretation is close to that of Schadewaldt (op. cit. in n. 1, esp. 368), and of Owen in *The Story of the Iliad* (186–9):

He lifts our eyes from their concentration upon the battlefield to the contemplation of other scenes which remind us of the fullness and variety of life; it is a breathing-space in the battle, in which we have time to look around us and remember that this is only an incident in the busy world of human activities, that though Troy may fall and Achilles' life be wrecked, the world goes on as before; and in that remembrance there is at the same time relief of emotional tension and yet a heightening of expectation through the holding back of the long-awaited crisis, and also a deepening of the poignancy of the tragedy by seeing it thus against the large indifferent background of the wider life of the world (Owen, 187–8).

But I hear the protest that this kind of interpretation is the product of

sentimental pacifism and is contradicted by the whole spirit of the *Iliad*.
The *Iliad*, it is claimed, is a poem of heroic war; it glorifies war and
glorifies those who kill most successfully. 'The *Iliad* is saturated in blood,
a fact which cannot be hidden or argued away, twist the evidence as we
may in a vain attempt to fit archaic Greek values to a more gentle code of
ethics. The poet and his audience lingered lovingly over every act of
slaughter' (Finley, *WO* 118). But not even Professor Finley can believe
that this is the only attitude to be found in Homer. We do not have to go
to the 'unheroic' Hesiod to find 'One kind of Strife fosters evil war and
battle, being cruel: her no man loves'.[31] Odysseus himself speaks of 'the
wars, and throwing spears with polished hafts, and the arrows, gloomy
things, which to other men are terrible' (*Od.* 14.225–6), and Menelaus
sitting at home in Sparta among the spoils of Troy laments,

> I wish I lived in my house with only a third part of all
> these goods, and that the men were alive who died in those days
> in wide Troy land far away from horse-pasturing Argos.
> (Od. 4.97–9)

But our standard authorities feel that such attitudes are alien to the
heroic ethos and to Homer proper. They write them off as later, anachronistic, and incongruous. Take, for instance, Finley (*WO* 97) on the
good king at *Od.* 19.107 ff. (quoted on p. 103 above): 'Everything that
Homer tells us demonstrates that here he permitted a contemporary note
to enter, carefully restricting it, however, to a harmless simile and thus
avoiding any possible contradiction in the narrative itself.' The Professor
of History abhors 'contradiction', and he sifts the poem for the history and
discards the contemporary or anachronistic accretions. For a historian this
may be legitimate method, but it has also been applied by a Professor of
Literature. This same strategy is even more fully worked out for the *Iliad*
by G. S. Kirk in his essay 'Homer: the meaning of an oral tradition'.[32] He
implies (11–12) that the unwarlike tone of the similes and the shield of
Achilles are foreign and somehow inessential: 'These intrusions are
morally and aesthetically permissible; they do not break the heroic mood
that must predominate before Troy because they are formally enclosed in
similes or in a digression about armour.' But he is well aware that such
attitudes are not only found on the shield and in the similes. On page 11
he nips through the greatest scenes in the *Iliad*—Hector and Andromache,
Achilles' rejection of the embassy, Priam and Achilles ('more unnerving'[33])—and concludes 'what is happening here is that the *subsequent
poetical tradition* [K.'s italics] has allowed these occasional flashes of
humanity to illuminate the severer architecture of the heroic soul'. The
metaphors are rather obscure, but presumably the 'heroic soul' is what the
Iliad is really about and 'heroic soul' is free from all contaminations of

'humanity'. These authorities, then, see anything that is not really 'heroic' and does not glorify war as 'subsequent' and detachable.

Chronologically speaking these divisions might be right, but as literary criticism they are invalid. Within a work of literature tensions, even contradictions, are inseparable parts of a complex whole. The strategy of Professors Finley and Kirk is in fact left over from the good old days of the multi-layered analysts: in these days of 'the monumental poet' we cannot split Homer into consistent layers so easily. I shall try to maintain that the shield of Achilles is much more than just 'a digression about armour' by looking at other ways in which in the *Iliad* war is set against a larger world view, other elements which confirm and give context to the striking effect created by the shield. It is, I suggest, as though there lay behind the *Iliad* the whole world of peace and ordinary life, but only glimpsed occasionally through gaps or windows in the martial canvas which fills the foreground.

This other world is seen most directly in Troy itself, since the Trojans still have to live in the setting of their former prosperity and joy. Troy as it was, as it might be were it not for the war, is envisaged most clearly in the scenes of Book 6—the palace of Priam (p. 101 above), its treasure-chamber (pp. 105–6 above), the whole scene between Hector and Andromache. But the peacetime Troy is glimpsed, subliminally almost, throughout the poem in the formulaic epithets: the city is spacious, well built, with fertile lands; it has fine horses and lovely women. The motif of the former wealth of Troy and of its royal house runs right through,[34] and it reaches its fulfilment, like so many of the motifs of the *Iliad*, in the scene between Achilles and Priam:

> And you, old sir, we are told that you prospered once . . .
> . . . of all these you were lord once in your wealth and your children.
> But now the Uranian gods have brought me, an affliction upon you,
> for ever there is fighting about your city, and men killed.
>
> (24.543–8)

We also glimpse the world that the Achaeans and the Trojan allies have left behind, the world they hope to win back to when the war is over (cf. the *Odyssey*). Again and again we are given fleeting glances of wives and families, native rivers, fertile estates, and beautiful treasures. They have left these to go to war, and many shall never return. These lost delights are evoked above all to emphasize the pathos of slaughter. Such passages are discussed in an essay of great insight by Jasper Griffin (see n. 19):

But in the *Iliad* the lesser heroes are shown in all the pathos of their death, the change from the brightness of life to a dark and meaningless existence, the grief of their friends and families; but the style preserves the poem from sentimentality on the one hand and sadism on the other. Stripped of the sort of passages here discussed, it would lose not merely an ornament, but a vital part of its nature (p. 186).

Thirdly, there are the similes. Many are drawn, of course, from the world of peace, of rural life, from the everyday life of ordinary people, the audience. What has to be further appreciated is that some of the simile-pictures derive their power from an actual *contrast* with the world of war which they are compared to.[35] What this contrast does is to oblige the audience to reconsider the context through the comparison, to look at it again in the light of the difference as well as the similarity. I hope to make the point simply by four illustrations. The tranquility of the snowscape at 12.278–86, spanning from mountain-top across the lowlands and out to sea, muffling all disturbance, throws us back with all the more shock into the din and violence of the Trojan attack on the wall. When the fire of Hephaestus sweeps through the vegetation on the banks of Scamander and even the fish are tortured, it is likened to a breeze that dries a newly irrigated plot and so delights the gardener (21.346–7). Agamemnon's wound hurts like a woman's labour pains (11.269–72), and when Gorgythion is killed his head droops like a poppy-head heavy with seed (8.306–7). Again and again pain and destruction and violent death are compared to fertile agriculture, creative craftsmanship, useful objects and tasks, scenes of peace and innocent delight. I quote the conclusion of a valuable article by D. H. Porter:[36]

The grimness and bloodiness of the battlefield are inevitably rendered darker and more tragic by the constant brief glimpses we get in the similes of a world where milk flows, flowers and crops grow in the fields, shepherds tend their flocks, and small children play. Conversely, these momentary glimpses of the world of peace are made more idyllic and poignant by the panorama of violence and destruction which surround them.

The similes thus let us—indeed make us—look through the war to the peace that lies behind it, to the peace that the warriors have abandoned and which many of them will never know again. The similes make us see war as wasteful and destructive, the blight of peace and pleasure. And this is, I suggest, what the shield of Achilles does, but on a far larger scale. *It makes us think about war and see it in relation to peace.* Achilles has just made the decision which will lead to Hector's death and then to his own; Hector has just made the decision which will lead to his death and then to the sack of Troy. At this point we are made to contemplate the life that Achilles has renounced and the civilization that Troy will never regain. The two finest things in the *Iliad*—Achilles and Troy—will never again enjoy the existence portrayed on the shield: that is the price of war and of heroic glory. The shield of Achilles brings home the loss, the cost of the events of the *Iliad*.

I trust I do not seem to be maintaining that the *Iliad* is an anti-war epic, a pacifist tract—that would be almost as much of a distortion as the opposite extreme which I am attacking. The *Iliad* does not explicitly condemn war nor does it try to sweeten it: indeed its equity is essential to its greatness. It presents both sides, victory and defeat, the destroyer and the destroyed; and it does not judge between them. The gain and the loss are put side by side without prejudice. In terms of quantity, of course, much more of the poem is taken up with war and killing, but the glimpses of peace and loss stand out all the more by contrast, as a simile stands out in a battle-scene, or the shield of Achilles in the poem as a whole.

The *Iliad* is a poem of war in which valiant heroes win glory in battle and prove their worth by killing the enemy. The poem is the product of a tradition of martial epic, songs of the κλέα ἀνδρῶν or 'glorious deeds of men'; and it does not deny—let alone condemn—the fundamental premiss of its own tradition, that mighty deeds of battle are fit matter for the immortality of song. Many early Greek epics may have consisted solely of narrative of the glorious exploits of Greek warriors,[37] but the *Iliad* is much, much more than that. The poem itself is the primary and incontrovertible source for what Homer regards as important, and it outweighs any amount of comparative material from other cultures or of synthesized versions of the 'Heroic World'. Homer shows what is important by conferring on it the immortality of song. Consider, after all, what it is that wins the major characters their immortality in the poem as it is. Hector may win glory by his victories in battle during the central books, but he is remembered above all for his scene with Andromache and for his failure and death in battle defending his fatherland.[38] Achilles is not immortalized for his massacre of Trojans in Books 20 and 21 so much as for his impending death before his time, for his rejection of the embassy in Book 9, and for his treatment of Priam.[39] Certainly some of the lesser heroes win their place in the poem for their deeds in battle, but there are others who are immortalized for what they do and say off the field, not only Thersites, Paris or Nestor, but Helen, Hecuba, and Priam. In fact, to cut a long story short, the great figures of the *Iliad* are great not because of the outstanding slaughter they inflict, but because of the quality of their suffering and the way that they bear it.

The *Iliad* owes its tragic greatness to Homer's ability to appreciate and sympathize with *both* aspects of heroic war. He shows how for every victory there is a defeat, how for every triumphant killing there is another human killed. Glorious deeds are done, mighty prowess displayed: at the same time fine cities are burned, fathers lose their sons, women lose their families and freedom. This is implicit in Achilles' own decision:

> Now I must win excellent glory,
> and drive someone of the women of Troy, or some deep-girdled
> Dardanian woman, lifting up to her soft cheeks both hands

to wipe away the close bursts of tears in her lamentation,
and learn that I stayed too long out of the fighting

(18.121–5)

—and explicit in his words to Priam in Book 24. He does not look after
his old father Peleus 'since far from the land of my fathers I sit here in
Troy, and bring nothing but sorrow to you and your children' (24.541–2).
Homer gives victory and prowess their due recognition, but he never loses
sight of the human cost, of the waste of what might have flourished and
brought joy. Human beings protect their dependants and win glory, and
thus war is important: human beings also suffer and endure, and war is a
great cause of this.

The scope of Homer's sympathy has perhaps never been more deeply
expressed than in Simone Weil's essay, *The Iliad, or The Poem of Force.*[40] It
was not written for scholars and is not argued in the academic mode: it
none the less conveys a fundamental understanding of the *Iliad*. A single
quotation will have to serve:

And yet such an accumulation of violences would be cold without that accent
of incurable bitterness which continually makes itself felt, although often
indicated only by a single word, sometimes only by a play of verse, by a run
over line. It is this which makes the *Iliad* a unique poem, this bitterness,
issuing from its tenderness, and which extends, as the light of the sun, equally
over all men. Never does the tone of the poem cease to be impregnated by this
bitterness, nor does it ever descend to the level of a complaint . . . Nothing
precious is despised, whether or not destined to perish. The destitution and
misery of all men is shown without dissimulation or disdain . . . and whatever
is destroyed is regretted.

The person who found this dimension in the *Iliad* was not some com-
placent pedant, but a young woman who renounced pacifism in 1939 and
died in 1943, consumed by regret for man's inhumanity to man.

Simone Weil understood the *Iliad* more fully than W. H. Auden. Auden
was disturbed that the great poem of war should include the shield of
Achilles, and insisted that art must present war in all its brutal inhumanity
without such loopholes. But the *Iliad* is not only a poem of war, it is also
a poem of peace. It is a tragic poem, and in it war prevails over peace—
but that has been the tragic history of so much of mankind.

NOTES

1. Little in this essay is new, though much may be unfamiliar to those brought up on the kind
of Homeric studies which have prevailed in Britain and America for some half a century now.
I have been especially helped by three essays on the shield: W. Schadewaldt, *Von Homers Welt
und Werk* (4th edn. Stuttgart, 1965) [hereafter *HWW*], 352–74 (first published in 1938),
K. Reinhardt, *Die Ilias und ihr Dichter* (Göttingen, 1961), 401–11 (first published in 1956), and
W. Marg, *Homer über die Dichtung* (2nd edn. Münster, 1971). Their influence has been pervasive

and I shall not try to single out every concurrence. For a list of those renegades who have taken the shield seriously in English see n. 30 below. I am indebted to Colin Macleod and Malcolm Willcock for some helpful suggestions and corrections.

2. For the contrasts between these two crucial decisions to fight see Schadewaldt's superb essay 'Die Entscheidung des Achilles', *HWW*, 234–67.

3. See J. Armstrong's excellent article on arming scenes, *AJP* 79 (1958), 337 ff., esp. 344–5. All the translations are Lattimore's, with slight alterations where necessary.

4. The useful introduction and commentary by C. F. Russo (2nd edn. Florence, 1965), esp. 29–35 date the poem to the sixth century. Anyone who has read the *Shield of Heracles* can hardly continue to believe that the *Iliad* and *Odyssey* were merely typical products of a tradition in which the author submerged his individual genius. I am not sure why Jasper Griffin does not make more use of this third-rate cyclic-type blustering in his excellent article 'The Epic Cycle and the Uniqueness of Homer', *JHS* 97 (1977), 39 ff.

5. See the useful pamphlet on the shield of Achilles by K. Fittschen in the series *Archaeologia Homerica*: Kapitel N, Bildkunst, Teil 1 (Göttingen, 1973), esp. 2; and compare the plates to be found on 93–109 and 181–3 of K. Friis Johansen, *The Iliad in Early Greek Art* (Copenhagen, 1967).

6. First published in *Poetry* for Oct. 1952. I can find no external reason to think the poem was written earlier than 1952.

7. 'Who would not live long', ὠκύμορος, μινυνθάδιος. The motif is introduced in Book 1 (352, 416 f.) and recurs throughout: see Schadewaldt, *HWW*, 260 f. 'Iron-hearted': the metaphor is rare in the *Iliad*, but is used by Hector of Achilles as he dies at 22.357 (otherwise only of Priam at 24.205, 521). 'Man-slaying': is it not likely that Auden derived the epithet from the phrase χεῖρας ἐπ᾽ ἀνδροφόνους at 18.317? The only other times the epithet is used of hands are also about Achilles: 23.18 and 24.479—the latter at the greatest moment of the entire *Iliad*.

8. For the less orthodox scholars see n. 30 below.

9. See Fittschen, op. cit., *passim*. For a bibliography of such views see Fittschen, 4–5.

10. 18.148–238 is the only fighting in between 18.1 and 20.156 ff.

11. Quoted from C. M. Bowra, *Tradition and Design in the Iliad* (Oxford, 1930), 126. I have found the most thoroughgoing and readable assertion of the paratactic approach the article by J. A. Notopoulos, *TAPA* 80 (1949), 1 ff. The notion has been adapted and updated by G. S. Kirk under the term 'cumulation', particularly in his paper 'Verse-structure and Sentence-structure' in *Homer and the Oral Tradition* (Cambridge, 1976) [hereafter *HOT*], 146 ff., esp. 167 ff. (originally in *YCS* 20 [1966], 73 ff.). Note this on 171: 'Arming scenes, descriptions of pieces of armour, developed similes, the description of minor figures and their genealogy whether or not in a catalogue—these are the typical *loci* for cumulation.'

12. Lessing, *Laocoon*, chs. 17–19. This point has been stressed by H. A. Gaertner, 'Beobachtungen zum Schild des A.', *Studien zum antiken Epos*, edited by H. Görgemanns and E. A. Schmidt (Meisenheim, 1976), 46 ff.

13. It would undoubtedly make most sense if line 483 ('land, heaven, sea') were a summary of the entire shield, and 484–9 the details of the first circle, showing only the heavens; this is maintained by Fittschen, op. cit., 10. But there are difficulties, above all the construction of line 484; this interpretation is impossible without emendation.

14. Cf. in various circumstances the rebukes and taunts at *Il*. 3.54, 15.508, 16.617, 16.745–50, 24.261.

15. Those who are inclined to fall for the stuff about women and wives in M. I. Finley, *The World of Odysseus* (2nd edn. London, 1977) [hereafter *WO*], 126 ff., should read *Iliad* Book 6 as an antidote. They might also take note of *Od*. 6.180–5 (overlooked by Finley).

16. See notably H. Hommel in *Palingenesia* iv (Festschr. für R. Stark, Wiesbaden, 1969), 11 ff., and Ø S. Andersen, *SO* 51 (1976), 5 ff., esp. 11–16.

17. Cf. Andersen, op. cit., 9.

18. Achilles had once come upon Aeneas herding on the slopes of Ida, but Aeneas ran and escaped (20.187 ff.). Achilles would often spare the Trojans he captured, like Lycaon whom he caught in Priam's garden cutting fig branches to make a chariot rail: but the death of Patroclus changes all that—see 21.99–113.

19. On pathos in the *Iliad* see the exceptionally perceptive and well-argued article by Griffin, *CQ* 26 (1976), 161 ff.

20. F. Solmsen, *Hermes* 93 (1965), 1–6. Further points against 535–8 are added by J. M. Lynn-George, *Hermes* 106 (1978), 396–405; Lynn-George defends 539–40 as Homeric, but unconvincingly to my mind. On the primitive notion of κῆρες ('doom') see J. Redfield, *Nature and Culture in the Iliad* (Chicago, 1975), 184 f.

21. For full details see S. West, *The Ptolemaic Papyri of Homer* (Cologne, 1967), 132–6.

22. It is often said that the division of the year into *four* seasons is not to be found before Alcman (fr.20). But all four of Alcman's seasons—ἔαρ, θέρος, ὀπώρη, and χεῖμα—are to be found in Homer.

23. Kirk, *HOT*, 12 asserts that the king is going to eat all the roast beef while the workers will have barley mash. I cannot see any reason for preferring this to the interpretation well argued for by Leaf. The heralds have performed the slaughter and jointing; the women are actually cooking it, and this involves sprinkling the meat with barley, exactly as at *Od.* 14.77.

24. Cf. Gaertner, op. cit., 61–3. For some examples of such *temene* or 'estates' in the *Iliad* compare 6.194 (Bellerophon), 9.576 (Meleager), 12.313 (Glaucus and Sarpedon), 20.184 (Aeneas).

25. Who is to say that it is pure coincidence that the unusual verb ὀαρίζειν also occurs at 6.516 used of the conversation of Hector and Andromache? See the good remarks of E. T. Owen, *The Story of the Iliad* (see n. 30 below), 121–2; cf. C. Segal, *The Theme of the Mutilation of the Corpse in the Iliad* (Leiden, 1971), 36.

26. J. Kakridis has produced comparative material which confirms that the main scene of an 'imagined ecphrasis' should come last; see *Homer Revisited* (Lund, 1971), 108 ff., esp. 123 (originally in *WSt* 76 [1963], 7 ff). Gaertner (op. cit., 53 n. 18) argues that the king's *temenos* is the climactic scene of the shield, but he does not refute Kakridis.

27. Most editors since Wolf have included the line and believed that it was wrongly ejected by Aristarchus. This rests on a long stretch of fictional pedantry in Athenaeus Book 4 (180a–181c). But all the experts on Aristarchus are quite clear that Athenaeus cannot have got his facts right—perhaps he did not try to. For full bibliography see *Scholia Graeca in Homeri Iliadem* IV, ed. H. Erbse (Berlin, 1975), 509. The case for the line must stand or fall without Athenaeus.

28. 141, ἀργεννῇσι ὀθόνῃσιν; 385, νεκταρέου ἑανοῦ; 419, ἑανῷ ἀργῆτι φαεινῷ. 3.385 surely gives extra point to Athene's taunt at 5.421–5: but at the time in Book 3 Aphrodite's treatment of Helen is no joke.

29. See Schadewaldt's brilliant essay on the death of Hector, *HWW*, 268 ff., esp. 331–2; also Segal, op. cit., 46–7.

30. Pride of place must go to Owen, *The Story of the Iliad* (Toronto, 1946, repr. Ann Arbor, 1966), 186–9; there is a quotation on p. 107. This admirable book is directed to students rather than research scholars, but that does not explain the unjust neglect of it. I suspect that it has been axiomatic that any Homeric study which does not take due account of oral composition must be totally valueless: I see no justification for this attitude. Other works in English which say things worth saying about the shield of Achilles are J. T. Sheppard, *The Pattern of the Iliad* (London, 1922), 1–10, esp. 8, C. H. Whitman, *Homer and the Heroic Tradition* (Harvard, 1958), 205 f., G. A. Duethorn, *Achilles' Shield and the Structure of the Iliad* (Amhurst, 1962), C. R. Beye, *The Iliad, the Odyssey and the Epic Tradition* (Garden City, 1966), 143–4, Redfield (see n. 20), 187–8. I find K. J. Atchity, *Homer's Iliad, the Shield of Memory* (Southern Illinois, 1978) disappointingly diffuse and fanciful.

31. *Works and Days* 14–15; see West's note on 15.

32. *HOT*, 1 ff. (first published in 1972); compare also *HOT*, 50–2 (first published in 1968).

33. 'Achilles' temporary compassion for Priam . . . is more unnerving . . . but then Achilles sees his own father in Priam, and in any case he rapidly suppresses the unheroic emotion and threatens a renewal of anger, the proper heroic reaction to an enemy.' This is not the place to explain why I take this to be a fundamental misconstruction of Book 24 and of the whole *Iliad*. It will have to serve for now to observe that what lines 560–70 do is to show what an *effort* of willpower it is for Achilles to overcome the 'proper heroic reaction'; but the whole point is that, unlike Agamemnon in Book 1, he succeeds. The lines do not mark the end of his compassion but its continuation (see especially 633 f., 671 f.).

34. See notably 2.796 f.; 18.288 ff.; 9.403, τὸ πρὶν ἐπ' εἰρήνης, πρὶν ἐλθεῖν υἷας Ἀχαιῶν, 'in earlier times, in peace, before the sons of the Achaeans came'=22.156 (see p. 106 above).

35. Only some similes, not all. I consider it a great mistake to try to isolate a single function for all Homeric similes: on the contrary Homer seems to expect his audience to be alert to a wide

variety. Far from providing relaxation the similes are especially taxing because of the very unpredictability of the relation of each to its context.

36. See in general Porter's excellent article 'Violent Juxtaposition in the Similes of the *Iliad*', *CJ* 68 (1972), 11–21 (the quotation is from 19); also Redfield (see n. 20), 186 ff. On the Agamemnon simile see also C. Moulton, *Similes in the Homeric Poems* (Göttingen, 1977), 98–9, on Gorgythion M. Silk, *Interaction in Poetic Imagery* (Cambridge, 1974), 5.

37. It is clear that the construction of battle narratives was highly traditional. This is one of many important points which receive interesting confirmation in B. Fenik, *Typical Battle Scenes in the Iliad* (Wiesbaden, 1968). The tradition was evidently chauvinistically pro-Greek: on Homer's departure from this see the fine essay 'Ἀεὶ φιλέλλην ὁ ποιητής;' in Kakridis (see n. 26), 54 ff. (originally in *WSt* 69 [1956], 26 ff.).

38. See the brief but telling remarks by Griffin (see n. 19), 186 f.

39. Note especially 24.110, spoken by Zeus to Thetis, αὐτὰρ ἐγὼ τόδε κῦδος Ἀχιλλῆι προτιάπτω, 'but I grant this glory to Achilles'. The κῦδος ('glory') is to pity Priam and accept the ransom, thus proving Zeus' estimate of him in 24.157–8 right rather than Apollo's in 24.39 ff.

40. Originally in *Cahiers du Sud* 1940–1, and reprinted in *La Source grecque* (Paris, 1952); translated into English as a pamphlet by M. McCarthy (New York, 1945, repr. 1967), and in the collection *Intimations of Christiniaty among the Ancient Greeks* (London, 1957) by E. C. Geissbuhler.

ADDENDUM

Contemporary Homeric scholarship in English has, happily, changed almost beyond recognition since the dreary days complained of in n. 30 and elsewhere. Apart from admirable commentaries on both the *Iliad* and the *Odyssey*, one might single out M. W. Edwards, *Homer, Poet of the Iliad* (Baltimore, 1987) and (from personal loyalty) *Homeric Soundings* (Oxford, 1992). Contributions specifically on the shield include F. Létroublon in *Poétique* 53 (1983) and T. K. Hubbard in *Arion* 2.1 (Winter 1992).

THE SUCCESSION ISSUE IN THE *ODYSSEY*

By JOHN HALVERSON

It is a commonly held view that the basic issue in the Ithacan sequences of the *Odyssey* is the succession to Odysseus' position as king. Thus J. V. Luce, for example, sees 'the outline of a power struggle with kingship as the prize for the most powerful noble'.[1] And M. I. Finley declares: ' "The king is dead! The struggle for the throne is open!" That is how the entire Ithacan theme of the *Odyssey* can be summed up.'[2] I should like to argue that this highly political perspective is unwarranted, that in fact there is no throne, no office of king, indeed no real Ithacan state, and therefore no succession struggle.

Finley's argument for a contest of succession is the fullest and has been the most influential. It starts out from the familiar exchange in Book 1 between Telemachus and the two leading suitors, Antinous and Eurymachus. There Antinous says tauntingly to Telemachus, 'May the son of Kronos not make you king (βασιλῆα) in sea-girt Ithaca, which thing is your patrimony by birth'; Telemachus, in response, allows that there are other βασιλῆες who might succeed to that position; and Eurymachus remarks that 'these things lie on the knees of the gods, who will be βασιλεύς of the Achaeans in sea-girt Ithaca' (1.384–401). According to Finley it is Penelope who has the power to determine who will succeed to that position: 'Let Penelope choose Odysseus' successor as king and spouse, and peace would be restored to Ithaca. The successful suitor would take the throne . . .'[3] The power to make this decision lies 'in the strangest place imaginable, in the hands of a woman' (91). Why Penelope has this power is acknowledged to be a mystery; 'Perhaps the Penelope situation became so muddled in the long prehistory of the *Odyssey* that the actual social and legal situation is no longer recoverable' (92). But in any case, 'virtually the whole aristocracy . . . were agreed that the house of Odysseus was to be dethroned' (93). Thus the argument assumes that Ithaca is a kingdom, that Odysseus has been its king, that succession to kingship will be determined by Penelope's remarriage, and that there is a hereditary dynasty in the process of being overthrown. None of these assumptions, I believe, can be justified.

Is Ithaca a kingdom? Though Finley allows for the uncertainties and insecurity of kingship and for the terminological 'oscillation between *basileus* as king and *basileus* as chief' (86), he evidently conceives of Odysseus as a monarch: e.g., 'When Odysseus returned there was no automatic resumption of his *royal* position. He had to fight . . . to regain his *throne'* (88, italics added). But though he uses the language of monarchy, he recognizes the extreme limitations of 'kingship'. As to royal functions, 'The king gave military leadership and protection, and he gave little else . . .' (101). Or again, 'The effective, powerful king gave protection and defense, by his dealings with kings abroad, by his organization of such activities as the building of walls, and by his personal leadership in battle' (ibid.). But can even such limited functions as these be ascribed to Odysseus? The text does not do so at any rate. Certainly we hear of no public enterprises such as the building of walls (nor of walls at all in Ithaca). There are no allusions to Odysseus as protector of the people against foreign attack (evidently what Finley has in mind by 'protection'). Military leadership might be inferred from Odysseus' role in the Trojan War, but that seems to have no political dimension: 'King Odysseus' does not mobilize 'Ithaca' and lead it to war; it is rather as a powerful individual that he has enlisted other individual warriors to participate in a military adventure. Obviously a great many Ithacan men were not persuaded to follow him (including Antinous' father, who disparages Odysseus' leadership and adventurism: 24.427–8). His dealings with foreign kings are also personal, without any suggestion of international diplomacy. A. G. Geddes, concluding a careful study of Homeric kingship, sums the matter up with the observation that Homeric kings 'seem to have no function in society'.[4] It would be just as accurate, perhaps more accurate, to say that Homeric society has no kings, in any meaningful sense of the word.

The *Odyssey* at least contains no indications that its hero's position was a 'royal' one or that he ever had or exerted political authority. To be sure he was a lord (ἄνασσε) to the people (2.234), but the verb need carry no more political connotation than does Telemachus' use of the noun when he is determined to be ἄναξ in his own household (1.397). Not only are there no allusions to Odysseus conducting affairs of state, there is not even a 'state' in evidence; Ithaca has no polity or even a corporate character. A good indication of this is the fact that it has got along for twenty years without any kind of general assembly let alone a king, implying that it is a land without any kind of central government. Apparently the Ithacans have gone about their business for nearly a generation in the absence of king, regent, or any political authority. Nor do we know that this is an anomalous situation. It is implied that when Odysseus was present, assemblies were sometimes called; or more accurately, it is implied that at least one assembly was called twenty years ago (one might well imagine that it was for the extraordinary purpose of recruiting for the Trojan expedition), and as far as the poem tells us, that may have been in turn the first in twenty years. In short, we have no grounds for assuming any but the most primitive kind of polity for Ithaca, least of all a functioning kingdom.

'King' therefore is surely the wrong word to translate βασιλεύς (even 'kinglet' and 'petty king' are misleading). Odysseus has indubitably been the leading man of his region, but this is a position of status, not an office, a position based above all on wealth, Odysseus' ζωή ἄσπετος ('means beyond telling', 14.96–7), and secondarily on personal ability and charisma. All of this is implied in the beginning exchange between Telemachus and the suitors. He does not therefore speak 'curiously' as Finley claims, when he refers to *other* βασιλῆες in Ithaca, 'not one of whom was a king' (86), for the word does not mean 'king'.[5] There are a number of big men in the region, and in the absence of the great Odysseus one of them might achieve a status of preeminence like his. But that is a matter of ability, enterprise, and chance; it is on the knees of the gods.

It is certain, however, that Telemachus cannot expect to become a βασιλεύς at all if the suitors continue to ravage his household; the daily consumption of over a hundred men will eventually destroy even Odysseus' great resources, as Telemachus is keenly aware. The suitors also understand this; it is precisely their strategy—not to ruin Telemachus, but to force remarriage on Penelope. It is the discovery of the weaving deception that leads to the occupation of Odysseus' home in the first place, and it is explicitly undertaken to put pressure on both mother and son to force her to choose a husband. That is why the suitors are there. Antinous tells Telemachus that they will continue to eat him out of house and home until Penelope chooses a husband. 'They will consume your livelihood and possessions just as long as she should hold this notion which the gods now put in her heart . . . . We shall not go to our lands or anywhere else before she marries that one of the Achaeans whom she wishes' (2.123–8). Eurymachus says the same thing shortly after: Telemachus' goods will be devoured as long as she keeps putting off the Achaeans about marriage (2.203–5).

From the suitors' point of view the solution to the problem is simple. Let Telemachus send his mother back to her father's home and let a marriage be arranged (2.195–7; cf. 1.275–8). The subject recurs frequently, and it is always clear that if she remarries she must leave Odysseus' household. Telemachus expresses his reluctance to thrust her out of the house (δόμων . . . ἀπῶσαι, 2.130; ἀπὸ μεγάροιο δίεσθαι, 20.343). Penelope herself sees her dilemma as a choice between remaining in her household and leaving it (μένω or ἕπωμαι, 19.525–8; 16.74–6). In Odysseus' own parting words, if he does not return, she is to remarry, 'leaving your house altogether' (τεὸν κατὰ δῶμα λιποῦσα, 18.270). Evidently Penelope's remarriage entails her separation from and renunciation of Odysseus' estate, which therefore cannot be a prize for a prospective suitor: it does not go with her. Telemachus' obligation 'to pay back' (ἀποτίνειν) her father seems to carry the same implication. But if the estate does not go with Penelope, neither *a fortiori* does Odysseus' position as βασιλεύς.

It is evident that Penelope in fact has no mysterious power to choose the next king. Neither the poet nor the characters attribute any such power to her, and there is no reason to think it exists. M. P. Nilsson, one of the first to make the suggestion, evoked the Oedipus myth as well as the *Odyssey* to claim that 'the throne when empty was given away with the hand of the queen-dowager'.[6] But the Oedipus story offers no real support for this contention. As Sophocles tells it anyway (*O.T.* 1198–204), Oedipus becomes king as the explicit result of removing the Sphinx, not by marrying Jocasta; the implication is that she goes with the kingdom rather than the kingdom with her. In another parallel from tradition, the marriage of Clytemnestra to Aegisthus, it is quite clear in both Homer and Aeschylus that Aegisthus' kingship is a usurpation, in no way legitimated by marriage; on the contrary, it must be established by intimidation and force.

On the other hand, kingship aside, it is possible that in the absence of offspring, the widow of a βασιλεύς would inherit his property, and if she remarried, her next husband would acquire control of the property and thus the power of a βασιλεύς, and perhaps the name as well. Only in such a circumstance would Penelope have any power of disposition, and it would not be mysterious. But while Telemachus is still alive, she has no power of any kind except a mother's moral and persuasive force. Neither, while Telemachus is alive, can the suitors aspire to Odysseus' social position, which is tied not to Penelope, but to his property, and this is Telemachus' legitimate inheritance, as all acknowledge. Eventually some of the suitors will plot his death, but not, it is fairly clear, for the purpose of acquiring Odysseus' 'throne'.

With Telemachus out of the way, the situation would presumably be quite different. But until Telemachus' voyage to the mainland, there is no plot to do away with him; it was evidently no part of the suitors' original intentions. At the time of his departure there is, in passing, a suggestion from one of the suitors that he might die on the trip and they could divide up his possessions (2.330 ff.). The suggestion is taken up in earnest a little later when they find that he has actually departed for Pylos. Later still, when Telemachus returns, having avoided the ambush, Antinous proposes the alternatives of murdering Telemachus or withdrawing from his house and ceasing their depredations (16.370 ff.). In both instances, the suggestion is to take possession of his livelihood (βίοτον) and properties (κτήματα), 'dividing them fairly among ourselves' (16.384–6). Now the division of Odysseus' estate, however extensive, among 108 people would certainly eliminate it as a potential power base for a would-be βασιλεύς. So even as they consider killing the rightful heir, it cannot be for the purpose of seizing power.

In fact it is explicitly out of fear of retaliation. Telemachus has openly threatened them: 'I will try how I may send evil death (κῆρας) on you, either going to Pylos or right here in this district' (2.316–17). He is mocked, but understood, one of the youths saying, 'Telemachus is indeed pondering our murder. He will bring some helpers from sandy Pylos or even Sparta . . .' (2.325–7). Later, when Telemachus has returned, the suitors are even more alarmed, fearing he will rouse the people against them and drive them into exile (16.374 ff.). It is at just these times that murder by ambush is proposed, and the motivation is both apparent and understandable.

Thus far, then, it seems clear that no aspirations to succeed Odysseus as βασιλεύς are attributed to the suitors. That rank or position would depend on and derive from the estate. If Telemachus is allowed to live, he will inherit the property. If he is killed, the estate will be disintegrated. Neither alternative allows for any of the suitors to succeed to Odysseus' position. Where then does the notion of a 'struggle for the throne' come from? Only one place that I can see (though not mentioned by any of its proponents), that is when the wily Eurymachus, in a desperate move to placate Odysseus' wrath before the final slaughter, tries to put all the blame on Antinous, whom Odysseus has just killed. It was Antinous, he says, who started everything, and not because he wanted the marriage but because of another idea, 'that he himself should rule (βασιλεύοι) the people/district of well-established Ithaca, having killed your son in ambush' (22.48–53). On the face of it this does sound like a usurpation plot. But in the first place, it should be noted that the implication is by no means a necessary one. After all, Antinous was one who proposed the division of Odysseus' properties, which, as already argued, obviously precludes a direct takeover of Odysseus' position. The assumption may therefore be no more than this, that with the dissolution of Odysseus' estate, Antinous, already a big man, a βασιλεύς, might well emerge as the new leading βασιλεύς in his own right. Not a usurpation then but a natural development. In the second place it must be asked whether the allegation is credible. We have already been told that Eurymachus is an accomplished liar. In Book 16 he protests eloquently to Penelope that no one shall ever harm Telemachus while he lives, but the poet comments, 'So he spoke encouragingly, but he himself was preparing his destruction' (16.434–8). He is quick-witted and self-serving, while Antinous, though arrogant and cruel, is not presented as a liar, but on the contrary is verbally at least very straightforward, and he himself expresses no thought of replacing Odysseus. It is possible that Eurymachus is betraying his own schemes here, since he has plotted the death of Telemachus and is also the front-running suitor. Telemachus seems to credit him with some such scheme, commenting that Eurymachus 'longs most to marry my mother and to have the γέρας ('prerogative') of Odysseus' (15.521–1). But at best Eurymachus would be the only one of the 108 suitors even to entertain the idea of succeeding to Odysseus' position—very far indeed from a 'power struggle', which even Eurymachus' testimony in no way suggests.

It should be noted too that after the first ambush has failed, Antinous' second proposal to kill Telemachus is not accepted by the other suitors. Amphinomus responds to it by deploring the idea of killing the scion of a βασιλεύς and urges that they learn the will of the gods before doing anything so extreme. The others agree. Unfortunately they do not consider further Antinous' alternative, to return to their own homes and court Penelope properly, but immediately go back to Odysseus' house and continue as before (16.394 ff.). Some time later, as the suitors are again discussing Telemachus' murder, an eagle carrying a dove appears in the sky on the left. Evidently this is the omen from Zeus they wished for, and Amphinomus interprets it as inauspicious: 'Friends, this plan, the murder of Telemachus, will not succeed for us. Let us rather think of the feast.' And again the words pleased them (20.240–7). Apparently they have given up any plan to kill Telemachus, but will continue to pressure Penelope by their presence in her house. We are entitled then to believe another suitor, Agelaus, when he later reasserts their original position to Telemachus and implicitly denies any designs on his person or inheritance. Tell your mother, he says, to marry whoever is the best man and brings the most gifts so that you may enjoy all your patrimony and she may care for another man's house (20.334–7).

We may conclude then that, with Telemachus out of the way, the person who married Penelope might well succeed to Odysseus' status as βασιλεύς. But this would be the result of acquiring Odysseus' property on which the status rests; he would not acquire the title simply by marrying the widow. It is possible that Eurymachus or Antinous secretly entertains such an ambition, since both plot the death of Telemachus. However, the overt position of all the suitors, frequently stated, is that if Telemachus should die or be killed, they will divide the estate among themselves, which would assure that no one succeeded to Odysseus' place; or if Telemachus remains alive, he will keep his patrimony when his mother remarries and leaves the household, which would allow the possibility that Telemachus or any of the other βασιλῆες—or no one—might become the leading man of the region, as implied by Telemachus at the beginning. But in no case is there any contest for a non-existent 'throne' or any general agreement 'that the house of Odysseus was to be dethroned'. There seems to be no good reason not to take the story at face value and admit that the suitors really are suitors, not political insurgents or conspirators. Whatever we may think of it, they do seem to be contending simply for Penelope herself.

This is not easy for everyone to accept. Thus W. K. Lacey, for example: 'It is impossible not to believe that the obtaining of Odysseus' οἶκος was in fact the suitors' main motive in coming to Odysseus' palace in the first place . . . . had they really only wanted to marry Penelope they would surely have welcomed Telemachus' initiative in seeking to ascertain the facts about her eligibility.'[7] He is referring to Telemachus' voyage to Pylos to try to find out if Odysseus is alive or dead, which would thus settle the question of whether Penelope is actually an eligible widow. But as we have seen, the suitors have every right to suspect other, very unwelcome motives for the voyage. Moreover, from their point of view, it could seem at best only another delaying action, since Penelope has already acknowledged to them that her husband is dead (ἐπεὶ θάνε δῖος Ὀδυσσεύς, 2.96). So Antinous reports her words anyway, and they are repeated verbatim by Amphimedon in Hades (24.131).

Finley too, in the course of asserting Penelope's power of deciding the next 'king', is reluctant to allow Penelope her own attractions: 'There was nothing about the woman Penelope, either in beauty or wisdom or spirit, that could have won her this unprecedented and unwanted right of decision as a purely personal triumph' (91). The implied assessment of Penelope here is certainly not shared by the suitors generally when their knees are loosened, their hearts impassioned, and each one prays to be in her bed, or Eurymachus specifically when he praises her as excelling all women in form and stature and balanced mind (18.212–50). For Finley it seems to be the 'mystery' of Penelope that explains the suitors' restraint. 'On the surface there is no good reason why they went on with the game for so many years.' They had the greater force; 'indeed there was no visible opposition'. Yet they 'refrained from murdering Laertes and Telemachos and seizing power', and 'publicly and repeatedly' conceded 'Telemachos' claim to his οἶκος' (90–1). There is more than a little question-begging here, for if there is no plot to seize power, the suitors' failure to do so requires no explanation. If one can bring oneself to accept the apparent *donnée* of the text, that the object of the suitors' suit is only Penelope herself, it becomes evident that these enigmas are manufactured. What is the difficulty in accepting it? Is it because she is a mature woman? Is it because the Greeks were so pragmatic about marriage? But no one applies such reservations about Helen. And in comparison to the genuinely fantastic elements of the *Odyssey* Penelope's desirability seems hardly problematic; it is merely a given of the romance, at most a rather mild hyperbole.

There is another political interpretation of the suitors that should be mentioned, one that would have them seen as young oligarchs and the Ithacan drama as a reflection of eighth-century historical conflicts between older monarchies and rising oligarchies.[8] It is possible that contemporary oligarchs may have furnished the poet with models of the 'corrupt life style' of the suitors, but there is nothing visibly political about the suitors' actions or aspirations. Clearly they are neither ruling Ithaca nor trying to do so in the present time of the story. Just as clearly, they are not plotting a *collective*, i.e., oligarchic, seizure of power in the future. Even on the reading—rejected here—that there is a political plot, the goal is the succession of *one* man to the 'kingship', not many. It is true that 'the suitors function regularly as a group' (136), but this need not be a sign of a proto-oligarchy; indeed it need not signify much of anything, for their only function is to entertain themselves, which is largely a group activity. In the process they are consuming Odysseus' household. This is Telemachus' complaint, not that he is being deprived of the 'kingship' of Ithaca; on the contrary, his attitude is plainly: Be *that* as it may, I will nevertheless be master of my own household (1.396–8). No one in the story, then, has any awareness of political issues; no one knows of any constitution to be overthrown or kingship to be usurped.

The possibility is not precluded, however, that the story might have been interpreted as a political allegory of the kind Rose suggests, and might even have been intended to be so interpreted. The likelihood rests on the historical contention that 'The most significant political phenomenon of the period is that the institution of monarchy was in the process of being displaced by oligarchy . . .' (132). Rose goes on to qualify these terms, so that oligarchy is 'collectively exercised control by the heads of large estates', and monarchy refers to a 'βασιλεύς, ruler of a relatively modest area including an "urban aggregate" through his personal prestige, wealth and prowess in war' (ibid.). But even with these sensible qualifications, there is considerable doubt that any change of this sort was in fact going on, as Robert Drews has recently shown in a thorough analysis of the available material.[9] Though he allows for the possibility of a few weak monarchies in 'Peloponnesian *ethne* which, after a fashion, survived the breakdown of the old order', he argues convincingly that 'At no time were kings in the *poleis* . . .' and that 'there was no tidal shift from monarchy to aristocracy in the eighth century . . .' (130). The earliest *poleis* were not under the rule of kings but were led by informal collectivities of leading men, βασιλῆες (he also denies the meaning 'king' for βασιλεύς, 129), and the changes that were taking place in the eighth century were simply in the direction of formalization and institutionalization of the earlier patterns. The Russian historian Juri V. Andreev,[10] arguing along similar lines, has also concluded that 'in der Homerischen Epoche die Monarchie als gewachsene und normal funktionierende Einrichtung in Griechenland noch nicht existierte' (383). Giving more specific attention to the *Odyssey*, he shares my view of the non-political character of the basic conflict: 'Der Grundkonflikt, um den herum die Fabel "unserer" *Odyssee* aufgebaut wird, ist ganz und gar nicht politischen Charakters' (371). If these views are correct, the kind of political allegory Rose suggests would be as improbable historically as it is textually.

If there is a succession issue at all in the *Odyssey*, it is at a politically primitive level very remote from the monarchic state. Ithaca and the adjacent islands are pictured as a region inhabited by farming people in which some families, because of their material wealth, tend to dominate. The heads of these families and their sons are the important men, the big men, of the region; they enjoy prestige and influence first because of their economic resources—they can grant and withhold favours—and second because of their manpower resources—they can marshal coercive force. It is in this way that they 'hold power' (ἐπικρατέουσιν) and 'lord it' (κοιραν-έουσιν) in the islands. These are words describing the suitors (1.245–6). Since there are over a hundred of them and the whole region is not extensive, individual spheres of influence would have to be, for the most part, very small indeed. It is evidently a manorial world. Odysseus, because he is by far the richest man in the islands— 'Not twenty men together have such wealth', says Eumaeus, perhaps with some prideful exaggeration (14.98–9)—is the most important man, the greatest βασιλεύς of the area. It is credible that, in his long absence and presumed death, others would aspire to that position. One of the suitors at least may be suspected of hoping to expropriate Odysseus' estates to such an end. Had one succeeded he would no doubt have become recognized as the leading man of the region (though not necessarily held in the highest esteem). But that is all the 'succession' would be about. If on the other hand Odysseus' estates were to be divided among the suitors, presumably the status quo of the last twenty years would continue, with power and influence distributed more or less evenly among the leading families. In that case there would be no immediate succession issue of any kind. But the outcome of any of the plans, including the one finally endorsed by the majority of the suitors, or all of them, to leave Telemachus with his inheritance, would be neither a monarchy nor an oligarchy, but the same stateless, manorial society the poet has consistently envisaged all along.[11]

NOTES

1. *Homer and the Homeric Age* (New York, 1975), 74.

2. *The World of Odysseus* (New York, 1965), 86.

3. Finley, op. cit., 87; cf. H. W. Clarke, who takes for granted that 'the kingship is to be awarded to whoever marries Penelope—hence the dynastic ambitions of the Suitors and their menace to Odysseus and Penelope', 'Telemachos and the *Telemacheia*', *AJP* 84 (1963), 129.

4. 'Who's Who in "Homeric" Society?', *CQ* 34 (1984), 31.

5. Cf. F. Gnschnitzer, 'ΒΑΣΙΛΕΥΣ. Ein Terminologischer Beitrag zur Frühgeschichte des

Königtums bei Griechen', *Innsbrucker Beiträge zur Kulturwissenschaft* 11 (1965), 99–112; and the just criticism of Robert Drews, *Basileus: the Evidence for Kingship in Geometric Greece* (New Haven, 1983).

6. *Homer and Mycenae* (London, 1933), 225.

7. 'Homeric Ἔδνα and Penelope's Κύριος', *JHS* 86 (1966), 63.

8. P. W. Rose, 'Class Ambivalence in the *Odyssey*', *Historia* 24 (1975), 129–49, developing an earlier suggestion by Cedric H. Whitman, *Homer and the Heroic Tradition* (Cambridge, Mass., 1958), 306–8.

9. Op. cit. (n. 5).

10. 'Könige und Königsherrschaft in den Epen Homers', *Klio* 61 (1979), 361–84.

11. Similar views may also be found in Sigrid Deger, *Heerschaftsformen bei Homer* (Vienna, 1970), 56; Oswyn Murray, *Early Greece* (Brighton, 1980), 40–1; W. G. Runciman, 'Origins of States: the Case of Archaic Greece', *Comparative Studies in Society and History* 24 (1982); Geddes, op. cit.; and Halverson, 'Social Order in the *Odyssey*', *Hermes* 113 (1985),129–45.

THE REUNION OF PENELOPE AND ODYSSEUS*

By CHRIS EMLYN-JONES

One of the most striking dramatic features of the climax of Homer's *Odyssey* is the lengthy postponement of the reunion of Penelope and Odysseus. The sequence of scenes which lead finally to recognition begins at 17.508, when Penelope asks the swineherd Eumaeus to summon the disguised Odysseus so that she may question him about her husband. But it is only at 23.205, after many diversions, that she breaks down in tears at the final realization that Odysseus is really home.

At first sight Odysseus' motivation for keeping his wife in the dark for so long may seem weak and implausible. During his extended conversation with Penelope in Book 19, he holds to his resolve even in the face of his wife's despair and grief. But what exactly is compelling him? In Book 11, he is advised by the spirit of Agamemnon, who has his own experience clearly in mind, not to reveal all to his wife and, above all, to return home secretly: ἐπεὶ οὐκέτι πιστὰ γυναιξίν ('Since woman are no longer to be trusted', 11.456).[1] Yet these warnings are themselves ambiguous, flanking, as they do, a tribute to Penelope in which Odysseus is assured: ἀλλ' οὐ σοί γ' Ὀδυσεῦ, φόνος ἔσσεται ἔκ γε γυναικός ('not that your wife, Odysseus, will ever murder you', 11.444). What does Odysseus learn about his wife's attitude and intentions? Earlier in the same book, the spirit of his dead mother, Anticleia, in response to an enquiry about whether Penelope has remarried, assures him that she remains steadfast in her grief (11.181–3). Admittedly, she goes on to describe Telemachus as administering the paternal estate 'without hindrance' (ἔκηλος, 184), whereas Odysseus has already heard from Tiresias, the prophet, about the suitors (11.115–17). But even if we ignore the chronological and structural problems of Book 11, Anticleia's view is echoed, with decisive authority, at 13.379–81 by Athene, who informs Odysseus that Penelope gives hope to all, and makes promises to each man, sending messages: νόος δέ οἱ ἄλλα μενοινᾷ ('but her mind has other desires'). Athene playfully ascribes Odysseus' caution to his nature: he is ἐπητής, ἀγχίνοος, ἐχέφρων ('persuasive, quick-witted, self-possessed'). But it is clear from 13.189–93 that the postponement of the recognition is part of the divine plan too: Athene brings down a mist over Ithaca, after Odysseus has landed and while he sleeps, to give her time to explain the situation to him and make him unrecognizable to his wife, townspeople, and friends, πρὶν πᾶσαν μνηστῆρας ὑπερβασίην ἀποτῖσαι ('until the suitors pay for all their transgression'). However the apparent necessity of including his wife in the category of people to whom he must not reveal himself[2] seems to lose its justification in Book 19.204 ff. Penelope has explained how much she longs for Odysseus' return and how much she hates the attentions of the suitors. When the beggar tells how he met Odysseus on his way to Troy, Penelope dissolves into tears of grief. But Odysseus: δόλῳ δ᾽ ὅ γε δάκρυα κεῦθεν ('hid his tears with guile', 19.212). Why, in Penelope's case, the δόλος ('deception')?[3] To say that Odysseus is obeying the instructions of Athene merely puts the problem back a stage; why did the poet choose what is, arguably, a weaker dramatic structure by developing the plot in this way?

One answer to this question, based on analytic premisses, is that the problem derives from the development of our *Odyssey* from an older poem in which the recognition of Odysseus by Penelope took place before the slaughter of the suitors in Odysseus' hall and the trial of the bow which precipitated the battle was the plan of Penelope and Odysseus acting in collusion.[4] This hypothesis was put forward to explain what have been seen as dramatic and psychological improbabilities in the plot of *Odyssey* 17–23.[5] Yet, even if the hypothesis is valid (and, as I shall demonstrate later, I do not believe that any of the so-called improbabilities point decisively in that direction)[6] it still does not furnish us with an explanation of why the poet of the *Odyssey* chose to expand in this way.

Another explanation of the problem, and one which has almost attained the status of orthodoxy in modern American Homeric studies, is that the recognition of Odysseus by Penelope is a gradual process, carried on at a largely subconscious or 'intuitive' level.[7] The *homophrosyne* of the beggar and Penelope develops and increases during their colloquy in Book 19.[8] Penelope is increasingly attracted towards the beggar, with his appearance and situation similar to that which she imagines for the 'absent' Odysseus, and with his authoritative predictions that her husband is about to return; Anne Amory argues that '. . . as she talks with him . . . Penelope becomes gradually certain that the stranger is in fact her husband. But, because she has so strong a fear of making a mistake in just this situation, she cannot rationally accept her interior certainty, and her recognition therefore remains largely subconscious.'[9] This subconscious feeling is, Amory thinks, strengthened by the prophecies, omens, and portents which increasingly occur in Books 17–20.[10] Despite her often expressed scepticism regarding signs and portents, Penelope is finally encouraged by them to trust to her intuition and institute the contest of the bow. As the most recent supporter of the 'intuitive Penelope' hypothesis, J. Russo, puts it, she is '. . . caught up in a swelling current of intuitions, intimations and half-believed hopes. It is the force of that current that led her to decide suddenly on the test of the bow.'[11]

Immediately before this decision, Penelope has related to the beggar a dream in which an eagle swoops down, kills the geese in her courtyard, and announces that he is her husband and that he will destroy the suitors. Having elicited the obvious interpretation from the beggar, that Odysseus will soon return and do just that, Penelope goes on to express scepticism, introducing the famous image of the gates of horn and ivory. This dream, Penelope thinks, came through the ivory gate and is therefore one of those, ἔπε' ἀκράαντα φέροντες ('bearing a message not to be fulfilled', 19.565).[12] Why, one may ask, does the decision of the bow follow such scepticism? Amory supposes that Penelope '. . . puts forward her suggestion about setting the contest, in a state of conflict and confusion. She genuinely feels that a decision is necessary, but she is very reluctant to make one. Seeking a further sign, she makes her reluctance plain, so that the stranger can discourage her plan if he is not Odysseus, but is really sure that Odysseus is coming soon. But the stranger does not merely repeat his assurance that Odysseus will return; he urges her to go ahead with the contest immediately because Odysseus will be there before it is completed. This assurance is so peculiarly explicit that Penelope must realise that Odysseus himself is speaking.'[13]

This is by no means the only plausible interpretation of the scene. It should be pointed out that the beggar has for some time been offering explicit assurances that Odysseus will soon be home, both to Penelope herself and others.[14] Likewise Penelope's scepticism in the face of dreams and omens has rarely wavered, only occasionally straying into the optative in the face of particularly convincing prediction.[15] It is difficult to see what can have brought about the change in her attitude at this point; certainly the beggar proves that he met Odysseus at the beginning of the Trojan War, but how does she make the jump from believing in this twenty-year-old meeting to having an 'intuition' of the truth of the often-heard prediction, that Odysseus will come home, let alone to believing that 'Odysseus himself is speaking'?

It is worth looking at how the scene ends. Odysseus has strongly supported her decision to hold a contest and given his assurance about her husband's return. Penelope concludes the interview by saying that she could listen to the beggar all night, but sleep is necessary. Amory interprets thus: '. . . Penelope is not yet ready emotionally to accept Odysseus' return, so she does not admit her recognition of him, but just gives up the whole problem for the moment. Understandably, in view of the variety and intensity of the emotions which she has undergone that day, she is overcome by a sudden weariness and a desire to return to her old condition of passive waiting.'[16] But, surely, it is equally plausible to see Penelope's appreciation of the beggar's ability to entertain her (τέρπειν, 590) as just that—a parallel to the cautious attitude of Eumaeus for whom Odysseus' entertainment-value as a storyteller was by no means accompanied by the guarantee that what he said was entirely true.[17] Admittedly, in Book 19 Penelope is greatly moved and becomes attracted to the beggar to the extent of confiding in him; but does this imply any suspicion that the beggar is Odysseus? At the end of the book Penelope's weariness in the face of 'variety and intensity of emotions' begs the whole question of exactly what those emotions were.

The 'intuitive Penelope' theory, like the analyst hypothesis before it, does attempt to offer an explanation of an apparent difficulty in the dramatic structure of the poem, namely: what motivates Penelope to decide on the contest of the bow—a decision that appears, it would seem, out of nowhere at 19.572? Yet the theory creates as many problems as it purports to solve; in order to accept the 'intuitive Penelope' interpretation, one has to assume that the poet is creating a psychological 'sub-text' in which what Penelope thinks and feels is increasingly governed by unconscious or semi-conscious desires and wishes; Homer is supposed to have postponed the reunion because he wished to explore a subtle interplay between conscious and unconscious mind, and the gradual emergence of conscious certainty that the beggar is Odysseus (though it should be noted that scholars who support this hypothesis differ widely as to when this 'certainty' actually emerges into Penelope's conscious mind).[18]

Because, according to the hypothesis, this activity takes place at a semi-conscious level it is particularly difficult to substantiate from the text. It follows from the theory that 'intuitive Penelope' often thinks and feels very differently from what she actually says. But on other occasions Homer appears not to need a 'sub-text', notably in Book 23, the final recognition of Penelope and Odysseus (see below p. 133f. and 138f.). The expression of Penelope's feelings at 23.85–110 provides conclusive evidence that Homer was perfectly capable of dealing directly with the psychological subtleties of mental and emotional confusion, when he so chose. Why then, one must ask, did he choose instead in Books 19–20 a technique so indirect and allusive as to require an interpretation which seems, on the face of it, to have more relevance to the novels of Henry James than to early Greek epic?

On a psychological level, it is surely more plausible to see Penelope's dream, as related at 19.535–53, as pure wish-fulfilment; her dream and her account of it is an expression, *not* of her belief or suspicion about the identity of the beggar but of her intense desire that Odysseus should come and extricate her from a terrible situation. Similarly, at the beginning of Book 20, when Penelope has one of her κακὰ ὀνείρατα ('evil dreams') that Odysseus is lying beside her (so vivid she thinks it is a ὕπαρ, 'a waking vision') and Odysseus lying in bed likewise has a vision of Penelope standing by his head, the poet is not '. . . doing his utmost to show both characters in the grip of an unusually powerful unconscious tug towards the full mental union that will not be possible for several books yet . . .'[19] but merely expressing Penelope's hope, forlorn, as she thinks, that her husband will come home, and allowing her, when awake, bitterly to contrast her dream with the, again as *she* thinks, almost certain fate of marrying one of the suitors; it is this contrast which makes the dream κακόν, 'evil'. On the other hand Odysseus' vision expresses his own strong anticipation of success.

But we do not need to read the scene primarily on a psychological level. The increasing frequency of dreams and omens which Amory noted (see above p. 127) is not so much an indication of the mental state of Penelope, as a device whereby the poet unifies his plot and increases dramatic tension by foreshadowing climactic events.[20] They are aimed at us, the audience, not as an external indication of some inner conflict which the poet hasn't the technique (or psychological knowledge?) to explain directly, but as a warning that the denouement is fast approaching. Thus, for example, in Book 20, immediately after Penelope and Odysseus have experienced dreams/visions of each other, Odysseus asks Zeus directly for a portent ἔκτοσθεν ('outside'); Zeus obliges with a thunderclap, and an omen (φήμη) is provided by a mill woman working outside who asks Zeus to grant her release from labour by making this the last day of the suitors' feasting (20.97–119).

Penelope's persistent scepticism about Odysseus in the face of what seems to be overwhelming evidence to the contrary enables the poet to exploit the dramatic irony in the contrast between seeming and reality. The obvious dramatic parallel is that of the *Oedipus* of Sophocles, as B. Fenik points out,[21] where the dramatist extracts the last drop of irony from Oedipus' inability to see the obvious truth.[22] Homer's dramatic irony, like that of Sophocles, is subtle and all-pervasive, present in small touches, e.g., 19.209, where Penelope's beautiful cheeks were streaming: κλαιούσης ἑὸν ἄνδρα παρήμενον ('weeping for her husband who was sitting beside her').[23] At 357–60, when bidding the old nurse Eurycleia to wash the beggar's feet, Penelope supposes that Odysseus must by now have hands and feet similar to those of the beggar: αἶψα γὰρ ἐν κακότητι βροτοὶ καταγηράσκουσιν ('for mortals age quickly in misfortune'). She is presumably to be seen as still listening immediately afterwards, when Eurycleia apostrophizes the 'absent' Odysseus in a way which initially suggests she is talking to the beggar.[24] The poet also causes Penelope to act in a manner which advances the plot and generates irony in the contrast between what she thinks she is doing and what is really happening. For example, in Book 21, when the suitors are trying unsuccessfully to string the bow, Penelope supports the beggar's request that he should be allowed to try the bow, ridiculing the implication that, if he were successful, he would have any marriage claim on her. If he is successful, she will give him clothing and transport to wherever he wishes to go.[25] Analysts and 'Intuitionists' are united in believing (on very different grounds) that at this point Penelope must be supposed to have guessed the beggar's identity. Why else would she support his request for the bow? Yet it is a characteristic of Homer's dramatic technique that he pushes to extremes the contrast between appearance and reality and exploits to the limits of plausibility what his characters in their ignorance may say or do.[26] At the approach of a climactic point in the poem it may be thought dramatically appropriate, if not psychologically entirely plausible, that Penelope should, in ignorance, assist her husband.

A third possible approach to the Penelope–Odysseus reunion comes from a rather different angle. Thus far, I have referred to dramatic appropriateness and psychological plausibility in comparative isolation from a broader context. It is, however, significant that postponement of reunion and recognition is not confined to Homer, or even Greek culture. It has been one of the achievements of the last fifty years of Homeric studies to show that the Homeric poems have their origin in a tradition of oral poetry which, in terms of both detailed composition and more general thematic structure, has a great deal in common with traditional poetry of other cultures.[27] In the case of thematic structure to which the emphasis has tended to shift during the last thirty-five years or so, researches have shown that the Homeric poet, as well as his non-Homeric counterpart was composing with repeated thematic elements, large-scale 'formulae'—a number of recurring associated motifs, which we might call a 'sequence'.[28] One group of motifs which reveals clearly the characteristics of a sequence is that of recognition in the *Odyssey*. If we consider the Penelope–Odysseus recognition in the context of the whole of Books 12–24, it will be apparent that it is merely the most elaborate of a whole series: with Telemachus, Eurycleia, Eumaeus, servants, suitors, and finally Odysseus' father Laertes (not to mention Odysseus' old dog, Argos). Common to the sequence are:

1. Odysseus in disguise.
2. A conversation in which Odysseus is pressed for his identity, in reply to which he tells a false story in which he claims to have seen Odysseus on his travels and predicts his early return. The other speaker refers frequently in conversation to Odysseus, usually introducing the topic very shortly after meeting him.
3. Odysseus tests the other's loyalty; the test is passed (or, in the case of the suitors and disloyal servants, failed).
4. Odysseus reveals himself.
5. The other refuses to believe.
6. Odysseus gives a sign ($\sigma\hat{\eta}\mu\alpha$) as a proof of identity.

7. Final recognition, accompanied by great emotion on both sides.
8. 'On to business'.

Despite great variety of length and treatment, some or all of these elements are recognizable in the various recognition scenes of the *Odyssey*.[29]
They are also common to the 'Return of the absent husband' theme in a
variety of poetic traditions, of which the *Odyssey* is recognizably one.[30] The
comparative material reveals that the element of postponement of recognition by means of false stories, tests, disbelief, and signs, is by no means
confined to the Homeric poems. A modern Greek ballad on the 'Return
of the long-absent husband' theme neatly illustrates, in the space of 43
verses, all the elements of the recognition sequence mentioned above in
the *Odyssey* context.[31] Notable is the apparent cruelty of the disguised
husband, who, on meeting his wife, pretends not only that he is dead but
that her dying husband's last wish was that she should marry the stranger.
Particularly interesting are the σημάδια or signs, tokens, which the dis-
believing wife demands from the husband; she requires knowledge of progressively more intimate details of courtyard, house, and bedroom until
finally her husband, by referring to marks on her body and also his amulet,
which she wears between her breasts, convinces her of his real identity.

What light can this exquisite miniature throw on the reunion of
Penelope and Odysseus? There is obviously a vast gap of scale and compositional technique; a recognition which the Greek ballad accomplishes
in 43 lines extends in the *Odyssey* to approximately six books, or 2,500
verses. Moreover, whereas in the ballad the vital conversations between
disguised husband and wife are laid out neatly and predictably in verses
which are structurally symmetrical, the Homeric dialogue follows a vastly
more complex pattern. Yet there are similarities. The element of, if not
cruelty, then a desire to provoke or upset is clearly in Odysseus' mind just
before his main conversation with Penelope at 19.45–6; he remains down-
stairs: ὄφρα κ' ἔτι δμῳὰς καὶ μητέρα σὴν ἐρεθίζω | ἡ δὲ μ' ὀδυρομένη εἰρήσεται
ἀμφὶς ἕκαστα ('so that I may further provoke the maids and your mother
who in her sorrow, will ask me about everything'). The plan of Odysseus
to provoke Penelope to tears[32] is clearly part of the traditional sequence,
stages 2 and 3 above, the questioning and false tale which test loyalty and
precede recognition, elements which Homer uses again, even less acceptably to conventional taste, in the Laertes recognition scene in Book 24.[33]

In the long conversation of 19.104–360, which is interrupted by
Eurycleia's own recognition of Odysseus' scar when she washes his feet,
the expectation is created in the audience that Odysseus will finally reveal
himself to Penelope, not only because this would seem dramatically the
obvious thing to do, but also because it would constitute a traditional
ending to the sequence.[34] Yet, in avoiding this solution, Homer exploits the

convention of the sequence in a curious way, by attaching all the major elements of stages 2–6 not to a genuine recognition sequence but to the goal of merely establishing that the beggar *has* met Odysseus. Thus, when Penelope has asked the traditional question: τίς πόθεν εἰς ἀνδρῶν; πόθι τοι πόλις ἠδὲ τοκῆες; ('Who are you and where do you come from? Where is your city and who are your parents?', 19.105), and has received a pre-dictably evasive answer, she refers immediately to her sorrow at the absence of Odysseus and her desperate attempts to keep the suitors at bay. This is followed by Odysseus' false tale (19.172–202). So far, this follows the normal sequence (scc, c.g., 14.185 359 in the Eumaeus recognition sequence). But at this point, Penelope breaks down at the mention of Odysseus and her tears are compared to the snow melted by the East Wind. Great emotion, accompanied by a simile, at this point in the sequence is elsewhere used for stage 7, the recognition itself.[35] But here Penelope weeps over a memory of her husband as he was twenty years pre-viously, on his way to Troy. Her husband, sitting beside her, as the text emphasizes (19.209), takes no active part in this. Penelope continues to maintain the illusion of a genuine recognition sequence by asking for a σῆμα ('sign') to prove, not the identity of the beggar (this is destined to remain a secret from her for some time) but merely that he has actually seen Odysseus. When the beggar supplies evidence by relating details of the dress which Odysseus and his entourage were wearing on this occa-sion, Penelope weeps again σήματ' ἀναγνούσῃ τά οἱ ἔμπεδα πέφραδ' Ὀδυσσεύς ('recognizing the certain signs that Odysseus had disclosed to her', 19.250). The extremes of irony and pathos in this scene arise not merely from the situation but from the poet's deliberate exploitation of all the elements of the sequence in a kind of 'spoof recognition', where the effect is obtained by using, and frustrating, the audience's undoubted knowledge and expectations.

The artistry of the final recognition scene in 23.1–240 in which Penelope and Odysseus experience difficulty in fully reuniting, has often been analysed (see also below pp. 138f.).[36] After so long a separation, husband and wife take time to discover an effective means of recognition on an appropriate level; the postponement here has to do with feelings and relationships and is acutely and movingly portrayed. Yet one can also look at the scene in terms of the working-out of the recognition sequence and what we may presume to have been audience expectations; stages 4–7 have not yet taken place: at the beginning of Book 23 Odysseus has not yet revealed himself, Penelope has not yet expressed disbelief and demanded her σῆμα. To have Penelope fly straight into Odysseus' arms would be not only far less effective; it would be antitraditional in a manner unthinkable for the Homeric poet, who exploited tradition but did not ignore it.

The revelation of the beggar's identity comes from Eurycleia; Penelope after initial joy falls back into scepticism but agrees eventually to come down to see the man who killed the suitors; the poet makes clear in subtle ways that her disbelief is not absolute.[37] Her disbelief is expressed directly to Odysseus in the form of silence; she and Odysseus find themselves only able to converse through Telemachus as a kind of mediator.[38] Penelope also uses Telemachus to indicate to Odysseus that she wants a σῆμα.

But it is, of course, Penelope herself who finally tricks the σῆμα out of an unwitting Odysseus. In ordering Eurycleia to make up a bed for him, and thus (for us, unthinkably) ending the scene yet again without full recognition, Penelope, in her turn, provokes Odysseus to anger and revelation of the secret of his bed, a σῆμα of particular appropriateness in this case.[39]

Thus the final elements of the sequence become a subtle game in which the two contestants toss the ball back and forth to each other.[40] The reversal of roles for the σῆμα where Penelope completely takes the initiative, is an appropriate final twist to the most extended and complex of Homer's recognition sequences. Perhaps it is not without deliberation that at the final recognition of 23.206, he repeats the formulaic line of the 'spoof-recognition' (19.250) when Penelope's knees and heart went slack: σήματ' ἀναγνούσῃ τά οἱ ἔμπεδα πέφραδ' Ὀδυσσεύς ('recognizing the certain signs that Odysseus had disclosed for her').

Thus far, an attempt has been made to answer the initial question of this paper—why the postponement of the Penelope–Odysseus recognition?— in terms of a poet using, and exploiting with great virtuosity and insight, the dramatic and thematic demands of his tradition, which were also, presumably, those of his audience. But we can, I believe, go a little further by looking more closely at the situation and attitude of Penelope herself.

At 18.158 Athene puts it into Penelope's head to descend so that she may inflame the suitors and seem more estimable (τιμήεσσα) in the sight of her husband and son than before. She laughs pointlessly (ἀχρεῖον, 163) and explains to her maid Eurynome that she wishes to show herself to the suitors and also to warn Telemachus about the dangers he faces from them. Eurynome approves the plan but suggests that Penelope should first wash herself and anoint her face, since nothing is gained by continual sorrow; for now Telemachus has come of age, which Penelope had always prayed for. Penelope rejects the advice, but Athene puts her to sleep and beautifies her. She then descends to the suitors and causes great passion among them. She then tells Telemachus off for the treatment of the beggar, and receives a conciliatory but firm answer. In reply to a compliment from Eurymachus, her chief suitor, Penelope says that her beauty departed when Odysseus left for Troy. Before leaving, he advised her to marry again when Telemachus should grow up. Penelope bewails the fact that this hateful marriage will now soon come and reproaches the suitors for their depredation of Odysseus' household. The disguised Odysseus, who has been sitting in the hall observing this scene, rejoices: οὕνεκα τῶν μὲν δῶρα παρέλκετο, θέλγε δὲ θυμὸν | μειλιχίοις ἐπέεσσι, νόος δέ οἱ ἄλλα μενοίνα ('because she enticed gifts from them and enchanted their spirits with blandishing words, but her mind had other desires', 18.282–3). Antinous, the ringleader of the suitors, promises gifts but reaffirms the suitors' intention of remaining until Penelope chooses one of them in marriage. The gifts duly appear and Penelope reascends to her upper room.

I have set out this scene in some detail because it is at the same time one of the most revealing and one of the hardest to interpret in the whole poem. There are two main problems, Penelope's motivation and Odysseus' reaction.

First, Penelope's motivation: why, at this point, does she suddenly decide to descend? Does she really want to inflame the suitors? She certainly cannot want to appear more estimable to Odysseus (161–2) since she doesn't know he is there. So it seems likely that both reasons given in 160–2 are those of Athene. The goddess beautifies the sleeping Penelope, if not against her will (but see 178–81) then without her knowledge. The most difficult detail is in 163, where ἀχρεῖον δ᾽ ἐγέλασσεν ('she laughed pointlessly') seems to suggest that she does not really know what she is doing or why.

If she is not a puppet, then she may be something worse; 'regina prope ad meretricias artes descendit' ('the queen stoops almost to the arts of the courtesan') has been the verdict of more than one commentator. This scene has also been cited by those who think Penelope is at least partly attracted to the suitors.[41] Her veil, it has been thought, is a sign of coquetry and note has been taken of Telemachus' characteristically harsh verdict, e.g., at 16.126–7: ἡ δ᾽ οὔτ᾽ ἀρνεῖται στυγερὸν γάμον οὔτε τελευτὴν | ποιῆσαι δύναται ('but neither does she refuse a hateful marriage nor can she make an end').[42]

Even more difficult is Odysseus' reaction. Why is he pleased at what Penelope is doing and how does he know that νόος δέ οἱ ἄλλα μενοίνα ('her mind had other desires', 283) if, in fact, he is even correct about Penelope's νόος here? The analytic hypothesis would see lines 281–3 as clear evidence of the imperfect adaptation of the earlier plot, in which Odysseus and Penelope were in collusion by this time.[43] On the other hand, Fenik, on the assumption that Penelope is *not* sincere in mentioning her approaching remarriage in this scene, states that Odysseus is 'simply made to know' this by the poet, who neglects strict motivation '. . . in direct proportion to the extent to which he develops his favourite situations with their special emotions and ironies'.[44]

These interpretations have in common the belief that Penelope's feelings and actions in this scene, whether partly autonomous or wholly directed by Athene, are essentially subordinate to the dramatic development of the plot, which is in the hands of Athene and Odysseus. U. Hölscher, however, in a comparatively neglected short article,[45] has argued that interpretation of this scene turns on the interpretation of the phrase νόος δὲ οἱ ἄλλα μενοίνα, which means, he maintains, not that 'she has something else up her sleeve' but that she wants something else passionately, namely the return of her husband.[46] This interpretation of the phrase, which would seem to have strong linguistic arguments in its favour,[47] removes any grounds for supposing that Penelope is tricking the suitors and clears the way for the key point in Hölscher's interpretation, which is that we should distinguish clearly between Athene's motivation in this scene and that of Penelope herself. Athene's motivation is fairly clear: she, and the poet, wish to arrange for Odysseus to obtain a first sight of Penelope, in all her beauty and dignity—his first sight for twenty years; at the same time Penelope unwittingly provides evidence that she is still faithful to him, not only in her distaste for the suitors but also in her reiteration of his advice, which he had given her before leaving for Troy—to remarry when Telemachus came of age (259–70). Thus Odysseus had reason to be glad that she was increasing his wealth with the suitors' presents while still, in her heart, longing for him.

But there is another strand of motivation here: that of Penelope herself. Telemachus has shown himself to be of age, independent, and authoritative, nowhere more so than in his reply to his mother's complaint about his ability to protect the beggar (226–42). Her descent can be seen as a preparation for a genuine remarriage, which, however distasteful to her, she feels compelled to make, both to remain obedient to her absent husband's advice and to relieve the intense pressure on Telemachus' and Odysseus' household.

Penelope's motivation has been obscured by Athene's aims in her beautification of the queen—a process which Penelope repeatedly and emphatically rejects: all her beauty departed, she says, when Odysseus left for Troy. The fact that this is not true (she is obviously highly desirable to the suitors) should not lead us to suppose that the poet wishes Penelope to be regarded as lacking in sincerity here.

The two strands of motivation in this scene mirror the ambivalence of the structure of the last half of the poem as a whole. The revenge plot, with its excitement, and suspense (Odysseus arriving in the nick of time) tends to overshadow Penelope, who often appears to do unmotivated or badly-motivated things. For example, there appears to be no obvious reason for her decision to decide on a new bridegroom by means of the contest of the bow at 19.572,[48] but the decision leads smoothly to the climax of Book 21. Even more awkwardly, the only way the poet can get Penelope off the

scene before Odysseus takes the bow and initiates the slaughter is to allow
Telemachus, somewhat unconvincingly, to send her upstairs (21.350–3).

Yet, helpless victim though Penelope sometimes appears, there are signs
that the poet also wishes us to be aware of her serious predicament
and appreciate her lonely and courageous decisions in the face of social
pressure, the δήμοιό τε φῆμιν ('voice of the people', 16.75) which sanctions
fidelity to her absent husband and is, at the same time, powerless to prevent the results of this fidelity—the rapacious suitors' actions.[49] Her predicament is precisely, if unsympathetically, summed up by Telemachus,
talking to the still-disguised Odysseus at 16.126–7: ἡ δ' οὔτ' ἀρνεῖται
στυγερὸν γάμον οὔτε τελευτὴν | ποιῆσαι δύναται ('but neither does she refuse
a hateful marriage nor can she make an end'), where Penelope's 'inability
to make an end' surely refers not to her personal preferences or to some
'feminine' weakness but to the social situation.

It has been observed that the return of Odysseus, that is, the plot of the
Odyssey, takes its motivation and precise starting-point from Penelope's
approaching crisis—the decision to remarry now that Telemachus has
come of age.[50] That the decision and choice of bridegroom appear to
belong to Penelope has been thought unusual and difficult to explain in
the context of Homeric social custom.[51] In fact, the exact situation with
regard to Penelope's prerogative in this matter is confused.[52] I would
suggest that the poet may have granted her what initiative she possesses in
the decision to remarry in order to focus our attention more closely on
Penelope and her dilemma.

Certain themes which illustrate this dilemma tend to recur. At
19.124–61, in conversation with the disguised Odysseus, Penelope
expresses them most acutely: her faded beauty, the attention of the suitors,
the trick of the winding sheet for Laertes, the maturity of Telemachus.[53]
She concludes (157–60):

> νῦν δ' οὔτ' ἐκφυγέειν δύναμαι γάμον οὔτε τιν' ἄλλην
> μῆτιν ἔθ' εὑρίσκω· μάλα δ' ὀτρύνουσι τοκῆες
> γήμασθ', ἀσχαλάᾳ δὲ πάϊς βίοτον κατεδόντων,
> γιγνώσκων.

'But now I cannot escape the marriage, nor can I find any other plan, but my
parents strongly urge me to marry and my son, understanding what is going
on, is distressed at their eating away of our livelihood.'

Pressure from others and the impossibility of escape are the predominant motifs of Penelope's situation. Unlike Odysseus, who has the ear of
Athene, Penelope has no help from the gods. Odysseus, too, has had a
long period of wandering in which he has endured without divine help;
but this is now over, whereas Penelope is forced to continue her well-
founded scepticism and endure alone.[54]

It has often been noted that Penelope and Odysseus have to endure in different ways: for Odysseus, it is the active endurance of the Cyclops' cave, the Laestrygones, and the Underworld; for Penelope it is the passive and confined waiting in her upper room of the palace, a siege in which she occasionally, with precautions (two attendants and a veil over her face), descends to face her besiegers.[55]

Homer explores the ambivalent attitudes of others to this endurance. Odysseus, when he enquires in Book 11 whether Penelope has remained faithful to him, receives the information from his mother Anticleia that his wife endures: τετληότι θυμῷ | σοῖσιν ἐνὶ μεγάροισιν ('with enduring spirit in your palace', 181–2).[56] But the endurance befitting her sex is also required by Telemachus at 1.353 ff. when Penelope objects to the bard Phemius singing a song about the mournful homecoming of the Achaeans: he tells her σοὶ δ' ἐπιτολμάτω κραδίη καὶ θυμὸς ἀκούειν ('let your heart and spirit be hardened to listen').

When the suitors have been slain and Penelope is informed that Odysseus is waiting for her downstairs (23.5 ff.), the incomprehension of Eurycleia and Telemachus is ironically reflected in their attitude to 'endurance': Penelope is reproached by Eurycleia for her θυμὸς δέ (τοι) αἰὲν ἄπιστος ('spirit always mistrustful', 72) and by Telemachus, ἀπηνέα θυμὸν ἔχουσα ('[you] having a harsh spirit', 97). In 100 he says that no other woman would keep distance τετληότι θυμῷ ('with enduring spirit') from a returning husband who had suffered so much: σοὶ δ' αἰεὶ κραδίη στερεωτέρη ἐστὶ λίθοιο ('you always have a heart harder than stone within you', 103). The effect is secured here not only by the ironic contrast between the uncomprehending judgements of Eurycleia and Telemachus and what is really going on inside Penelope, but also by the use of the word for 'endure'; to persist τετληότι θυμῷ is no longer a commendable stance now that Odysseus is home! Note also how Eurycleia and Telemachus project these qualities into the past (Penelope was always [αἰεί, 72, 103] like this) and so, by implication, pass judgement on her long endurance and scepticism.

The eventual encounter between Penelope and Odysseus (see also above pp. 133 f.) is interrupted by a conversation (23.117–51) in which Odysseus and Telemachus decide how to act in the face of imminent vengeance from the relatives of the slain suitors. This was long regarded as an interpolation;[57] Fenik, in rejecting the interpolation theory, attempts to show how 'interruptions' of this sort are a normal feature of Homeric composition; there is no need for us to presume a tense, waiting Penelope 'on the stage' since epic does not, as a rule, consider the presence of 'silent characters'; during this interruption Penelope ceases to exist.[58] Fenik makes a plausible general case, but I feel that, just as this whole scene (23.1–240) is exceptional in a number of ways,[59] so in this particular case, it is unlikely that an audience, having waited for the recognition for about 2,000 verses, and apparently faced with yet another postponement, would simply forget Penelope and her situation.[60] But there is another reason why the poet does not intend us to forget Penelope; at the end of the passage, Telemachus and the servants carry out Odysseus' instructions to wash, put on clean clothes, sing, and dance so that neighbours and other outsiders will think that a wedding is taking place. We are then given the reaction of the outsiders—the δήμοιο τε φῆμιν ('voice of the people', 16.75) on Penelope: σχετλίη οὐδ' ἔτλη πόσιος οὗ κουριδίοιο | ἔρυσθαι μέγα δῶμα διαμπερές ἧος ἵκοιτο ('hard hearted, she did not hold out to preserve the great house of her wedded husband, until he should return', 23.150–1). The δῆμος, in its censure of what it supposes Penelope to have done, applies, like Telemachus and Eurycleia, the double standard of 'endurance'.

When the scene is resumed and Odysseus has had a bath and has been made handsome again by Athene, husband and wife now talk directly to one another. Odysseus had offered provocation at 116 by accusing Penelope (through Telemachus) of slighting him because of his dirty and ragged appearance. But now (166) he loses patience and repeats word for word Telemachus' accusation of 100–2 (=168–70) and echoes 103 in 172: ἦ γὰρ τῇ γε σιδήρεον ἐν φρεσὶν ἦτορ ('indeed, this woman's heart is iron within her'). The final condemnation comes, albeit in semi-humorous indignation, from the mouth of Odysseus himself.

⋆　　⋆　　⋆

Penelope is the most elaborately and searchingly portrayed of Homer's female characters. She is a great queen who exceeds in wisdom and insight the great heroines of old (2.117–21), receiving a fulsome tribute from Agamemnon (24.192 ff.) for her *aretē*. Yet the poet's ironic play on different attitudes to, and associations of, Penelope's *aretē*—her fidelity and endurance—brings into the foreground the ambiguity of her situation and enables the poet to explore the personal and social pressures upon her sympathetically and at some depth. I would therefore maintain that in rejecting a version of the *Odyssey* in which Penelope and Odysseus defeat the suitors in collusion after an early recognition, and instead, deciding[61] on a late recognition after the slaying of the suitors, Homer's purpose was not only to exploit the dramatic possibilities inherent in a major extension of the recognition sequence but also to give himself time to establish the recognition of Penelope and Odysseus as the other, and perhaps equally important, climax of the *Odyssey*. It is the placing of this recognition, clear of the other main climax of the death of the suitors, which enables the poet to conclude in fitting manner his extended and searching portrait of the noble queen.

NOTES

* This article has its origin in a paper presented to the London branch of the Classical Association on 10 February 1983. I am grateful to Malcolm Willcock and Ronald Willetts for helpful comments on an earlier draft.

1. Cf. 13.383 ff., where Odysseus acknowledges Athene's intervention as having preserved him from the fate of Agamemnon, who was killed by his wife Clytemnestra and her lover Aegisthus (related by Nestor [3.255–75; 303–10] and Menelaus [4.512–37] to Telemachus). On the influence of the Agamemnon 'Return' on the *Odyssey*, see U. Hölscher, *Die Atridensage in der Odyssee* in Festschrift Richard Alewyn (Köln-Graz, 1967), 1–16.

2. Odysseus includes Penelope in his instruction to Telemachus not to reveal his identity, at 16.300–4.

3. B. Fenik, *Studies in the Odyssey, Hermes* Einzelschr. 30, Wiesbaden, 1974, 40 thinks that O. 'has sound practical reasons for maintaining his disguise . . .'. I cannot see what these reasons are in Penelope's case, unless Fenik is thinking of the presence of serving-maids during the interview —surely not a strong psychological or dramatic motive for the postponement.

4. This is, in fact, how one of the dead suitors, Amphimedon, explains the recent events to Agamemnon in the Underworld at 24.167–9.

5. For a summary of the analytic position on this question, see G. S. Kirk, *The Songs of Homer* (Cambridge, 1962), 245–8.

6. See p. 135 below.

7. The starting-point was the thesis of P. W. Harsh, now generally regarded as highly improbable, that Penelope fully recognizes Odysseus in Book 19 and that all her subsequent words and actions must be seen in this light ('Penelope and Odysseus in *Odyssey* XIX', *AJP* 71 [1950], 1–21). The basis for more recent modifications of this thesis was A. Amory, 'The Reunion of Odysseus and Penelope' in *Essays on the Odyssey: Selected Modern Criticism*, ed. C. H. Taylor, Jr. (Bloomington, 1963), 100–36. See also C. H. Whitman, *Homer and the Heroic Tradition* (Harvard, 1958), 303; C. R. Beye, *The Iliad, the Odyssey and the Epic Tradition* (London, 1968), 178; and recently N. Austin, *Archery at the Dark of the Moon* (California, 1975), 200ff.; J. Finley, Jr., *Homer's Odyssey* (Harvard, 1978), 3ff.; T. van Nortwick, 'Penelope and Nausikaa', *TAPA* 109 (1979), 269–76; and J. Russo, 'Interview and Aftermath: Dream, Fantasy and Intuition in *Odyssey* 19 and 20', *AJP* 103 (1982), 4–18.

8. Some, e.g., Whitman, op. cit., 303, Amory, op. cit., 131 n. 6, and Austin, op. cit., 208 ff. put Penelope's suspicions concerning O's identity as far back as 18.158ff., when, on the prompting of Athene, Penelope descends to the suitors (on this scene, see pp. 134–5).

9. Op. cit., 105.

10. Prophecy of Theoclymenus the seer: 17.151–61; Omen of Telemachus' sneeze: 17.539–47; Dream of Penelope: 19.535–53; Vision of Theoclymenus: 20.345–57. There are others at which Penelope is not present (15.525–38; 19.36–40; 20.98–121; 20.240–6).

11. Op. cit., 17.

12. On this image, see the interesting hypothesis of Amory, 'The Gates of Horn and Ivory', *YCS* 20 (1966), 1–57.

13. Amory, 'The Reunion of Odysseus and Penelope', 106.

14. See 19.300–7 (to Penelope) and 14.152, 14.391ff. (to Eumaeus); 18.145–6 (to Amphinomus, one of the suitors); 20.232–4 (to Philoetius, an oxherd).

15. We are also given to understand that Penelope has made a habit of consulting wayfarers and has often been deceived (e.g., Eumaeus at 14.124–30). Her scepticism is most notable at the beginning of Book 23, when she persists in asserting that Eurycleia, in believing that Odysseus is really home, is being tricked by some god.

16. Ibid.

17. Cf. Eumaeus to Odysseus at 14.361–89, following a prediction by the beggar of O's return. See also Eumaeus to Penelope at 17.513–16.

18. See above refs. at n. 8.

19. Russo, op. cit., 6. An extreme psychological interpretation of the dream of the eagle and the geese suggests that Penelope's sorrow at the slaughter of the geese and her relief that they are

in reality unharmed, shows that her unconscious mind is considerably less hostile to the suitors than her conscious (Russo, op. cit., 9; van Nortwick, op. cit., 276; for the theory, see G. Devereux, 'Penelope's Character', *Psychoanalytic Quarterly* 26 [1957], 378–86). This, in the face of her continual emphatic assertions that she loathes the suitors and their attentions! This hypothesis represents a curious reversion, in the name of modern psychological interpretation, to the Victorian idea that Penelope did not entirely dislike the suitors (see S. Butler, *The Authoress of the Odyssey* [London, 1897], 130–1). On the dream, see the sensible remarks of J. Finley, op. cit., 19 n.7.

20. See the pertinent remarks of A. J. Podlecki, 'Omens in the *Odyssey*', *G & R* 14 (1967), 12–23, esp. 21–2.

21. Op. cit., 46.

22. It is perhaps worth noting that Sophocles' play has also provoked a thesis that Oedipus comes to know the truth at an early stage in P. Vellacott, *Sophocles and Oedipus* (London, 1971), 104.

23. Cf. also the often-observed irony in O's address to P. in 19.107: ὦ γύναι = 'lady' or 'wife'.

24. 19.361–74. In 362 the omission of an addressee is surely deliberate here (R. Lattimore, in his otherwise excellent translation, *The Odyssey of Homer* [New York, 1965], includes a 'to him', mistakenly). Homer further exploits the ambiguity in σέο, τέκνον (363) for which the most likely addressee is the beggar. It is only when Eurycleia reverts to addressing Odysseus in the third person and the stranger as 'you' (370–2), that this ambiguity is resolved.

25. Penelope has also given promises, in less detail, during their colloquy at 19.310–11.

26. On this characteristic, see U. Hölscher, *Untersuchungen zur Form der Odyssee*, Hermes Einzelschr. 6, Berlin, 1939, 61.

27. I take this position, in the general form I have stated it, to be uncontroversial. The basic work was done by Milman Parry, 'The Making of Homeric Verse', *Collected Papers*, ed. A. Parry (Oxford, 1971), see esp. 'Whole Formulaic Verses in Greek and South Slavic Heroic Song', 376–90 and A. B. Lord, *The Singer of Tales* (Harvard, 1960).

28. The idea of the sequence as a compositional device in Homer has been thoroughly explored in certain limited contexts by, e.g., B. Fenik, *Typical Battle Scenes in the Iliad: Studies in the Narrative Technique of Homeric Battle Description*, Hermes Einzelschr. 21, Wiesbaden, 1968; T. Krisher, *Formale Konventionen der homerischen Epik* (Munich, 1971).

29. So far as I am aware, there has, as yet, been no major study of recognition scenes in the *Odyssey* comparable in scope with those of Fenik and Krisher on the *Iliad* (seen n. 28 above). For some discussion of the recognition sequence as a species of 'Testing' see A. Thornton, *People and Themes in Homer's Odyssey* (Otago, 1970), 48 ff.

30. For the modern Serbocroatian tradition, see Lord, op. cit., and especially Appendix III, 242–59, 'Return Songs'.

31. Conveniently quoted, with translation, in J. T. Kakridis, *Homer Revisited* (Lund, 1971), 151–3 (in the context of the Penelope–Odysseus recognition).

32. On ἐρεθίζω see LSJ ad loc. The word has clear overtones of unfriendly provocation (Lattimore's 'stir up' is rather weak).

33. 24.226–350. On the element of cruelty in this recognition, see the remarks of P. Walcot, 'Odysseus and the Art of Lying', *Anc. Soc.* 8 (1977), 1–19 (reprinted in C. Emlyn-Jones, L. Hardwick, and J. Purkis, edd., *Homer: Readings and Images*, London, 1992, 48–62).

34. But n.b. the Eumaeus sequence, when an extended conversation in Books 14–15 (Eumaeus' loyalty is tested on several occasions) is put on ice, as it were, until Book 21 when, in a rather abbreviated version of the sequence, Odysseus finally reveals himself. It is hard to find a plausible explanation for the postponement except, perhaps, that there are more important people, such as Telemachus, to come first. Moreover, if, at the beginning of Book 16, Eumaeus is 'in the know' much of the irony of the Telemachus recognition would be lost.

35. 16.213–19 (Telemachus); 23.231–40 (Penelope). The paucity of similes in the *Odyssey* (as opposed to the *Iliad*) may perhaps allow us to read significance into the positioning of several of them immediately after final recognition.

36. The most sensitive and acute commentary on this scene is still W. Schadewaldt, 'Die Wiedererkennung des Odysseus und der Penelope' in *Neue Kriterien zur Odyssee-Analyse*, Sitz. der Heidelberger Akad. der Wiss. Phil.-hist. Klasse (1959).

37. Schadewaldt, op. cit., 13. 23.86–7 betray nicely Penelope's confusion, inclining towards a

belief that she is hearing the truth. W. B. Stanford (*Homer's Odyssey* [London, 1957], note on line 86) is surely mistaken in supposing that there is any ambiguity in φίλον πόσιν ('dear husband') here, in view of the following line.

38. See Schadewaldt, op. cit., 16, on Telemachus' role as a 'Vermittler'.

39. Stanford, op. cit., note on 188–9 acutely suggests that the idea of the σῆμα of the bed, namely its immovability (23.188–202) only gradually suggests itself to Odysseus in the light of a real σῆμα in the sense that Penelope requires, in the course of this speech, i.e., at 202. Cf. also 206.

40. So, Schadewaldt, op. cit., 16.

41. See above n. 19 for the psychological theory of Penelope's unconscious attraction to the suitors.

42. On the significance of δύναται here, see below p. 137. At 15.20ff. Athene hurries Telemachus back from Sparta with talk of the fickle θυμὸς ἐνὶ στήθεσσι γυναικός ('spirit in the breast of a woman').

43. See Kirk, op. cit., 246.

44. Op. cit., 120. Note also that Athene informed Odysseus of Penelope's νόος at 13.381.

45. 'Penelope vor den Freiern' in *Lebende Antike: Symposion fur R. Sühnel*, edited by H. Meller and H.-J. Zimmerman (Berlin, 1967), 27–33.

46. The phrase occurs also at 2.92 and 13.381, in the context of Penelope making promises to the suitors but νόος δὲ οἱ ἄλλα μενοίνα. Hölscher's interpretation fits these contexts as aptly as 18.283. Moreover, it is unlikely that the poet would have singled out one example of a formulaic phrase of this kind for special meaning. Thornton, op. cit., 98 assumes that the words refer to the forthcoming interview Penelope has arranged with the beggar; but this seems to be reading back significance into a meeting which, at the time, cannot have seemed to her to hold out any more hope than her previous encounters with strangers claiming to have met O. (See 14.126–30.)

47. See H. Frisk, *Griechisches Etymologisches Wörterbuch* (Heidelberg, 1970), q.v. μενοινάω 'heftig verlangen' (cf. μένος). Other Homeric uses of the word (see LSJ ad loc.) support this interpretation. On νόος, see K. von Fritz, 'νόος and νόειν in the Homeric Poems', *CP* 38 (1943), 79–93, where the word is closely connected with inward vision of what is absent.

48. This, like the story of the spinning and unpicking of the shroud for Laertes (2.93–110; 19.138–56), is clearly a folk-tale element in the story. It is perhaps significant that there is a slight discrepancy in Homer's account: at 21.1ff. it is Athene who puts the idea of the bow contest into her mind.

49. M. I. Finley, *The World of Odysseus* (London, 1962), 108 emphasizes the essentially passive role of the *demos* in the struggle over Penelope's marriage and Telemachus' inheritance.

50. See Hölscher, 'The Transformation from Folk-Tale to Epic', in *Homer: Tradition and Invention*, ed. B. Fenik (Leiden, 1978), 51–67.

51. See Finley, op. cit., 102–5: 'That prerogative mysteriously belonged to Penelope' (104). Thornton, op. cit., 108–10 thinks that Penelope has the right of choice by virtue of Odysseus' decree in his parting words to her before he left for Troy (18.259–70). But this seems to be placing too much emphasis upon a private conversation between husband and wife (hardly a 'decree') which would surely have cut little ice with the Ithacan *demos* or the suitors, even if they can be supposed to have known about it before Penelope's revelation at 18.25ff.

52. Certain contexts suggest that Telemachus has the right to send Penelope back to her parents, but refuses to do so for financial, religious, and social reasons (e.g., 2.130–7 where he is replying to Antinous' request that he do just that, so that she may marry τῷ ὅτεῳ τε πατὴρ κέλεται καὶ ἁνδάνει αὐτῇ, 'whoever her father instructs her to and whoever pleases her', 2.114). Elsewhere the suitors seem to suppose that Penelope has the sole, or at least, the deciding choice (see 18.288–9).

53. See also 2.91–110, where the themes are associated by Antinous, the suitor.

54. To this extent, Amory's picture of Penelope as looking 'at things only intermittently' (op. cit., 104) is correct; but, as I made clear above (p. 128) I cannot accept the psychological implications of Amory's thesis for the reunion; Penelope's inability to see things clearly stems entirely from her situation—its causes are wholly external to her.

55. I am not forgetting Odysseus' confinement on Calypso's island; but this is not given major emphasis in the *Odyssey*.

56. Repeated by Eumaeus to the returning Telemachus in 16.37–8.

57. See Schadewaldt, op. cit., 19.

58. Fenik, op. cit., 66–70.

59. See Schadewaldt, op. cit., p. 13 ff. on the dramatic structure, and especially on the element of 'übereckgespräch' (16) involving Penelope, Telemachus, and Odysseus.

60. None of Fenik's parallels (op. cit., 68) are really comparable to the *Odyssey* Book 23 example in terms of dramatic suspense and importance of the character who has 'dropped out of sight'.

61. I have assumed that the choice was Homer's; but I would not thereby wish to exclude the possibility that the poet of the *Odyssey* was working within a tradition in which this late recognition was normal. Of course, the evidence (or rather, the lack of it) does not allow us to decide.

ADDENDUM

For update and further bibliography see pp. 153–4.

TRUE AND LYING TALES IN THE *ODYSSEY*

By CHRIS EMLYN-JONES

What is truth and what are lies in the *Odyssey*? Odysseus in his lying story to Eumaeus (14.192 ff.), just as the sea-nymph Eidothea in her true advice to the weather-bound Menelaus (4.383 ff.), claims to be speaking μαλ' ἀτρεκέως, 'quite precisely'. As all politicians are aware, if you wish to stand a chance of being believed it helps to emphasize the accuracy of what you are saying; this introductory line was as much a formula for Homer as it is today.[1]

Yet, listeners in the *Odyssey* often do not seem to care very much whether what they hear is actually delivered μαλ' ἀτρεκέως, as promised. It is perhaps understandable that Telemachus should not resent Athene's brief fictional autobiography, which she claims to deliver μαλ' ἀτρεκέως, when she visits him in disguise at the beginning of the *Odyssey* (1.179 ff.); after all, divinities are a law unto themselves. But in other circumstances, too, regard for truth may take second place. In 14.508 ff. Eumaeus, in his reception of Odysseus' lying story (a lie within a lie) of his resourcefulness on a cold night underneath the battlements of Troy (14.463 ff.), seems unconcerned with truth or falsity; for the swineherd, the tale is an αἶνος ἀμύμων (14.508), an 'excellent story',[2] the chief quality of which is that it is not παρὰ μοῖραν, 'inappropriate', nor an ἔπος νηκερδές, 'an unprofitable speech' (509), but a story which secures the teller a warm cloak for the night and implies, incidentally, his former status as leader of an ambush at Troy along with Menelaus and Odysseus.

What Eumaeus approves of, both in the Odysseus of the tale and the man sitting in front of him, is initiative in producing the story and skill in telling it. Listeners may be promised truth and accuracy but what they want most of all is to be entertained. For King Alcinous, in the short interlude of Odysseus' long tale at the Phaeacian court, the truth of what he is being told is, apparently, guaranteed not only by Odysseus' φρένες ἐσθλαί, 'good sense', but also (illogically to us) by his μορφὴ ἐπέων, 'elegance of words', which matches the skill of an ἀοιδός, a professional singer (11.367–8).

In 4.239 in Menelaus' palace, Helen announces that she will delight the guests with ἐοικότα concerning a past encounter with the absent Odysseus. In one sense these reminiscences are 'fitting', i.e., effective, like her medicines, in cheering her guests up after their melancholy thoughts about the lost Odysseus; but the word also has a connotation of 'plausible', calling to mind Odysseus' lies to Penelope in 19, where: ἴσκε ψεύδεα πολλὰ λέγων ἐτύμοισιν ὁμοῖα (203), 'he knew how to say many lies which resembled truth'. For Homer, both senses of the word are operative at 4.239; plausibility and appropriateness are designed to meet the artistic and social expectations of the listeners.

That these qualities are not exclusively at the service of truth is shown by Odysseus who demonstrates speech κατὰ μοῖραν in both his true and lying tales throughout the *Odyssey* and receives an equally enthusiastic reception for either. As Peter Walcot has shown, lack of moral scruple concerning the telling of lies is shared by Homeric society not only with later Greek but also with more recently observed peasant communities where lying functions as an acceptable form of social assertion.[3] On a practical level, stories referring to 'broad Crete' were sufficiently far removed geographically from the knowledge of the audience in the *Odyssey* to avoid any danger of the validity of claims being questioned.[4] We might note that Odysseus swiftly goes 'off the map' in the presence of the much travelled Phaeacians, giving, perhaps, an unintended irony to Alcinous' distinction between his guest and men who make up lying stories, ὅθεν κέ τις οὐδὲ ἴδοιτο (11.366), 'from sources which no one could see (i.e., test) for himself'![5]

The question of truth and lies, however, goes deeper than this. It is only when we get to Thucydides that a clear and explicit distinction is made between matter and manner, truth and presentation, in historical narrative (1.21). The tendency to blur these two aspects, clearly seen in Alcinous' compliment to Odysseus (above p. 144), is a natural consequence of the all-pervading Greek rhetorical tradition, with its roots in Homer and culmination (Thucydides notwithstanding) in classical Athenian orators and sophists.

Yet, it would obviously be absurd to suggest that, in the *Odyssey*, the audience is always indifferent to the truth or otherwise of information received; Eumaeus is wary of, and Penelope too often taken in by, lying beggars who spin a yarn in return for board and lodging. But what Eumaeus objects to, and Penelope all too readily believes, are predictions that Odysseus is on his way home—the one part of Odysseus' lying tale in 14.199–359 (ironically, the only essentially true part) which the swineherd does not believe.[6] From this and other instances we can infer that fairly strict standards of truth are required where the immediate interests of the audience would be adversely affected by lies. So, when Telemachus is advised by Nestor to visit Menelaus to find out news of his missing father (3.317 ff.), the old man feels the need to assure Telemachus that Menelaus will not lie to him, the implication being that, while good story-tellers may embroider or invent, when it comes to matters of vital importance to the welfare of their audience, they can be relied upon (the disguised Athene says the same to Telemachus about Nestor at 3.20).

Basic reliability is only, however, the negative side of telling a tale κατὰ μοῖραν, 'appropriately'. It is also important for the teller to point a moral (cf. Odysseus' αἶνος ἀμύμων [14.508], see above p. 144) and to project himself in a chosen favourable light—two aspects of the tale which often come to the same thing. The teller is also, on occasions, enabled to test the listener by noting whether the implications of the story are grasped and acted upon. In 17, Antinous, the evil ringleader of the suitors, fails to take the point of Odysseus' lying tale, in which the beggar's alleged experiences illustrate the importance of liberality, the dangers of *hybris*, and the unpredictability of fate (17.419–44, on which see below p. 150).

Odysseus' fictional autobiographies vary according to the image he wishes to project.[7] As a beggar in Ithaca he comes across as a man not deficient, despite his present abject appearance, in the assertive qualities of Homeric *aretē* (explicitly claimed at 14.212). Yet, in a sense he meets the same test in 6.162–7 where, with a story, he reassures and subtly flatters the young princess Nausicaa, and later in 9–12 where, although accepted by the Phaeacians and restored to his normal appearance, he still feels the need to present his past in such a way that they will be further impressed and supply him with still more gifts.

All guests, in Homeric society, need to have ready a convincing answer to the question τίς πόθεν εἰς ἀνδρῶν, 'what man are you and where do you come from?', which invariably follows the courtesies of *xenia*, or guest-friendship; indeed, providing a convincing story, at least passably presented, is one of the obligations of the guest according to the ritual of hospitality. Moreover, the standard of performance may hold the clue to future treatment. The need to lie may, as the scholium on 13.294 suggests, be more pressing when travelling abroad and among enemies; certainly Odysseus, unsure of whom he can trust, displays his resourceful intellect (νόον πολυκερδέα, 13.255) in continually and subtly adjusting the details of a basic theme to suit situation and audience, and much of his narration is designed to keep him one jump ahead, notably in the most clearly 'improvisatory' of his stories, to Athene at 13.256–86.[8] Yet there is a sense in which the youthful and inexperienced Telemachus at Sparta faces the same social hurdle. Whether his story is true or false (often as in the brief story the shipwrecked Odysseus tells to Nausicaa at 6.162–7 [see above] the question of truth or falsity is meaningless in the dramatic context [see further below pp. 150–1]), the important thing for the guest is to combine exciting material with a skilled delivery in order to create the best possible impression and gain the greatest possible advantage.

Much of the dramatic suspense in the *Odyssey* arises from the postponement of autobiography inherent in the conventions of *xenia* (the guest is not questioned until after supper). This is particularly marked in the second half of the poem, where Odysseus' series of false tales are an integral part of a repeated thematic sequence which leads ultimately to recognition or revelation of true identity.[9] But, as B. Fenik has noted, the 'retardation' consequent upon the telling of the false stories is also to be seen in earlier parts of the poem where Odysseus' reticence about personal details and reluctance to tell the whole truth (not amounting to a 'lying tale') gives dramatic weight to his final announcement of identity at the beginning of 9.[10]

To turn from the social context to the content of stories; just as true and false stories are generated by the same social pressures and are required to meet the same criteria of excellence, so, in the *Odyssey*, true and false stories share thematic material and presentation. It has often been noted that themes of hardship, restless wandering, capture by pirates/traders, abandonment on a strange shore, hospitality offered (son of King Pheidon, 14.316–20) and violated (Cyclops, 9.252 ff.; Laestrygones, 10.100 ff.) are not only common to true and false tales but also relate to incidents in the main action of the poem.[11] Menelaus, just like Odysseus in his beggar's guise, gained much wealth from Egypt (4.90 ff. and 14.285–6). Odysseus *in propria persona* suffered the same shipwreck as the beggar (12.415 ff. = 14.305 ff. verbatim). This repetition of motifs is even found in the most elaborate of Odysseus' lying stories (to Eumaeus, 14.199–359), within the individual tale: the 'deceitful pirate/trader' theme is employed twice in the same story, firstly of a Phoenician whose attempt to sell Odysseus is foiled by a storm (288–309) and secondly, to explain his presence on Ithaca, where he claims to have escaped from dishonest Thesprotian traders who were, like the Phoenician earlier, plotting to sell him into slavery (334–59).

Presentation of stories also follows a pattern; when there is time, the announcement that the truth is about to be divulged is preceded by an introduction in which the teller emphasizes the extent to which hardship has been suffered and the time it would take to complete a recital of woes (reassurance to the audience, perhaps, that a full evening's entertainment was guaranteed!), compliments his host, and remarks on the pleasantness of the occasion. The two most elaborate introductions illustrate the point that, with true or false stories, there is need for careful preliminaries; in 9.2–38, the elaboration indicates the thematic importance of the very long story to follow. But here Odysseus also needs to establish himself as a person of stature. In 19.107–71, on the other hand, the elaboration comes from Penelope's need to confide in the stranger (124–61) and his attempt to evade her question: τίς πόθεν εἰς ἀνδρῶν; πόθι τοι πόλις ἠδὲ τοκῆες; (19.105), repeated with more insistence at 162–3. In Odysseus' evasion we can see him not only in character as a beggar paying her traditional compliments but also as her husband, wishing to find out her feelings and circumstances.[12]

On the whole, motifs are repeated largely, verbatim, e.g., the storm and shipwreck sequence (12.415 ff. = 14.305 ff.) or in a manner whose level of generality does not allow comparison between treatments of stories. One incident, however, an ill-fated piratical expedition, does allow us to compare different examples of presentation of the same story in the light of the personal circumstances and situation of the teller, and reveals some of the subtleties of the poet's technique in the treatment of detail.

Right at the beginning of his mammoth tale of 9–12, Odysseus describes an abortive raid on the Ciconians at Ismarus in Thrace. For Odysseus and his companions this was the first incident after their departure from Troy, demonstrating the piratical activity which was an integral part of formal warfare in Homer.[13] After sacking the city, killing the men, enslaving the women, and collecting booty, Odysseus' companions, neglecting his advice to make good their escape, got drunk and were eventually forced to fight a Ciconian force which had been assembled to counter-attack. After a hard-fought battle, Odysseus and his depleted company were forced to flee 'from death and destruction' (9.39–61). This incident recurs, with changed location but strikingly similar detail, in Odysseus' lying story to Eumaeus (14.257–84). In his *persona* as a beggar, Odysseus describes his successful life in war after a somewhat disadvantaged start as the illegitimate son of a Cretan, Castor, and how restlessness after the Trojan War drove him to make an expedition to Egypt. Here events similar to the 'real' raid on the Ciconians occurred.

It is not profitable, or even meaningful, to ask which is the original story. Probably, the story of an unsuccessful raid was a 'floating' tale which could be changed and adapted to fit a number of different contexts in the oral recitation of a poem such as the *Odyssey*[14] (it recurs again at 17.419–44, on which see below p. 150). However there are differences between the versions in 9 and 14 which give interesting insights into how the teller adapts the story to the circumstances in which he tells it. In 9 Odysseus describes the sacking of Ismarus with something of the dispassionate objectivity of a military commander. The Cicones had been Trojan allies (*Il.* 2.846) and so the operation could almost be seen as part of the war; emphasis is put on proper shares of booty (cf. *Il.* 1.163 ff.) and a controlled battle in which only towards the end of the day (for the Iliadic imagery see *Il.* 16.777–9) were the Greeks forced to retreat. Even in extremis Odysseus insists on proper mourning for the dead before the journey is resumed (9.64–6). In 14 the picture is somewhat different. The plundering takes place after, and against, Odysseus' warning, it is described as a much less controlled operation (οἱ δ' ὕβρει εἴξαντες ἐπισπόμενοι μένεϊ σφῷ, 'But they, yielding to *hybris*, giving the rein to their passion', 14.262), and the plight of the victims is given greater prominence (ἐκ δὲ γυναῖκας ἄγον καὶ νήπια τέκνα, 'they carried off the women and innocent children', 263).[15] The counterattack of Egyptians, when it comes, does not meet, as in 9.54–5, with sustained resistance. The Greeks go into a panic (φύζαν . . . . . κακήν, 269) and are either killed or enslaved, all except the narrator, who casts off his armour, throws down his spear, and supplicates the King of the Egyptians, who, honouring Zeus Xenios, saves him from the hostility of the angry Egyptian soldiery (14.266–84).

The detailed differences in the two stories reflect the creation, by the teller, of subtly different *personae*. In 9 Odysseus, in his own *persona* as an aristocratic commander of the Ithacan force at Troy (mentioned in the *Catalogue, Il.* 2.632 ff.) describes the sack without emotion or excuse (piracy, especially in time of war, would not necessarily have been disapproved of by the aristocratic Phaeacian audience) and emphasizes failure to obey his orders as the cause of the disaster, as well as κακή Διὸς αἶσα, 'evil destiny of Zeus' (9.52). In 14, on the other hand, by transposing the order of events (putting the giving of advice before the marauding) and emphasizing the fate of the non-combatant Egyptians (women and children), the disguised Odysseus contrives to give quite a different impression: namely that he was not totally in favour of the raid (he carefully avoids spelling out the purpose of the expedition at 14.246), has sympathy with the victims in the face of the *hybris* of his companions (*he* was not involved), and was unsurprised at their total rout (there was no battle: 269–70). His final action in supplicating his enemy (behaviour reserved in the *Iliad* for minor Trojans and those whose lack of heroic *aretē* Homer wishes to emphasize—cf. *Il.* 21.40 ff.) is not one which the real Odysseus would have contemplated in that situation.

The cumulative effect of the differences in the two passages suggest that the contrast is not accidental. In 14 Odysseus, while emphasizing his prosperous origins and ability, is at pains to project himself, not as a major Homeric hero engaged in a military operation, but as someone involved in an exploit which gets out of hand. This is surely calculated to appeal to Eumaeus no less than Odysseus' action in supplicating the Egyptian King at 276 ff., and the pointed reference to *Zeus Xenios* in 283 drives the point home.

Clearly the episodes in 9 and 14 must be seen in their contexts as part of a bigger whole (in 9 immeasurably bigger)—namely, the total story; but, at the same time, it appears that each episode is aimed κατὰ μοῖραν at its very different audience: in the one case, aristocratic Phaeacians, for whom Odysseus is a famed celebrity and, in the other, a simple, albeit nobly born, swineherd, whose sympathy and finer feelings the beggar must consider in order to survive and whose conception of what constitute either plausible or fitting exploits for the wretched figure sitting in front of him, largely decides the nature and course of the story.

Odysseus uses this episode once again as a lying story in 17.419–44, this time as the sole incident. The tale is not 'after supper' but inserted into a highly dramatic episode when Odysseus, having made his first contact with the suitors, is begging food from them in his own palace. He addresses Antinous, the ringleader and most violent of the suitors, and asks him for food (17.415–19). The begging is explicitly designed to test the suitors' liberality (17.413), and Odysseus leads into the story (which is repeated almost verbatim, 17.427–41 = 14.258–72) by praising Antinous' lordly appearance which should, Odysseus maintains, imply a more lavish donation. He recalls his past prosperity which went hand in hand with liberality (not a quality he attributes to himself in Bk. 14)—all of which Zeus spoiled by putting it into his head to go on a pirate expedition (explicitly mentioned here—ληϊστῆρσι πολυπλάγκτοισιν . . . ἰέναι, 'to go with far-wandering pirates', 425–6). The ending of the story is very different: instead of pardon, Odysseus was sold into slavery, the remainder of his adventures being passed over as πήματα πάσχων, 'suffering woes' (444).

The reason for changing the end of his account of what happened to him as a result of the raid is not difficult to see. Odysseus is not here so much concerned with Zeus Xenios (though he might well be) as with the consequences of *hybris*. The story, which opens with remarks about liberality, is mainly about violence. The details are repeated verbatim, but the changed dramatic context in which Odysseus tells the story throws a different emphasis. This time there is to be no mercy, either for the beggar in the story or, in reality, for the suitors. The *hybris* of Odysseus' companions takes on considerable importance in the context of Antinous' threat of physical violence to Odysseus (17.409–10) and its fulfilment when Antinous throws a footstool at Odysseus and hits him (17.463–4), both of which passages frame the story. But circumstances change, Odysseus is saying: Zeus can bring ruin. The story is intended as an object-lesson and a warning for Antinous, an αἶνος—one which, however, he does not heed. It is also intended for the suitors as a whole, whose *hybris* in plundering Odysseus' estates and courting his wife is often emphasized (e.g., 1.368, 4.321, 15.329, 17.565, etc.).[16]

The changes in emphasis between versions in 9, 14, and 17 demonstrate that the story *can* be used by the teller to convey subtly facts about himself and different aspects of his personality, as well as to convey warnings and suggest paradigms for behaviour.[17] In respect of these functions there is no difference in the *Odyssey* between true and false stories (nor between biographical and autobiographical, though it might be thought that the latter, being based on personal experience, carry more weight).[18] The concepts of truth and falsity relate not to some supposedly 'real' historical context, but to the artistic demands of the poem.[19] Indeed, as Peter Walcot suggests, the lying stories do contain truth on a higher level in that, while the details may be 'false', in the dramatic context the underlying *persona* of the teller is accurately portrayed (and, it may be added, the lesson conveyed to the listeners timely and relevant to their situation).[20]

★   ★   ★

The basic story material is the vast backdrop against which the *Odyssey* plot is developed. It represents a complex body of themes which extends ultimately to the total world and experience of the Homeric age—a vast resource upon which the singer, professional or amateur (Demodocus or Odysseus), could draw.[21] Stories of past suffering are capable of almost infinite lengthening through elaboration and reduplication of themes and, at the same time, compression to the two-line summary. That the *Odyssey* uses only a fraction of the story material which would have been available to the Homeric bard is clear from the odd fragments of stories otherwise unknown, e.g., at 18.138–40, where in a highly compressed $\alpha\hat{i}\nu o\varsigma$, intended as a warning to the 'good' suitor Amphinomus, the disguised Odysseus introduces the fragment of a story element otherwise unknown to the *Odyssey*: Odysseus confesses that once he gave way to force and violence—$\pi\alpha\tau\rho\acute{\iota}\ \tau$' $\dot{\epsilon}\mu\hat{\omega}\ \pi\acute{\iota}\sigma\upsilon\nu o\varsigma\ \kappa\alpha\grave{\iota}\ \dot{\epsilon}\mu o\hat{\iota}\sigma\iota\ \kappa\alpha\sigma\iota\gamma\nu\acute{\eta}\tau o\iota\sigma\iota$, 'relying on my father and brothers'. Similarly at 1.198 Athene, without apparent motive, introduces an alternative to an otherwise true account of Odysseus' detention on an island, kept captive by *savage men*—possibly a thematic variant on the Calypso-detention.[22] The poet demonstrates, in the context of oral composition (on which almost all would now agree the Homeric poems are based), the ability to create multiple variations by rearrangement of detail within the framework of recurring story-patterns.

The later stories of Odysseus have come in for some harsh criticism for failing to equal the dramatic quality and thematic interest of those of 9–12;[23] it is certainly an exaggeration to suggest that they are among the dramatic high spots of the poem. They are less elaborated, contain less dramatic interest or scope for extended incident; the most elaborate lying story, that to Eumaeus in 14, maintains its pace by means of expressions conveying the passage of time (e.g., $\dot{\epsilon}\xi\hat{\eta}\mu\alpha\rho$ . . . $\dot{\epsilon}\beta\delta o\mu\acute{\alpha}\tau\eta$, 'for six days . . . on the seventh', 249–52) and other connectives.[24] These are elements which occur also in the *Nostos* material (Books 3–4, doubtless related to the *Nostoi* of the other heroes, a poem composed reputedly by Agias of Troizen) and Odysseus' recital in Books 9–12, but in the latter the variety of detail is greater, the speed more leisurely, and dramatic structure tighter.

It seems that this artistic difference is related to the social status of the tellers. The *Odyssey*, distinguished by its sympathetic portrayal of humble characters, nevertheless shares the predominantly aristocratic ethos of the Homeric tradition. What has happened to Nestor, Menelaus, Agamemnon, Odysseus, and other heroes returning from Troy is more important and more noteworthy than the tribulations of lesser mortals, albeit men who claimed the friendship of the great (cf. Odysseus at 14.470). This is nowhere more obvious than in the relationship to the gods revealed by the narrators. Odysseus, *in propria persona*, enjoys the personal protection of Athene and, in his travels, encounters Hermes and other divine and semi-divine figures (cf. Menelaus in his Egyptian adventure: 4.351 ff.). For Odysseus the beggar, the world is a lonelier place, through which he travels without the personal support (or even opposition) of powerful divinities, but at the mercy of the remote and impersonal whims of the gods and evil fate (cf. 14.198, 227, 348, 357), and in the mundane world, vulnerable to the chance schemes of pirates. Moreover, however long it may take, the great heroes usually reach home; for lesser mortals, like the beggar and Eumaeus, not forgetting Eumaeus' Phoenician abductress (who, after all, was only trying to get home herself, 15.425–36), displacement is complete.[25]

NOTES

1. It should be noted that Odysseus explicitly claims ἀλήθεια only for the actual truth (e.g., 16.226), but it is doubtful whether the poet intended this to be significant; when giving Penelope a version of his activities since she has last seen him which omits any hint of Odysseus' presence, Telemachus claims, notwithstanding, to be speaking ἀληθείην (17.108).

2. αἶνος = 'story with a moral' or here more appropriately, 'with an ulterior motive'.

3. See *Ancient Society*, 8 (1977), 1–19.

4. See scholium on 14.199 quoted in C. R. Trahman, *Phoenix* 6 (1952), 31–43.

5. This translation, supported by a scholium on 11.366, seems preferable to Lattimore's 'from which no one could learn anything'.

6. Yet note that Eumaeus describes this part of Odysseus' tale as οὐ κατὰ κόσμον (14.363), a description which although clearly implying its supposed falsity, nevertheless also contains an underlying implication concerning its artistic arrangement: 'not in order.'

7. See Walcot, op. cit., 1 ff.

8. For a subtle analysis of this story see Walcot, op. cit., 10 ff.

9. See my discussion of the recognition sequence, *G & R* 31 (1984) 1 ff. (= pp. 126–43 in this collection), and focusing on evidence from the scholia, N. J. Richardson, *Liverpool Latin Seminar* 4 (1983), 219–35.

10. See *Studies in the Odyssey* (Wiesbaden, 1974), 5 ff.

11. Ibid. 168 ff.

12. See my discussion, op. cit., 7–8 (=pp. 132–3 in this collection).

13. Cf., e.g., *Iliad* 1.366–8.

14. The intrusive third persons (ἐμάχοντο / βάλλον: 9.54–5) in a first person context might suggest a variant form of the narrative or a 'floating tale' (see W. B. Stanford, *Homer, Odyssey* [London, 1958], note ad loc.).

15. Stanford, op. cit., note on 14.262, thinks that *hybris* does not refer to the act of piracy but to the neglect of suitable safety precautions, on the grounds that piracy, as 'quite a gentleman's profession in the Heroic Age', would not be so described. This is surely wrong: (1) *Hybris* is a word closely related to gratuitous violence or the threat of violence (see LSJ ad loc. and N. R. E. Fisher, *G & R.* 23 [1976], 177–93); (2) Odysseus in his beggar's *persona* could not count on Eumaeus having the same attitude to piracy as the 'gentleman' heroes of the *Iliad* (*hybris* is

not mentioned in the Book 9 version of the story, delivered to the aristocratic Phaeacians); (3) Odysseus goes out of his way, in this episode, to dissociate himself from the attack which he might, therefore, quite consistently condemn as *hybris*.

16. The need to test also applies to friendly listeners and extends well beyond the exigencies of the situation (see my discussion, op. cit., 8 [=p. 133 in this collection] and Walcot, op. cit., 19–20).

17. This paradeigmatic function is also notable in the *Iliad*, e.g., Phoinix at 9.524–99; Nestor at 11.655–761. It passes, more formalized, into Greek lyric and elegiac poetry.

18. For examples of a true story related to an αἶνος, see Nestor using Agamemnon's fate as a warning to Telemachus not to stay too long away from home (3.313–16), and Menelaus deprecating comparison between his palace and Olympus by recounting briefly the trouble he has undergone to amass his treasures (4.78–93).

19. For preoccupation with the 'real' stories, see W. J. Woodhouse, *The Composition of Homer's Odyssey* (Oxford, 1930).

20. Walcot, op. cit., 9.

21. Homer, not without irony, one supposes, twice likens Odysseus in his stories to an *aoidos* (Alcinous at 11.368 and Eumaeus at 17.518). This and other references suggest that the poet was using his hero's narrative skill as a reflection of his own.

22. Likewise the Aetolian wanderer who lied to Eumaeus at 14.379–85 represents a variant on the 'I have seen Odysseus and he will soon be home' theme.

23. See esp. G. S. Kirk, *The Songs of Homer* (Cambridge, 1962), 360. In talking of 'flagging tempo' and describing one such story as a 'digression', Kirk seems to me to misconceive the essentially paratactic structure and leisurely pace of Homeric epic.

24. See J. H. Gaisser, *HSCP* 73 (1969), 26–32, who remarks on the lively staccato style of 13.256–86 (the most 'improvisatory' of Odysseus' stories: see above n. 8) and also the elements of structure in 14.199–359.

25. The author wishes to thank Desmond Costa for reading a draft of this paper and making a number of helpful suggestions.

ADDENDUM

There has been a number of significant developments on the related topics of Deception, Disguise, and Recognition in the *Odyssey*. Richardson has explained the dramatic and emotional effects of Aristotelian *anagnorisis* in relation to the *Odyssey*, with special attention to the literary criticism to be found in the scholiasts. A major study of Recognition has been undertaken by Cave, extending throughout European poetics from Aristotle to Barthes and Shakespeare to Conrad.

Narratological analysis of Penelope's role is found in Felson-Rubin and especially Murnaghan (which runs parallel to analysis in terms of an oral-poetic 'recognition sequence'), e.g., in M.'s idea that Penelope participates in a number of conflicting plots of which she is unaware and that she acts out a kind of recognition of Odysseus in 'recognition scenes that have gone underground' (52). Again in connection with Penelope, Katz has recently developed an argument that *Odyssey* 17–23 explores the 'indeterminacy of narrative direction' (192) in juxtaposing Penelope's indecision with the Clytemnestra and Helen paradigms which 'function . . . as an alternative narrative structure . . .' (ibid.).

The arguments in 1984 against the idea of an 'intuitive recognition' of Odysseus by Penelope have proved controversial; in the introduction of his

recent major commentary on *Odyssey* 17–20, Russo has restated the arguments for the psychological interpretation against what he believes to be a
'minimalist' or 'literalist' approach. On the interpretation of Penelope's dream
at *Odyssey* 19, 535–53, I think it can be disputed that P.'s bitter weeping over
the slaughter of the geese '*can only point* (my italics) to some ambivalence in
her true feelings towards (the suitors) . . .' (13 n. 13); see esp. Katz's careful
interpretation, 145–8. For restatement of objections to the 'psychological
interpretation', see Jones, 172–4 and especially Rutherford (2), who makes
the point (35) that subconscious recognition reduces much of the subtle irony
and pathos of the encounter of Penelope and Odysseus in *Odyssey* 19. Further
exploration of the functional role of the language of the *Odyssey* as medium of
disguise and identity can be found in Goldhill, especially Ch. 1 of his (2).

BIBLIOGRAPHY

T. Cave, *Recognitions: a Study in Poetics* (Oxford, 1988).
I. J. F. de Jong, 'Between Words and Deeds: Hidden Thoughts in the *Odyssey*' in de Jong and
    J. P. Sullivan (edd.), *Modern Critical Theory and Classical Literature* (Leiden, 1994), 27–50.
N. Felson-Rubin, 'Penelope's Perspective: Character from Plot' in J. M. Bremer, I. J. F. de Jong,
    and J. Kalff, (edd.), *Homer: Beyond Oral Poetry* (Amsterdam, 1987), 61–83.
S. Goldhill, (1) 'Reading Differences: the *Odyssey* and Juxtaposition', *Ramus* 17.1 (1988), 1–31.
——(2) *The Poet's Voice: Essays on Poetics and Greek Literature* (Cambridge, 1991).
P. V. Jones, *Homer's Odyssey: a Companion* (Bristol, 1988).
M. A. Katz, *Penelope's Renown: Meaning and Indeterminacy in the Odyssey* (Princeton, 1991).
S. Murnaghan, *Disguise and Recognition in the Odyssey* (Princeton, 1987).
N. Richardson, 'Recognition Scenes in the *Odyssey* and Ancient Literary Criticism', *Liverpool*
    Latin Seminar 4 (1983), 219–35.
J. Russo, M. Fernández-Galiano, and A. Heubeck (edd.), *A Commentary on Homer's Odyssey*, Vol.
    3 (Oxford, 1992).
R. B. Rutherford, (1) 'The Philosophy of the *Odyssey*', *JHS* 106 (1986), 145–62.
——(2) (ed.), *Homer, Odyssey XIX and XX* (Cambridge, 1992).

ODYSSEUS AND THE RETURN OF THE SWALLOW

By E. K. BORTHWICK

δεξιτερῇ δ' ἄρα χειρὶ λαβὼν πειρήσατο νευρῆς·
ἡ δ' ὑπὸ καλὸν ἄεισε, χελιδόνι εἰκέλη αὐδήν.

(Then he took the bow in his right hand and proved the string;
and it sang beautifully, in tone like a swallow)   *Odyssey* 21.410–1

I

In an article in *CP* 80 (1985), 33–4, entitled '*Odyssey* 21.411: the Swallow's Call', Luis A. Losada drew attention to the apparent oddity that the sound of Odysseus' bow-string, as he twanged it after stringing it in the presence of the suitors, is compared to the note of the swallow, since for the most part, the swallow's twittering cry, in terms of sound quality, is traditionally associated in much of later Greek literature with either barbarian unintelligibility, loquacity, or sometimes lamentation—none of which is at all appropriate here.[1] He suggests instead that a 'thematic connotation' was alluded to by Homer, the migratory cycle and vernal return of the swallow, and concludes that 'the swallow and its call might well be called a quintessential metaphor for the idea of returning . . . No more appropriate bird call exists—the singing bowstring heralds the hero's return.'

I think that he is right, and that the theme can be developed even further than he does, as well as having a wealth of parallels drawn from a variety of later sources, which suggests a long-established and persistent symbolism in both folk-lore and poetic tradition, as I will go on to illustrate in the second half of this article. It may be that Odysseus' return is represented as coinciding with the coming of spring (the most ubiquitous of all swallow associations): Losada refers to the accumulation of pertinent detail in Norman Austin's *Archery at the Dark of the Moon* (California, 1975, 246 ff.), about how 'the air suddenly becomes alive with intimations of spring', beginning with Penelope's comparison of her grief for Odysseus' loss to that of the nightingale 'when spring is newly come' (19.519), a seasonal reference less obviously appropriate to that bird.[2] But a striking feature of the swallow's return is not merely the season, nor even its reappearance in the same general locality (it is φιλόχωρος, 'loving its own place', Artem. *Onir.* 4.56), or house (in relation to men it is 'house-sharing', πέδοικος Aesch. fr. 53, σύνοικος Aesop. 39a, 255H., πάροικος Babr. 118.1, 'domesticated and friendly', σύντροφος καὶ εὔνους Arr. *An.* 1.25.8, 'intimate', συνήθης Dion. *Av.* 1.21), or roof (it is 'roof-sharing', ὁμώροφος Babr. 18.14, cf. *A.P.* 10.2, Theoc. 14.39, Ael. *N.A.* 1.52, etc.), but specifically in the old familiar matrimonial nest. This is frequently *within* the house itself, indeed close to the domestic hearth, for the swallow is the ἐφέστιος ὄρνις ('bird of the hearth', Himer. *Or.* 6.3), μερόπεσσι συνέστιος ('sharing the hearth with men', Nonn. 3.12).[3] One recalls the Odyssean *leitmotiv* of Odysseus' repeated oath concerning his own impending return by the ἱστίη τ' Ὀδυσσῆος ἀμύμονος ἣν ἀφικάνω ('the hearth of blameless Odysseus to which I am come') in 14.159 (to Eumaeus), 19.304 (to Penelope herself), 20.231 (to Philoetius), and his ultimate return αὐτὸς ζωὸς ἐφέστιος ('I myself, alive, at my own hearth', 23.55). When Athene too suddenly transforms herself into a swallow and sits watching the final victory of her favourite hero, observe that the central roof-beam of the megaron on which she perches (22.239) is called —uniquely here—sooty (αἰθαλόεντος), that is, it is close above the *eschara* or 'hearth', where Odysseus had first sat with his wife in disguise (19.389), where, after the revelation of his identity, they next meet (23.89), and where in the light of the fire (164–5) the ultimate recognition appropriately takes place. (Incidentally, as the contrast of their return to hearth and home of Agamemnon and Odysseus is one of the foremost themes in the structure of the *Odyssey*, note that Agamemnon's death ἐφέστιος ['at his hearth'] at the hands of his wife and her paramour is stressed at 3.234, a motif which Aeschylus made most effective use of at *Ag.* 851, 968, 1056, 1310.)[4]

The presence of swallows within the house was obviously familiar to the Greeks, and the subject of a much-quoted note by J. G. Frazer in *CR* 5 (1891), 1–3 and 230–1. Surprisingly however he never alludes to the Homeric material, nor, in his citing the generally favourable[5] response to their presence in diverse regions such as modern Greece, Austria, China, and Japan, does he adduce examples from our own literature, such as verses by the nature poet John Clare's *On seeing two swallows* 'twittering as wont above the old fireside', and (from *The Swallow*) 'in the sooty chimney pop / where thy wife and family / every evening wait for thee'.[6] The notable devotion of the swallow to the family unit appears often in Greek literature: it is called 'child-loving' (φιλόπαις *A.P.* 10.16, φιλότεκνος ibid. 10.4).[7] But to be noted particularly, for its appropriateness to the Odysseus–Penelope conjugal relationship, is Artemidorus' statement (2.66) that to dream of a swallow is ἀγαθὴ . . . μάλιστα πάντων πρὸς γάμον· πιστὴν γὰρ τὴν οἰκουρὸν ἔσεσθαι τὴν γύναικα σημαίνει ('Good above all for marriage, for it indicates that the wife will be a faithful keeper of the house').[8] For in the *Odyssey* surely Penelope above all is the archetype of the faithful housewife. According to E. A. Armstrong,[9] the very songs of swallows 'tend to be relevant to the pair-bond', and 'they sing before coition, and perhaps during it'.

It is singularly apposite, then, that when Odysseus, like the swallow, has returned to the old domestic hearth, and holds for the first time in twenty years his own treasured possession, the κειμήλιον ἄνακτος of 21.9, his stringing and 'tuning' of the bow should be signalled by the swallow's note.[10] It is thus virtually one of the series of *sound* omens which at important junctures confirm the impending return of Odysseus (Telemachus' sneeze at 17.541, Zeus' thunder at 20.103, the mill-grinder's prayer at 20.120), signal the approval of the gods (thunder again at 21.413), and end the conflict (the thunderbolt at 24.539). Eustathius in his commentary on our passage was puzzled by the bowstring's note being called καλόν ('beautiful') by Homer, because of the often pejorative associations of the swallow's cry, and concluded that it does not mean ἡδύ ('sweet'), but that the testing of the string proved it to be not dry and useless, but in good condition. But surely καλόν here can have the overtones of the *favourable* omen, just as at 11.130 ῥέξας ἱερὰ καλά ('having sacrificed fair victims') does not mean that the sacrificial victims are beautiful, for the adjective is common in this context: see LSJ s.v. II.2, and the use of καλλιερεῖν of auspicious portents in Herodotus, Xenophon, etc.

Another structural feature of the *Odyssey* is how comparisons to various birds are interwoven at emotionally charged points in connection with the hero's return, and with the relationship of Odysseus, Penelope, Telemachus, and their guardian Athene: I think of the sympathetic sea-nymph Ino, who saves him from near fatal shipwreck 'like a shear-water' (5.337, 353);[11] of the likening of the Phaeacian ship carrying the sleeping Odysseus back to Ithaca (perhaps the most romantic moment in all classical poetry) to the flight of the speeding falcon (13.86–8); of the recognition of father and son in the simile of the crying of sea-eagles or vultures (16.216);[12] of the lament of Penelope compared to that of the nightingale (19.518); of her dream of the eagle-Odysseus and the geese-suitors (19.536), prefigured by the similar omen to Telemachus (15.160); of the omen of eagle and dove which frustrates the plot against Telemachus (20.242); of the pursuit of the suitors likened to eagles pursuing small birds (22.302); of the last charge of Odysseus himself like an eagle (24.538). Athene's non-human transformations in the Ithacan palace are into an ὄρνις ἀνοπαῖα—taken to be a swallow by some ancient authorities (1.320),[13] a φήνη (lammergeyer, 3.372: cf. the Odysseus/Telemachus simile referred to), and finally a swallow (22.240); and Carrol Moulton observes: 'The short swallow similes unobtrusively underline her partnership with Odysseus and the certainty that she will champion his cause', concluding 'Much of the bird imagery in the *Odyssey* is related to the hero's homecoming.'[14] J. M. Boraston, in a somewhat neglected article on 'The Birds of Homer' in *JHS* 31 (1911), 244, comments on 'Homer's choice of the swallow to represent Athene in the house of Ulysses because of the close attachment of this goddess to the domestic fortunes of Ulysses' household'.

II

The swallow as emblematic of domestic bliss and fidelity recurs in a wide variety of literatures of different periods. In reporting Plutarch's strange myth of Isis transformed into a swallow (*Mor.* 357c), Otto Keller characterizes the goddess as 'die Schirmerin häuslichen Glücks und ehelicher Liebe'.[15] Aelian (*N.A.* 10.34) reports τιμᾶται δὲ ἡ χελιδὼν θεοῖς μυχίοις καὶ Ἀφροδίτῃ, μυχίᾳ μέντοι καὶ ταύτῃ ('the swallow is held in honour by the gods of the house and Aphrodite, for she too is one'), combining deities of love and the domestic hearth.[16] Theophylactus Simocatta (*Quaest. Nat.*, in J. L. Ideler, *Physici et Medici Graeci Minores* i. 168) refers to the swallow's song around the house in terms of an *epithalamium*: διδάσκουσι (sc. χελιδόνες) προσᾴδειν ἀνθρώποις καὶ περιλαλεῖν θαλάμοις ᾠδὴν εὐαρμόνιον ('Swallows teach how to sing in harmony with man, and to chatter a harmonious song round the bed chambers').[17] In his *de Mirabilibus Mundi*, Albertus Magnus acknowledges the accepted swallow symbolism: et quia hirundo multum diligit, ut dicunt philosophi, ideo multum eligunt eam ad excitandum amorem ('and because the swallow loves greatly, as philosophers say, therefore they choose it especially for stirring love'); and according to Beryl Rowland, 'some Church Fathers saw the swallow as the symbol of maternal care and domestic contentment'.[18] Armstrong (op. cit., 182) quotes the 16th-century writer Gerard Leigh, *Accedence of Armorie* (London, 1562): 'Wheresoever he (the swallow) breedeth, the goodman of the house is not there made cuckolde.' One cannot fail to notice the irony implicit in the conversation of Duncan and Banquo in *Macbeth* 1.6, as, following on the scene of altercation between Macbeth and his lady, and before the fatal night, they approach the castle redolent, it would seem, of domestic harmony, and so singled out by 'the temple-haunting martlet' for the 'love-mansionry' of his 'pendent bed and procreant cradle'.[19]

In the passage just quoted, Albertus goes on to refer also to the amorous proclivities of *turtur*, *columba*, and *passer*, but the love associations of the swallow seem to lack the more lecherous overtones at least of the sparrow (the turtle-dove is of course notoriously chaste or faithful), although the theme of frustrated yearnings of lovers, as well as spouses, occurs. The well-known Anacreontic poem (25 West) σὺ μέν, φίλη χελιδών compares the continual torments of the lover with the regular nest-building of returning swallows, a theme I notice too in an aria from Handel's Italian *cantata a tre* (librettist unknown), *Cor fedele: Clori, Tirsi e Fileno*, beginning 'Come la rondinella dall' Egitto / benchè offesa, ritorna al nido antico', which compares the swallow's return to the consistently recurring pangs of love. I take it that the allusion to the swallow's love-song ('motus amoris musicos') at the end of the *Pervigilium Veneris*, when the eager lover asks 'quando fiam ut chelidon, ut tacere desinam?' ('When shall I become like the swallow, that I may cease to be silent?'), associates, more optimistically, its spring song with the return of love. The theme of the little song 'Oh swallow, swallow flying, flying south' in Tennyson's *The Princess* is that of the swallow as the conveyer of a message of love.[20]

The swallow's song as an epithalamium appears as a striking motif in the works of the Italian poet and novelist Gabriele D'Annunzio. In his *Primo vere*, the section entitled *Connubii vespertini* includes the lines

> da l'oriente la stella di Venere
> ti vibra il raggio pronubo,
> mentre le gaie rondini cinguettano
> per te l'epitalamio.

('From the east the star of Venus flashes for you its nuptial ray, while the merry swallows twitter for you the epithalamium')

The same theme is interwoven by D'Annunzio into the story of his novel *L'innocente* (1892)[21] of a married couple who attempt reconciliation, after a period of infidelity and estrangement, by a sentimental revisiting in April of the villa where once they had spent their honeymoon. The swallows in their old nests under the gutters are represented as awaiting the couple's arrival (132), the husband, Tullio, daydreams, and, as their deafening chatter increases, suggests they go to the old bridal chamber (135), to be greeted by a gathering of excited birds, almost touching them as they fly like arrows (140), which have looked after the secrets of the house (150), faithfully enveloping it (155), so that the couple marvel at their activity 'around our nest of times gone by' (156). The chatter intensifies as they enter, and one swallow flies through a broken window-pane (157). After their love-making, the birds flutter incessantly (164), increasing always through the twilight (168, 173). There can be no doubt that the swallow symbolism has been carefully articulated by D'Annunzio and happens to coincide with the same motif in George Meredith's 'Modern Love', poem 47, 'We saw the swallows gathering in the sky', where the sudden gathering of these birds appears to reconsecrate a pair of estranged lovers in their former harmony.

As striking an example as any of such swallow imagery is the nostalgic yearning of the fifth poem ('Es kehret der Maien . . .') of the song-cycle

An die ferne Geliebte (Op. 98) of Beethoven to whom nature, Homer's *Odyssey*, and the theme of '*l'amour conjugal*' were all alike so dear. The coming of May is suggested in the accompaniment at the transition from the previous song by piano trills (the swallows) punctuated by cuckoo calls in the pictorial style of the Pastoral Symphony, then the lover's ardent song, as he sits gazing from his distant hill, continues:

> Die Schwalbe, die kehret zum wirtlichen Dach,
> Sie baut sich so emsig ihr bräutlich Gemach,
> Die Liebe soll wohnen da drinnen.
> Sie bringt sich geschäftig von Kreuz und von Quer
> Manch weicheres Stück zu dem Brautbett hieher,
> Manch wärmendes Stück für die Kleinen.
> Nun wohnen die Gatten beisammen so treu,
> Was Winter geschieden verband nun der Mai,
> Was liebet, das weiss er zu einen.

('The swallow which returns to the hospitable roof builds so diligently her bridal chamber—love shall dwell there within. Busily she brings from every nook and cranny soft scraps for her bridal bed, warm scraps for her little ones. Now the pair lives faithfully together. What winter has parted, now May has united. May knows how to bring lovers together')

Joseph Kerman[22] has drawn attention to the fact that the words of the poem (by the little-known young medical student, Alois Jeitteles) were composed in close conjunction with Beethoven's own wishes, and almost certainly with his own celebrated *Unsterbliche Geliebte* (now identified most convincingly with Antonia von Brentano) in mind,[23] and that 'the domestic bliss recorded corresponds to a nostalgic wish that he often voiced'.

To revert finally to Greek swallow literature and symbolism, in a somewhat speculative article,[24] F. Adrados has attempted to relate the most famous of swallow songs, the Rhodian *Chelidonismos* ἦλθ' ἦλθε χελιδών ('the swallow is come', *Carm. Pop.* 848 Page), and also the Samian *Eiresione* lines (attributed to Homer himself in the Herodotean *Vita*) νεῦμαι τοι νεῦμαι ἐνιαύσιος ὥστε χελιδών ('I come yearly like the swallow'), to an ancient ritual of a symbolic celebration of a *hieros gamos*, drawing attention also to the popularity of swallow motifs in Mycenaean art. Austin (op. cit., 200) then went so far as to compare the *Odyssey*'s theme of the 'beggar' returning to possess himself of the lady of the house to the jovial threats of the beggar boys in the masquerade of the *Chelidonismos* to do this very thing, if not rewarded.

By an odd irony, the Rhodian song was introduced as a theme with exactly the *opposite* symbolism by Giovanni Pascoli in his *Ultimo Viaggio*,[25] who, like Dante, Tennyson, and Kazantzakis, uses the Tiresias prophecy of *Od.* 11.119 ff. to portray Odysseus as the persistent, unsatisfied wanderer, who on his return to Ithaca feels stifled by his humdrum life by the domestic hearth with an ageing Penelope and tedious Telemachus. After ten years of such boredom, he hears the songs of swallows which herald the beginning of the sailing season (a familiar *topos* of the *Greek Anthology*), takes down the helm from above the hearth, and joins his old comrades on the beach waiting to leave for new adventures. As they set sail, the Ithacan minstrel Phemius accompanies them on his lyre as they sing the Rhodian *Chelidonismos*. Another twist to the swallow theme (which also has a slight flavour of the basic *Odyssey* story) is contained in an anonymous 18th-century version of an earlier Byzantine popular song, 'Black Swallows from the Desert',[26] in which an unfaithful husband instructs the swallows to fly away to his home to tell his wife that he will *not* be returning. She may become a nun, or marry again, for he has been detained by the daughter of an Armenian witch, who casts spells on ships so that they will not sail, and upon himself so that he cannot return.

Another more modern swallow song, however, which most closely resembles its ancient counterpart, from which it must surely derive, is no. 307a in Passow's *Popularia Carmina Graeciae Recentioris*, ἦρθεν, ἦρθε χελίδονα. This too is addressed to the lady of the house, the καλὴ οἰκοκυρά ('fair housewife'), a phrase strikingly recalling the πιστὴ οἰκουρός ('faithful housewife') of Artemidorus' swallow dream interpretation, which first alerted me to the richness of the symbolism attached to the theme of the swallow's return to the matrimonial nest, adding, I believe, a special warmth to our appreciation of the simile of *Od.* 21.411.

NOTES

1. Both the lamentatory and barbarian associations of the swallow (first attested in Hesiod and Aeschylus respectively) seem to be chiefly the product of the gruesome Attic Procne-Philomela-Tereus legend, which differs from the earlier myth alluded to in *Od.* 19.518ff., and which tarnished the otherwise generally favourable swallow lore.

2. See M. L. West on Hes. *Works and Days* 569, where this phrase's only other occurrence refers to the return of the *swallow* in spring.

3. Philip S. Robinson, *The Poet's Birds* (London, 1883), 439–40 comments that in the western tradition the swallow is especially 'the bird of the hearth'. Peter Tate, *Swallows* (London, 1981), 75 reports that the same is true at the other extremity of its migratory life: in southern Africa swallows are called *intaka zomzi* (birds of the home). For the swallow as friend of man, Aelian (*N.A.* 1.52) quotes lines from the *Odyssey* (15.72–4) about giving hospitality to a guest and speeding him on parting.

4. Note too the irony in Eur. *H.F.* of Heracles' return to the domestic hearth at 523 to save his family, only to kill them subsequently by the very *eschara* (922ff.).

5. The exceptional embargo on swallows in the house contained in the Pythagorean dictum χελιδόνα οἰκίᾳ μὴ δέχου ('receive not a swallow in the house'), variously interpreted, was doubtless due to the sage's dislike of their interruption of his treasured silence.

6. For a modern example of swallows' access to the house itself even in colder climates, see E. M. Nicholson, *Birds and Man* (London, 1951), 210: 'at one ancient house near Oxford where windows and doors were open throughout the summer, swallows regularly flew through the large hall.' Tate (op. cit., 51) reports that during a cold English autumn in 1979 'swallows hurled themselves at house windows in East Kent, apparently in an attempt to get inside out of the cold'.

7. Cf. Oppian, *Hal.* 5.579–86, Plut. *Mor.* 982 f.

8. It is true that Artemidorus also has a *less* favourable interpretation of swallow dreams, that they may presage θάνατον ἀώρων σωμάτων καὶ πένθος καὶ λύπην μεγάλην ('untimely death, lamentation, and great grief'), but, although the sequel in the *Odyssey* produced 108 such deaths, this does not seem to me such apposite symbolism as the Odysseus–Penelope conjugal reunion.

9. *A Study of Bird Song* (Oxford, 1963), 136, 159.

10. By a curious mis-recollection, Ann Amory ('The Reunion of Odysseus and Penelope' in *Essays on the Odyssey*, ed. C. W. Taylor, Indiana, 1963, 116) attributes the swallow note, not to the moment of stringing, but of actual shooting: 'the first arrow sings like a swallow.' This comparison is indeed not uncommon: cf. Shakespeare, *2 Hen. iv* 4.3.36 (Falstaff), 'Do you think me a swallow, an arrow, or a bullet?', Longfellow, *Hiawatha* xxi. 72, 'Homeward shoots the arrowy swallow', and Mary Howitt, 'The martin and the swallow / are God Almighty's bow and arrow'. In D'Annunzio's *L'innocente* (see below), swallows chase through the air 'with the speed of arrows', and 'with a sharp cry, like arrows from a bow'.

11. For the association of the αἴθυια with Athene, see D'Arcy Thompson, *Glossary of Greek Birds* (Oxford, 1936), 29.

12. Both αἰγυπίος and φήνη, said by Aelian (*N.A.* 12.4) to be sacred to Athene, are noted for φιλοστοργία ('family affection': see D'Arcy Thompson, s.vv.). For στοργή as the *mot juste* for Odysseus and his family, see schol. *Il.* 2.292. Gilbert White, in his account of *hirundines* nesting in chimneys, twice cites the word to characterize the natural propensities of swallows (*Natural History of Selborne*, Letters 18–22).

13. Whether it is actually a bird name, or refers to a bird leaving the hall through the ὀπή which lets out the smoke from the hearth, the swallow is obviously the appropriate bird to think of here. Boraston (loc. cit., 245) observes: 'The swallow is mentioned thrice by Homer, and always in the house of Ulysses; no other bird is made to appear there, and the swallow occurs nowhere else.'

14. *Similes in the Homeric Poems* (Göttingen, 1977), 139.

15. *Die Antike Tierwelt* (Leipzig, 1909), ii. 115.

16. According to A. de Vries (*Dictionary of Symbols and Imagery*, London, 1974, 449) swallows were sacrificed to the *Lares* because of their nests in the houses they guarded, and, to Tate (op. cit., 69), those injuring them were punished because they were sacred to the *Penates*. In neither case is a reference for the statement given, and I should be glad if any reader of this study can provide them.

17. Users of D'Arcy Thompson's *Glossary* may like to correct the mysterious reference (317) to Theoph. Samos. (without numerical location). I am grateful to Mr Nigel Wilson for identifying the correct passage for me.

18. *Birds with Human Souls: a Guide to Bird Symbolism* (Tennessee, 1978), 165. Unfortunately, she cites no references, but doubtless much derives from famous swallow references in *Ier.* 8.7 and *Ps.* 84.4. Ambrose (*Hex.* 5.17, vol.14 Migne) devotes a chapter *de hirundinis sedulitate, industria et pietate in filios* ('concerning the swallow's solicitude, its industry, and piety towards its children').

19. Staunton's emendation *love* for *lov'd* is convincing. It is not agreed whether Shakespeare's martlet here is the house-martin or the swift, but the former in particular shares many of the characteristics of the swallow in traditional beliefs. The association of swallows and temples is of course familiar in classical literature: e.g., Ar. *Lys.* 774, Eur. *Ion* 171, Clem. Alex. *Protr.* 4.52, and cf. *Ps.* 84, quoted above, on the swallow finding a nest for herself in the tabernacles and altars of the Lord.

20. It is incidentally curious that the lines following this song describe the reaction of the listeners, who 'like the Ithacensian suitors in old times / stared with great eyes, and laughed with alien lips', an allusion, of course, to the Theoclymenus prophecy of *Od.* 20.347, but the context of which closely parallels the description of the suitors' reaction to the stringing of the bow and its swallow note at 21.412.

21. I am indebted to my colleague Brian Phillips for the references in this paragraph, which are to the edition of *L'innocente* of Mondadori (Milan, 1979). For D'Annunzio's preoccupation with swallows, see also the curious details in the biography by T. Antongini (London, 1938), 328, 446. Nostalgia for the 'matrimonial nest' also lies behind Frederick Delius's calling the third movement of his String Quartet 'Late Swallows'—with reference to the happy associations of his wife's rural home at Grez. I might refer here to the fact that Puccini's opera *La Rondine* derives

its name symbolically from the theme of the ultimate return to the domestic hearth of an unfaithful woman who had 'flown away'.

22. *Beethoven Studies*, ed. Alan Tyson (New York, 1973), 123 ff. Beethoven was passionately devoted not only to the *Odyssey*, but to the severely pious nature almanac of C. C. Sturm, *Beobachtungen über die Werke Gottes im Reiche der Natur und der Vorsehung*, for whose observations about the instinctive powers of swallows to return to their old nests without compass to steer or direct, and their family devotion, see his entries for April 27, May 1 (both marked by B. in his own copy). About this same period he wrote down in his *Tagebuch* the unidentified Italian lines 'Scherz' amando la Rondinella, / lieto gode la tortorella, / io sola misera non io goder'—the familiar contrast of the happy state of the most faithful of birds, and the yearnings of the frustrated lover. (See *Beethoven Studies*, ed. Tyson III, Cambridge, 1982, 220.) For a curious comparison of the therapeutic qualities of B.'s own music to the swallow's family contentment, see J. D. M. Rorke, *A Musical Pilgrim's Progress* (Oxford, 1921), 10, 91–2.

23. 'No one can hear these songs adequately sung without feeling that there is something more in that music than the mere inspiration of the poetry', A. W. Thayer, *Life of L. van Beethoven* (New York, 1921) II, 343.

24. *Emerita* 42 (1974), 47 ff.

25. From his *Poemi Conviviali* (1904), of which W. B. Stanford gives a sympathetic résumé in *The Ulysses Theme* (London, 1963), 205–8.

26. Μαῦρα μου χελιδόνια ἀπ' τὴν ἔρημο, no. 259 in C. A. Trypanis, *The Penguin Book of Greek Verse* (1971). The appeal is addressed also to περιστέρια (doves), the other traditionally faithful birds.

'BUT WHY HAS MY SPIRIT SPOKEN WITH ME THUS?': HOMERIC DECISION-MAKING[1]

By R. W. SHARPLES

It has been argued, above all by Bruno Snell,[2] that there is lacking in the Homeric poems any notion of the 'self' as an integrated whole; the individual is regarded rather as an assembly of more or less independent psychic forces. There can thus, it is argued, be no making of decisions by individuals in the Homeric poems, because there is no such thing as a psychic whole which could decide; in his *Scenes from Greek Drama*, Snell argues not only that Homer in the *Iliad* does not explicitly present Achilles as *deciding* to avenge Patroclus and die young, but also that there are differences in outlook between Homer and Aeschylus which mean that Homer *could not* portray such a decision, whereas Aeschylus could.[3]

It may well be felt that there must be something wrong with an interpretation which leads to so paradoxical a conclusion. What I want to do here is to consider another way—suggested by Voigt in 1934—of looking at one group of passages which can be seen as supporting it, those in which a character is represented as conversing with his spirit or *thumos*, and then to go on to draw some contrasts and parallels with later, philosophical writers. The group of passages follow a conventional formulaic pattern, but it should not be supposed that their wording lacks significance for that reason alone; we may begin by considering two of them.[4]

And in distress (Odysseus) spoke to his great-hearted *thumos*: 'Alas, what will become of me? It is very bad if I flee fearing their numbers; but more chilling if I am captured alive; the son of Cronus has put the other Greeks to flight. But why has my *thumos* spoken with me thus? For I know that it is cowards who flee the battle, and whoever is best in battle, he must hold his ground valiantly, whether he is wounded or wounds another.' While he was pondering these things in (his) *phrēn* and (his) *thumos*, the ranks of the shield-bearing Trojans came on . . .   (*Iliad* 11.403–12)

And in distress (Hector) spoke to his great-hearted *thumos*: 'Alas, if I enter the gates and walls, Polydamas will be the first to reproach me, who indeed told me to lead the Trojans back to the city before this terrible nightfall, when Achilles came on. But I was not persuaded; it would indeed have been much better. Now, as I have caused men to be lost by my presumptuous folly, I am ashamed before the Trojan men and the Trojan women with their trailing robes, in case someone else inferior to me should say, "Hector trusted in his own strength and caused men to be lost." That is what they will say; it would then be far better for me to meet Achilles face to face and either return after slaying him or perish myself gloriously before the city. But if I put my bossed shield and strong helmet down, and leant my spear against the wall, and myself were to meet noble Achilles and promised to give him Helen and goods with her to take to the sons of Atreus, all that Paris brought in his hollow ships to Troy—and that was the beginning of the dispute; and at the same time to give other things to the Achaeans, all that this city conceals; and if at the same time I took an oath from the Trojan elders not to hide anything, but to divide equally all the possessions that the lovely city contains within it—but why has my *thumos* spoken with me thus? If I went up to him he would not pity or respect me, but would kill me there and then unarmed like a woman, when I had taken off my armour. It is not now possible to converse with him from rock or tree in the way a young man and a maiden, a young man and a maiden converse with each other. It is better to meet in battle as soon as possible; let us know to which of us the Olympian will give the victory.' So he pondered as he waited, and Achilles drew near to him . . .   (*Iliad* 22.98–131)

Firstly, it should be noted that in both these passages the speaker makes reference to 'me' as well as to the *thumos*. The passages in fact display the same pattern. The argument on one side is put, and this is rejected with the words 'but why has my *thumos* spoken with me thus?'—where 'my' translates *philos*—and a statement of the considerations that lead to the course of action eventually adopted. The situation is slightly more complex in *Iliad* 22, in that there yet another course of action—return to Troy—has been considered and rejected before the choice between parleying with Achilles and fighting is made; but the basic pattern is the same.[5] It might indeed be argued that the choice between parleying and fighting is no real choice at all, the former being impossible; but that is a reflection of the situation, not a sign that Hector is not an individual person and capable of making decisions. The rejection of flight in both passages rests on what one may broadly call moral grounds; it is typical of Homeric values that the issue is presented in terms of loss of face, explicitly in Iliad 22,[6] and that it is stated in terms of what is a *bad*, or a *better*, course of action.[7] A broadly similar process of decision-making is presented, in the third person this time and without reference to the *thumos*, in a passage from *Odyssey* 22—though here what is 'better' or 'more profitable' is more obviously a matter of self-interest even to our way of thinking:

(Phemius) pondered two ways in his *phrenes*, whether he should go out of the hall and sit as a suppliant by the well-built altar of great Zeus of the Enclosure, where Laertes and Odysseus had burned many thighs of oxen, or whether he should rush up to Odysseus and entreat him by his knees. And this way seemed more profitable to him as he pondered, to clasp the knees of Odysseus son of Laertes . . .   (*Odyssey* 22.333–9)

In both of the *Iliad* passages—as Hermann Fränkel pointed out in the case of that from *Iliad* 11[8]—the discussion is introduced as an address *by* the person *to* his *thumos*; it is only subsequently that the very same words are described by the person involved as something his *thumos* has said *to* him. And in each case the passage is summed up by a description of the person as pondering these things *in* his *thumos*. These fluctuations, it would seem, are not purely arbitrary. Rather, what we have in the two *Iliad* passages is a milder form of that distancing of certain actions and impulses from the self that can be seen as underlying Homeric references to *menos* and *atē*.[9] With hindsight, a character finds it difficult to regard certain actions as his own—either because he would not normally be capable of them, or because they now seem foolish; so he ascribes them to forces outside himself.[10] Somewhat similarly, the description of what was *introduced* as a course of action contemplated by the character himself rather than as a course of action suggested *to* him *by* his *thumos* can be seen as an expression of his repudiation of it. It is true, of course, that 'he spoke to his great-hearted *thumos*' are the poet's own words as narrator, while 'why has my *thumos* spoken with me thus?' are words that he puts in the mouths of his characters; but, rather than supposing that a contrast should be drawn between the poet's way of understanding such internal debates and that which he ascribes to his characters, it seems more plausible to suppose that the shift of expression reflects the fact that we have reached a different stage in the decision-making process as the poet presents it to his audience.

This interpretation may also explain another Homeric passage which is cited as evidence for the lack of the notion of an integrated self in Homer:

I purposed in my great-hearted *thumos* to go up to (the Cyclops) drawing my sharp sword from beside my thigh, clutch it in my hand and pierce him through the breast, where the midriff surrounds the liver. But another *thumos* held me back. For we too would have perished utterly there; for we would not have been able with our hands to push away from the door the huge stone which he had placed against it. So for a while, grieving, we waited for the holy Dawn . . .   (*Odyssey* 9.299–306)

Surely the point here is that the eventual decision, to wait for the dawn, is one which Odysseus takes only reluctantly; thus, he presents it not simply as his judgement of the situation, but as a force holding him back against his inclination, even though the force is one which reflects his own sound judgement. One might of course object that Hector's decision to fight in *Iliad* 22 is also a reluctant one; but that, perhaps, is to forget Homeric values—it is a good thing to fight your enemy, even if you perish in the process, but it is not a good thing to have to refrain from attacking your enemy, and do nothing at all, because you are dependent on him for your survival.

While Snell argued that Homeric man is not a single integrated self but an assemblage of more or less independent psychic forces, Fränkel argues that Homeric man in fact seems remarkably *simple*; his actions are actions of the whole man, even if—or, perhaps, *because*—the dividing line between self and the external world is less clear than for us.[11] It is in fact precisely because Homeric man can so easily distinguish from his 'self' or contrast with it the sources of impulses which he rejects, that that 'self' can remain simple. There is indeed, as Snell pointed out, no *term* for this 'self' in Homer;[12] but the first person personal pronoun serves to indicate it, as it does for us when we are not reflecting on these issues at a second-order level. And, it must be stressed, the situation is always a *dynamic* one; the boundaries of the self are not fixed, but fluctuate, even within the course of a single decision-making process.[13]

Snell's picture of Homeric man as a collection of psychic forces, with its consequent difficulty concerning exactly who or what it is that makes a decision, might with more justice be attributed, not to Homer, but to Plato. In *Republic* 4 the soul is divided into three parts, reason, *thumos*, and desire; and internal conflict is explained in terms of conflict between these. But if these are in conflict, suggesting different courses of action, what is the self that actually takes the decision? Plato is, of course, drawing an analogy between the three parts of the soul and the three classes in his Ideal State—the rational rulers, the spirited soldiers, and the acquisitive productive class. He has often been criticized, notably by Popper,[14] for adopting the 'organic' view of the state as a kind of super-person—to the interests of which those of the individuals in it must be subservient, as those of the parts of the body must be to the whole. But he may also be criticized, conversely, for adopting a 'political' view of the individual soul.[15] There is no 'state' that takes decisions other than, over and above, the classes within it; and, similarly, it is not clear how there can be a self other than, over and above, the three conflicting parts of the soul. What we regard as the making of a decision will in fact be the prevailing of one part, because it is stronger, over another, which is weaker; and that, it may be argued, is not so much a description of decision-making as we know it, as in fact something else which is not decision-making at all. Further, whereas Homer's accounts of decision-making are not intended to form part of a systematic psychological theory, Plato's account of the tripartite soul is;[16] and for that very reason it is the more open to the objection that it seems in fact to do away with the deciding self altogether.[17]

At *Laws* 1 644c ff., indeed, as Adkins points out,[18] Plato, portraying man as a puppet of the gods worked by the strings of judgement, pleasure and pain, and fear and confidence, says that *we* should always yield to the pull of the golden cord of judgement, while resisting the others. Here there is certainly a unified, deciding self—as Adkins points out, the picture is not a deterministic one, since we have the power to resist the pull of the cords. But the unification of the deciding self is only achieved by placing outside us, in the image at least, those impulses that were in the *Republic* attributed to the parts of the soul; the strings are not parts of the puppet. Even if we do not press the image, but regard the psychological forces represented by the strings as parts of the self,[19] no explanation is given of how the part that actually decides—the puppet itself—relates to them. And, furthermore, judgement is placed on the same level as the other impulses; this may be satisfactory in the context in the *Laws*, which is concerned with obedience to law as the civic embodiment of judgement, but would it satisfy Plato in other contexts, seeing that he regards the individual's reason as the highest part of the soul, and, in the *Timaeus* at least, as the only part which is immortal?[20]

Snell's picture of man in the Homeric poems, then, seems to apply to Plato, in some passages at least, rather than to Homer. Aristotle and the Stoics took a different view of internal conflicts from Plato; and it is not without interest that there are certain points of similarity between *their* views and the Homeric poems.[21] Aristotle, in *Nicomachean Ethics* 7.3, attempts to explain how there can be moral weakness—how a man can know what he should do, but yet act otherwise—by suggesting that the knowledge is temporarily rendered inoperative in the presence of a more immediate temptation;[22] as to *why* this happens in some cases and not in others, he seems in one passage at least to suggest that the ultimate explanation is a physiological one (1147b 6–9). Although he distinguishes between the man who fails to abide by his resolution once formed and the man who acts impetuously (ibid. 7.7 1150b 19ff.; 7.8 1151a 1ff.; 7.10 1152a 27ff.), his general treatment does seem more suited to moral weakness in the form of a temporary lapse—one might almost say a temporary moral blindness—than to a conscious struggle between conflicting impulses in which the better impulse eventually fails; and this may seem not unlike Homeric *atē*,[23] with the difference that there is now no implication that its source is outside the agent.

The early Stoics argued that moral conflict is not a tension between different parts of the soul; rather, it is a rapid oscillation between conflicting judgements (Plutarch, *Moralia* 441c = H. von Arnim, *Stoicorum Veterum Fragmenta* 1.202, 3.459).[24] The ruling part of the soul (as opposed to the reproductive soul, the five senses, and the power of speech) is a unity. This Stoic picture can be seen as an improvement on Aristotle; where his analysis is more suited to a temporary lapse than to an actual moral conflict, the Stoics are able, by appealing to the rapidity of the oscillation between judgements, to explain the appearance of conflict and tension without sacrificing the unity of the soul.

This Stoic theory differs from the Homeric accounts of decision-making, the conversations with the *thumos*, precisely in that it is clear, and indeed emphasized, that in the Stoic view it is a single entity, the ruling part of the soul, which entertains the conflicting judgements. But there does seem to be a certain affinity, not only between the Stoic theory and the temporary blindness of Homeric *atē*, but also between the Stoic theory and the presentation of alternative viewpoints in the debate of the Homeric hero with his *thumos*. For, while the Homeric account does not consistently attribute the presentation of the different viewpoints to a single self, it does not *consistently* attribute a particular viewpoint to the *thumos* and another to the self either. The Stoic view, emphasizing the alternation between different judgements, may thus have more in common with the Homeric view of the matter than does Plato's analysis in *Republic* 4.

NOTES

1. Versions of this paper were read to the Classics Staff Seminar at the London Regional Office of the Open University, and to a seminar on Homer in University College London. I am most grateful to all who were present on these occasions for their comments and suggestions.

2. *The Discovery of the Mind*, tr. T. G. Rosenmeyer (Harvard, 1953), ch. 1; cf. E. R. Dodds, *The Greeks and the Irrational* (Berkeley, 1951), 15 ff. The view is criticized by H. Lloyd-Jones, *The Justice of Zeus* (1971), 8 ff.

3. B. Snell, *Scenes from Greek Drama* (Berkeley, 1964), 1 f. My colleague James Hooker suggests to me that *Iliad* 9 can be seen precisely as an extended depiction of the making of a decision by Achilles, the stages of the process being presented in his successive speeches.

4. Other passages which exhibit a similar pattern are *Iliad* 17.90 ff. (Menelaus) and 21.552 ff. (Agenor); C. Voigt, *Ueberlegung und Entscheidung bei Homer* (Berlin, 1934), 92, 94. I have translated as literally as possible, with no attempt at elegance; for discussions like the present, where it is with the details of the wording that we are concerned, this seems most appropriate.

5. In the passage from *Iliad* 11, as in that from *Odyssey* 22 (below), the course eventually adopted is one of those mentioned before the decision is taken; in that from *Iliad* 22 it is not—which has the effect of heightening the pathos.

6. Dodds, above n. 2, 17 f.; A. W. H. Adkins, *Merit and Responsibility* (Oxford, 1960), 46 ff.

7. From Homer to Aristotle (and beyond), the tendency of Greek thought is to formulate decisions in terms of assessing what is the best course for the individual to follow. This applies both to the conduct of life as a whole—the central question of ethics being 'what way of life is most conducive to *eudaimonia*?' (Adkins, above n. 6, 253)—and to individual decisions. Socrates' approach to decision-making in terms of the comparison of the consequences for oneself of different courses of action (Plato, *Protagoras* 356 ff.; Xenophon, *Memorabilia* 3.9.4) is only the generalization of the approach we already find in *Iliad* 22, even if the criteria by which the consequences are assessed differ from one context to another.

8. *Early Greek Poetry and Philosophy*, tr. M. Hadas and J. Willis (Oxford, 1975), 79 n. 11.

9. Dodds (above n. 2), ch. 1, especially 13 ff.

10. Cf., on *Iliad* 11.403 ff., Voigt (above n. 4), 89 f. I am not here advocating a reductivist approach—one that would claim that the significance of references to divine intervention in Homer can be exhausted by their explanation in terms of the individual's psychology. But the attempt to relate aspects of the Homeric presentation of these occurrences to features of our own experience may assist us in understanding it. In the study of ancient thought in general, whether in technical philosophical writers or elsewhere, there is a place both for the synchronic approach —comparing the responses of ancient and modern thinkers to what are often essentially the same issues—and for the historical one; the important thing is to be aware of the difference between them.

11. Fränkel (above n. 8), 79 ff.

12. Snell, loc. cit. (above n. 2); Dodds (above n. 2), 15 f.; Fränkel (above n. 8), 76 ff. *Psuche*, the later term for the 'soul' of the living man, is only used of the dead or dying in Homer.

13. It should also be pointed out, with Adkins (above n. 6), 314 n. 12, that there are passages in Homer where there is no suggestion that it is anything other than the self that is taking the decision; e.g., *Iliad* 1.189 ff.

14. K. R. Popper, *The Open Society and its Enemies*[5] (London, 1966), i. 79–81.

15. Cf. Popper, op. cit., 79 n. 32.

16. It is, after all, repeated in the *Timaeus* (69c ff.) and in the myth of the *Phaedrus*. At the same time, there may be a danger of seeing Plato as more committed to a particular analysis than he in fact is; he does introduce the doctrine of the tripartite soul in the *Republic* in a particular context and for a particular purpose, and it may be a mistake to see him as concerned to give a definitive account of the soul there in the way that Aristotle, for example, is in the *de Anima*.

17. It is true that other passages, such as *Republic* 6 486d, give a rather different picture; but it is not clear how they are to be reconciled with *Republic* 4. It is also true that in the Ideal State —or the philosophical individual—there is no problem; reason, or the Guardian-Rulers, rule and take the decisions. Further, Plato in the *Republic* still holds, with Socrates, that all wrong-doing is the result of ignorance; if a person's desires triumph over his reason, that is because the person as a whole lacks knowledge (586a; cf. *Timaeus* 86b). But it is precisely the interpretation of the outcome of moral conflict as the prevailing of one force over another, with no 'self' actually deciding between them, which raises the objection. At the same time, it must be recognized that there will be decisions which do not involve a conflict between the parts of the soul, and that these do not raise a problem; presumably, in these cases whichever part of the soul is predominant in a given individual will do the deciding.

18. Adkins, above n. 6, 302.

19. Cf. 'these emotions in us', 644e 1.

20. 69c ff.; above n. 15. Cf. W. K. C. Guthrie, 'Plato's Views on the Nature of the Soul', *Entretiens Hardt* 3 (1955), 2–19, reprinted in G. Vlastos (ed.), *Plato* (Garden City, N.Y., 1971), Vol. II ch. 15.

21. The position of the historical Socrates on this issue was idiosyncratic, and hence best treated in a footnote. Unlike Plato, it seems clear that he regarded the soul as a unity; as for Homer, Aristotle, and the Stoics, so for Socrates at any given time there is only one answer to the question 'which course of action does X think best?' But, uniquely among Greek thinkers (for the Stoics did not confine their attention to the sage) and notoriously, Socrates does not seem to have countenanced weakness of will or temporary lapses at all; if Agamemnon suffered a temporary lapse and acted, by taking Achilles' prize, in a way he later regretted, then that would be a sign for Socrates that *as a general truth* Agamemnon did not possess the knowledge that would have told him how to behave.

22. On this chapter see the discussion by W. F. R. Hardie, *Aristotle's Ethical Theory*[2] (Oxford, 1980), 258–93.

23. Above n. 9.

24. Posidonius reverted from this view, holding that even if there were not distinct *parts* of the soul, as Plato had said, there were distinct rational and irrational *faculties* which could be in conflict with each other (cf. Galen, *On the Opinions of Hippocrates and Plato*, 5.5.32–5, 5.7.3, and 6.2.5; respectively *Corpus Medicorum Graecorum* vol. 5.4.1.2 p. 324.2–23, 336.23–6, and 368.20–6 de Lacy).

ADDENDUM

See further Richard Gaskin, 'Do Homeric heroes make real decisions?', *CQ* 40 (1990), 1–15, and Bernard Williams, *Shame and Necessity* (Berkeley, 1993), 21–49.

HOMERIC SURVIVALS IN THE MEDIEVAL AND MODERN GREEK FOLKSONG TRADITION?

By G. M. SIFAKIS

The basis of comparison between the Homeric poetry and modern Greek folksong is that in either case we have a body of poetic texts behind which stretches a long tradition of oral composition; they both have existed, roughly, in the same geographical area, including mainland Greece, Asia Minor, the islands of the Aegean and the Ionian Sea, Crete, and Cyprus; and they are cast in cognate language forms. But the two bodies of poetry are separated by a great time distance, though how great it is difficult to determine because whatever we can say about the origins of modern folksongs is hypothetical and uncertain.

Origins of folksongs

The only songs for which we have a *terminus post quem* are the historical ones (for example, all the songs about the Fall of Constantinople must have been composed after 1453, when the Polis fell to the Turks), although they may include earlier formulae and motifs. But when we look, say, for the origin of the songs of the 'Akritic' cycle, i.e., the songs about the struggles of the guards of the eastern frontiers (ἄκραι) of Byzantium against, chiefly, Arab invaders, we enter, as it were, the mists of prehistory and myth. The origins of Akritic songs are thought to coincide with the events to which they refer (from the 8th to the 11th century), but in the course of the oral epic tradition the historical personages of the songs assumed mythical proportions, and very seldom they, or the events told in the songs, can plausibly be referred to historical events and personalities known from written historical sources.[1]

When we proceed to probe into the origins of ballads, we find ourselves in the land of timeless folktale. Yet it may be worthwhile to mention here an influential theory proposed about forty years ago by the late Stilpon Kyriakides.[2] According to him, the origins of the ballads go back to the performances of the so-called 'dancers' or 'pantomimes' of Late Antiquity. The pantomimes were also called 'actors of tragic dancing' because they represented, by means of their dancing which was a solo performance, tragic stories, while a group of musicians, comprising both singers and instrumentalists, accompanied them by singing a simplified and shortened version of a tragedy. What these accompanists did was called τραγῳδεῖν and the singers themselves, by a strange sort of poetic justice, were called τραγῳδοί. These performances, highly praised by such representatives of the Second Sophistic as Lucian and Libanius, brought the history of tragedy to a lyric exodos, so to speak, just before tragedy became extinct. And as prior to the time of radio broadcasting and the gramophone, the stage of musical theatre and variety shows was the source of songs that would be picked up by the spectators and eventually become fashionable and popular, so the performances of tragic singers and dancers were the source of songs that have come to be what we know today as folk ballads.

Ballads do contain such motifs as a woman killing her own child and serving his flesh to his father to eat, a woman being sacrificed to secure the success of a great undertaking, and so on; but are such motifs tragic, as Kyriakides thought, or merely mythical, i.e., what we nowadays call motifs of folk literature? Ballads do not show strings or configurations of motifs that would suggest derivation of modern songs from specific tragedies.[3] On the other hand, the modern Greek words for singing and song, τραγουδῶ (a late form of τραγῳδέω) and τραγούδι (from τραγῴδιον, diminutive of τραγῳδία), lend support to Kyriakides's theory and point unmistakably to Late Antiquity. Yet, more work remains to be done on paratheatrical performances and popular entertainers in Hellenistic and Roman times before we can either accept without reservation or reject the main line of argument of this theory.

Literacy and oral tradition

However, even if we extend the origins of whole categories or of specific songs into Late Antiquity[4] there still remain several centuries that separate them from Homer's time—*though by no means from people familiar with Homeric poetry*. I cannot go into the question of Homer's *Nachleben*, but I should like to point out, in the first place, that it began shortly after the eighth century B.C. and coincided with the commitment of his epics to writing. This is what made them accessible for public performance at festivals all over the Greek world, as well as for reading at schools in antiquity (and in Byzantine times). We may confidently extend E. G. Turner's assertion that 'Homer continued to be the best-read author' in Graeco-Roman Egypt to the whole Greek-speaking world in antiquity.[5]

Be that as it may, we should not underestimate the importance of oral tradition even in times of (relatively) widespread literacy. In fact, literacy in antiquity was widespread only in the sense that it was not confined to professional scribes but was part of the basic education available to children (mainly to boys) in most Greek cities. But this kind and level of literacy has nothing to do with our own concept and the uses of literacy we take for granted. Large sections of the population were illiterate, others were semi-literate but had neither the opportunities nor the ability to read for pleasure.[6] We must, therefore, understand that oral tradition in antiquity (as well as in medieval times) is a concept much wider than the tradition of *aoidoi*, the early epic singers,[7] and involves many aspects of ancient culture and masses of population, spread over large geographical areas, throughout many centuries.

Another point that must be made here is that limited literacy, confined as it was to a relatively small percentage of the population which nevertheless included rhapsodes, actors, and popular entertainers such as *homeristai* (paratheatrical performers of the epics in later antiquity, apparently a variety of mimes),[8] broadened the horizon of oral tradition and enriched it. Stated simply, oral tradition (in the wider sense of an orally transmitted multifaceted culture) could not come to an end for as long as there were illiterate people in adequate numbers to use it and function as its carriers.

Cultural circumstances, in Early as well as in Late Antiquity (with the possible exception of classical Athens), could hardly be taken to have been more favourable to the spread and applications of literacy than in many Greek-speaking areas in, for example, the 17th or 18th century, when modern folksong was fully operative as a system of poetic expression and communication. The type of society to which Greek-speaking communities (more precisely perhaps the ones outside a few major cities) belonged, being basically medieval in character,[9] was not illiterate though its traditional literature was oral. The Church, on the other hand, employed the ancient language in its services,[10] public administration was conducted with the help of writing, legal transactions were conducted by means of written documents, as was official, commercial, and some private correspondence. It was society, then, which was fully aware of the power of the written word; but only a small percentage of its members were aware of written literature, or read certain types of literary works. Otherwise, the great majority (a considerable part of which was completely illiterate) was unaware or made no *direct* use of written literature.

'Direct' is a significant qualification because in addition to purely oral creations such as folksongs, fairy tales, animal tales, *ætia*, and the like, it is more and more recognized nowadays that several works of Byzantine and post-Byzantine vernacular literature had a parallel oral transmission: read aloud on various occasions by literate persons, they were picked up by members of an illiterate (or half-literate) audience, and were eventually written down again from memory or dictation; and while this theory seeks to explain wide divergences in the manuscript tradition of Byzantine works,[11] it is a fact that short versions or extended passages of works of

Cretan Renaissance literature, such as *The Shepherdess, Erotokritos,* and *Erophile,* have been recorded by scholars in Crete and elsewhere in recent times.[12]

The case of *Erotokritos,* the monumental narrative masterpiece of Cretan literature, is of particular interest for our discussion. Written in the idiom of eastern Crete by Vitsenzos Kornaros, a learned poet, who probably composed his work in the early seventeenth century (not very long before the fall of Crete to the Turks), it became during the period of Turkish occupation extremely popular not only in Crete but in many other areas as well; and the characters of its protagonists, Erotokritos and Aretousa, 'entered the realm of modern Greek popular mythology'.[13] I doubt if any villager could be found on Crete, up to the middle of this century, who would not know the story of Erotokritos or would not be able to sing or recite some lines of the poem. But if contemporary Cretans are mostly literate we may be sure that their forefathers in the previous two centuries were quite the opposite.[14]

Language evolution and oral poetry

The above considerations hardly suffice to suggest a *continuous* oral poetic tradition from antiquity to modern times. But if they help us, as I submit they do, to assume that a certain degree of familiarity with Homeric poetry was, throughout antiquity, a part of the cultural background of the average Greek, regardless of his or her schooling, it may then be legitimate to imagine that bits of poetry survived and were transmitted in the same way and by the same process by which the Greek language evolved after the end of antiquity. After all, plain language and traditional oral poetry are two overlapping systems of communication utilizing the same units of signification, except that poetry combines and binds them together into larger units (formulae, metaphors, images, etc.), operating as it does at a secondary level of meaning and communication.

This comparison of poetry with language implies that potential survivals of poetry should not be expected to be entire poems or discrete fragments of poems but rather formative elements of poetic expression, which may have survived as such although they have undergone linguistic changes; or, to put it in more technical terms, which retained their character as poetical signs while they underwent transformation or even translation as verbal signs. To this general category of formative elements motifs and motifemes[15] also belong; indeed, it is to this field of research, i.e., to the identification of motifs of folk literature in Homer, and their comparison with similar motifs in other literary genres, mainly the folktale, that significant contributions have been made.[16]

The study of thematic motifs in Homer looks very promising, particularly if modern methods of narrative analysis should be brought to bear upon it, but limitation of space prevents me from going into it (although a brief reference to it will be made in the last section of this paper). I shall, therefore, concentrate on smaller elements of poetic discourse, in which form and content are examined as a unit. These elements are *signs*, in the linguistic (and semiotic) sense of the term, occupying part of a line (ancient hexameter or modern fifteen-syllable iambic), sometimes a whole line. My examples are roughly classified into *common speech expressions*, *representations of common practices*, *metaphors and similes*, and *idealized images*.

Common speech expressions

Perceptive readers have not failed to notice a considerable number of expressions in Homer and in folksongs, which correspond exactly in meaning;[17] e.g.:

1a. ἀλλήλους τ᾽ εἴροντο (*Od.* 17.368)
(They asked each other).

1b. κι ὁ γ-εῖς τὸν ἄλλο ἀναρωτᾶ (Crete, B 177)
(They asked each other).

2a. κλαῖον ὀδυρόμενοι (*Od.* 10.454; cf. 8.577, *Il.* 24.48)
(They cried and lamented).

2b. ἔκλαιεν καὶ ὀδύρονταν κι ἐτράβα τὰ μαλλιά της
(Rhodes, Mart. 40; cf. *Digenis Akritis*, E version, 182)
(She cried and lamented and tore her hair).

3a. ἐπὶ γούνασι θῆκε (*Od.* 19.401; cf. *Il.* 21.506)
(She put him on his knees).

3b. στὰ γόνατα τὴν ἔβαλε (Epirus, B 27)
(She put her on her knees).

4a. βαρὺ στενάχων (*Il.* 1.364, 4.153, etc.)
βαρέα στενάχοντα (*Il.* 7.334, *Od.* 4.516, etc.)
(Groaning heavily).

4b. καὶ βαριαναστενάζει (Karpathos, etc.)
βαριὰ κι ἀναστενάζει (Chios, Promp. I, 23)
(Groaning heavily).

5a. αἴ κέν μοι δώῃ Ζεύς . . . (*Il.* 8.287)
αἴ κέ ποθι Ζεὺς | δῶσι (*Il.* 1.128–9)
(If ever Zeus would grant me).

5b. ἂν δώσει ὁ Θεός . . .; νὰ δώσει ὁ Θεός . . .(common)
(If God should grant . . .).

5c. μὴ τοῦτο θεὸς τελέσειε (*Od.* 17.399)
     (God may not do that).

5d. ὁ Θεὸς νὰ μὴν τὸ κάμει (Crete)
     (God may not do it).

6a. χαίρει δέ μοι ἦτορ (*Il.* 23.647)
     γήθησε δέ μοι φίλον ἦτορ (*Od.* 7.269)
     (And my heart is happy).

6b. καὶ νὰ χαρεῖ ἡ καρδιά μου (Man. II, 68)
     καὶ νὰ χαρεῖ ἡ ψυχή της (*Digenis* E, 997)
     (And my heart/her soul be happy).

7a. ἐμοί γε κατεκλάσθη φίλον ἦτορ
     (*Od.* 4.481, 538, 10.496; cf. 9.256, 10.198, etc.)
     (My heart was broken).

7b. κι ἐμὲ ἡ καρδιά μου ἐρράγη (Syros)
     ἐρράην ἡ καρδιά μου (Karpathos; Promp. II, 83)
     (My heart was broken).

Although these parallel phrases—and many others that could easily be added to them—are very similar in form and meaning, it is difficult to know whether they are directly related as verse parts, because they are expressions apparently used in many historical periods of the Greek language; so they could also have been used in poetry time and again—though we cannot tell whether their use in everyday language was due to poetry, or vice versa. Their significance lies in that they testify to the continuity of spoken Greek; on the other hand, they are idiomatic enough to merit our attention in relation to the phrase groups mentioned below.

Representations of common practices

Poetry, Aristotle says, is an imitation of life, a representation of πράττοντες, men and women in action. It is to be expected, therefore, that certain typical practices, or characteristic actions, would be represented by poetry; e.g.:
    Grief is often expressed by tearing one's hair:

8a. ἡ δέ νυ μήτηρ / τίλλε κόμην . . . (*Il.* 22.405-7)
     τίλλοντό τε χαίτας (*Od.* 10.567)
     (His mother tore her hair . . . They tore their hair).

8b. ἔκλαιεν καὶ ὀδύρονταν κι ἐτράβα τὰ μαλλιά της
     (Rhodes, Mart. 40)
     ἔσερνε τὰ μαλλιάν τση
     (Crete, B1, 117; more examples cited in Promp. II, 110)
     (She cried and lamented and tore her hair/She tore her hair).

Striking one's thighs was another gesture of agony and desperation:

9a. ὤμωξέν τ' ἄρ' ἔπειτα καὶ ὢ πεπλήγετο μηρὼ
     χερσὶ καταπρηνέσσ', ὀλοφυρόμενος δ' ἔπος ηὔδα
     (*Il.* 15.397–8; cf. 113–14)
     ([Patroklos] groaned aloud then and struck himself on both thighs
     with the flats of his hands and spoke a word of lamentation
     [Lattimore]).

9b. ἐκλούθα κι ὁ παπὰ-Βαρδῆς κι ἔδερνε τσὶ μερούς του
     (Crete, B1, 160)
     (Father Varthis followed and kept smacking his thighs).

The horrible punishment of cutting off the nose and ears of traitors and enemies seems to have been known to Homer as well as to poets of Byzantine Akritic songs:

10a. τοῦ δ' ἀπὸ μὲν ῥῖνάς τε καὶ οὔατα νηλέϊ χαλκῷ | τάμνον
     (*Od.* 22.475–6; cf. 18.86)
     (They cut off his nostrils and ears with the pitiless bronze).

10b. κόβκει τοῦ Τρεμοδάχτυλου τὴ μύτη καὶ τ' αὐκιά του
     (Naxos, etc., Promp. I, 21)
     (He cuts off Tremodakhtylos' nose and ears).

Young women *go down* to a spring or fountain to fetch water:

11a. ἡ μὲν ἄρ' ἐς κρήνην κατεβήσετο καλλιρέεθρον (*Od.* 10.107)
     (She came down to the fair-flowing spring).

11b. μιὰ λυγερὴ κατέβαινε στὴ βρύση νὰ γεμίσει (Crete, A 19)
     (A slim girl was coming down to the fountain to fill [her pitcher] up).

It is a question, however, whether we have here independent reflections of a common practice in each case—and a landscape feature at that!—or poetic expressions, which have been transformed and adapted to different contexts. The latter seems to me at least as likely as the former.

Metaphors and similes

Metaphors and similes, common to Homeric poetry and modern folksongs, can easily be found. Thus, a little boy or a pretty girl are likened to a star (*Il.* 6.401; Sporades, Lüd. 46); the arms of a brave fighter appear to glow as he moves (*Il.* 4.432, 13.245, 22.26, 32; Crete, Lüd. 128; Kerkyra, Man. II, 40, 102); fighters resemble wild beasts (*Il.* 3.449, 11.546; Crete, Jean. 37; Kerkyra, Man. I, 206), spring at their enemies like a lion (*Il.* 11.129, 20.164, etc.; Peloponnese, *Laogr.* 1 [1909] 222; Cyprus, Lüd. 216; more examples cited by Promp. I, 91), fall down when they are killed like felled trees (*Il.* 4.482 [poplar], 5.560 [fir-tree], 13.178 [ash],

13.389–90 [oak, pine trees]; Fauriel I, 20 [cypress]); a man's or a woman's
heart burns (rather than bleeds) for someone suffering or being far away
(see below); a man wishes that the earth might swallow him rather than be
disgraced (Il. 4.182, 6.282, 8.150, 17.416; Crete, Promp. I, 132); a palace
or house shines like, or is to its owners, the sun and the moon (see below);
stars and leaves are the greatest of multitudes to which any large number
of objects or people can be compared (Il. 8.555 [stars], 2.800 [leaves];
Cyprus, Chios, Thrace, etc., see Petr. 359); a man's or woman's tears flow
like a fountain (see below), or like a river (Od. 19.207–8; Crete, Petr.
365), and so on.

Such figures are not necessarily significant by themselves, because some
of them may be universal; they may represent, that is, universal crystal-
lizations of human experience into concrete images. Some others may be
culture-bound but, although it is poetry that more often than not creates
them, they subsequently enter everyday language, whence they can re-
enter poetry at any time. However, in some cases ancient and modern
expressions are so close that they suggest a direct relationship. Take, for
instance, the following examples:

12a. ἀλλά μοι ἀμφ' Ὀδυσῆϊ δαΐφρονι δαίεται ἦτορ (Od. 1.48)
(But my heart burns for wise Odysseus).

12b. νὰ μὴ θωρῶ τοὺς φίλους μου καὶ καίετ' ἡ καρδιά μου
(Chios, Promp. I, 27)
(that I may not see my friends, and my heart burns).

13a. ὥς τε γὰρ ἠελίου αἴγλη πέλεν ἠὲ σελήνης
δῶμα καθ' ὑψερεφὲς Μενελάου κυδαλίμοιο
(Od. 4.45–6; cf. 7.84–5)
(A luminescence like that of the sun or the moon was over the high-
roofed palace of noble Menelaus).

13b. Μάνα μου, τὸ παλάτι μας εἶν' ἥλιος καὶ φεγγάρι
(Chios, Kan. 38; cf. Promp. I, 69)
(Mother, our palace is [like] the sun and the moon).

14a. δάκρυα θερμὰ χέων ὥς τε κρήνη μελάνυδρος
(Il. 16.3; cf. 9.14)
([Patroklos] stood by him and wept warm tears, like a spring dark-
running [Lattimore]).

14b. ἐτρέχαν τὰ ματάκια ντου σὰν τὴν κατάχλυα βρύση
(Naxos, Promp. I, 89)
(His eyes were running like a spring shrouded in darkness).

Tears flowing like a spring, in example 14, may be a universal image, but
a dark-water spring is not. Lattimore's translation here is not perhaps very
successful, for it is the spring itself which is dark either because it is
assumed to be in a rock cavity (or cave) or because the water is collected

in a deep cavity that looks dark to those who bend down to drink. The word κατάχλυα, a rare poetic gloss not used in casual speech, is synonymous to μελάνυδρος and cognate to Homeric ἀχλύς (mist, fog) and ἀχλύω (to be or grow dark).[18] I think, therefore, that we may have here an ancient image maintained and transmitted by poetry.

Another simile for shedding tears in Cretan folksongs has been taken as a survival from Homer rather than as an independent creation because of a partial, possibly formulaic, correspondence:

15a. ὡς δὲ χιὼν κατατήκετ᾽ ἐν ἀκροπόλοισιν ὄρεσσιν (. . .)
ὡς τῆς τήκετο καλὰ παρήϊα δάκρυ χεούσης
(Od. 19.205, 208)
(As the snow melts on lofty mountains . . . so her cheeks melted as she wept).

15b. ὡς λιεῖ τὸ χιόνι στὰ βουνὰ ἤβαλ᾽ ἀρχὴ καὶ λιώνω
(Crete, Petr. 364)
(As the snow melts on the mountains, so have I begun to melt).

Idealized images

In addition to metaphors and similes, we also find similar images of another kind, namely idealized conceptions and representations—i.e., artistic imitations in Aristotle's sense—of certain aspects of life. They are not parts of any figures of speech but thematic motifs that belong directly to the narrative. I realize that this is too general a definition and applies to all content motifs of which the fabric of traditional narrative is made. I may have a few more words to say about motifs later on, but at this point I would like to quote the following examples:

The enchanting voice of a young woman working at her loom and singing as she weaves attracts the attention of one or more passers-by; this motif, which leads to a meeting and dialogue, is found in Homer (the goddess Circe) as well as in many modern songs:

16a. ἔνθα δέ τις μέγαν ἱστὸν ἐποιχομένη λίγ᾽ ἄειδεν,
ἢ θεὸς ἠὲ γυνή
(Od. 10.254–5; cf. 221, 226)
(Here someone was moving to and fro at a great loom and sang in a clear voice, either a goddess or a woman).

16b. Κοράσιο στὴν Ἀνατολὴ ἔφαινε κι ἐτραγούδειε
(Crete, A 415)
. . . ἔφαινε καὶ γλυκοτραβουδοῦσε
(Thrace, Laogr. 1. [1909] 606; cf. Promp. I, 12, for other examples)
(A girl in the East was weaving and singing / . . . she was weaving and singing sweetly).

In a time when different hygienic conditions from our own prevailed, the look of a man or a woman coming out of a bath could create a sensation:

17a. ἔκ ῥ' ἀσαμίνθου βῆ δέμας ἀθανάτοισιν ὁμοῖος
      (*Od.* 3.468; cf. 23.163, 24.370)
      (He [Telemachus] came forth from the bath and his appearance was like that of the immortals).

In folk ballads, the seduction of the unfaithful wife by her brother-in-law (or vice versa) is introduced by the following line:

17b. ἐβγαίν' ἡ κόρη ἀπ' τὸ λουτρὸ κι ὁ νιὸς ἀπ' τὸν μπαρμπέρη
      (Chios, Kan. 32; other examples cited by Promp. I, 21)
      (The girl comes out from the bath and the young man from the barber's).

The image of a man leaning on his staff as he addresses a gathering of people is common to Homer and to folksongs:

18a. τῷ ὅ γ' ἐρεισάμενος ἔπε' Ἀργείοισι μετηύδα
      (*Il.* 2.109; cf. 8.496)
      (Leaning on it [his sceptre] he [Agamemnon] spoke and addressed the Argives).

In the New Year's carols, Saint Basil leans on his staff to recite, as he is asked, the alphabet:

18b. καὶ στὸ ραβδί του ἀκούμπησε νὰ πεῖ τὴν ἀλφαβήτα (common).

Several other images could be adduced here, from the simple image of an olive tree stretching its foliage widely (about which see below) to more complex ones, such as the tremor of mountains and trees caused by the passage of a god or another supernatural creature (*Il.* 13.18–19; Sinope, A 336), or a sailor's grave to be dug on the shore in accordance with the wish of the dead or dying man (*Od.* 11.75; Dodecanese, B1, 244–5; Lüd. 213); but such images merge with larger motifs and motifemes.

Motifs

Motifs are notoriously difficult to define, and include actions (dynamic motifs), descriptions (ἐκφράσεις), characters, attributes, objects, etc. They belong to an equally vague and unspecified domain, the so-called 'folk-literature', which is considered, somewhat incongruously, both as a time-less narrative universe and as an open set of culture-bound and overlapping traditional narrative systems. The latter view presupposes an historical growth and interaction among these systems but, either because their origins are considered lost in the mist of prehistory or because early attempts at tracing them have not been successful, historical orientations are completely out of fashion in contemporary folklore and anthropology.

When we encounter, therefore, motifs common to Homer and folksongs we cannot tell whether they are historically related or whether their similarity is due to chance, or to some obscure line of development. In addition to the images mentioned above, I mean motifs such as horses talking to their masters (*Il.* 19.404 ff.; Thrace, *Laogr.* 622; Cyprus, Lüd. 73), or crying for the death or the forthcoming death of their riders (*Il.* 17.427; Crete, Zan. 11), three-headed snakes (*Il.* 11.40; Karpathos, A 431; Cappadocia, etc., Promp. I, 86), monsters with several heads and mouths displaying batteries of close-set teeth (*Od.* 12.91; Crete, A 21), heroes boasting that they fear no one (*Il.* 7.196, *Od.* 2.199; Crete, A 55; Thrace, *Laogr.* 593), travellers arriving unexpectedly at a place where people are having dinner or the feast (this is idealized timing, *Od.* 4.3, 10.61, 452; Cyprus, Sak. 22; Cephalonia, *Laogr.* 257), recognition tokens and tests (*Od.* 21.217, 23.73 ff., 24.328 ff.; common in folksongs [Zan., Promp. II. 91]), and so forth. Yet, close scrutiny of the form of such narrative units, as well as their context, would, I think, produce plausible results.

Restrictions of space prevent me from engaging in this kind of enquiry but I should like to conclude this paper by mentioning just three pairs of examples, in which content and form are equally significant. Firstly, in the *Iliad*, Ajax prays to Zeus to deliver the Achaeans from the dark fog that has enveloped them, to clear the sky and let them see again:

19a. Ζεῦ πάτερ, ἀλλὰ σὺ ῥῦσαι ὑπ᾽ ἠέρος υἷας Ἀχαιῶν,
   ποίησον δ᾽ αἴθρην, δὸς δ᾽ ὀφθαλμοῖσιν ἰδέσθαι (17.645–7)
   (Father Zeus, free from the mist the sons of the Achaeans, make the
   air bright, and give sight back to our eyes).

In a lament from Epirus we find a very similar prayer to God (although in a different context):

19b. Θέ μου, καὶ πάψε τὴ βροχή, σκόρπισε τὴν ἀντάρα,
   νὰ ἰδοῦνε τὰ ματάκια του, ν᾽ ἀκούσουνε τ᾽ αὐτιά του (Lüd. 234)
   (My God, make the rain stop, disperse the fog, so that his eyes may
   see, his ears may hear).

My second example is from Odysseus' false account to Penelope, before their actual recognition. She wants to find out who is Odysseus:

20a. Ξεῖνε, τὸ μέν σε πρῶτον ἐγὼν εἰρήσομαι αὐτή·
τίς πόθεν εἰς ἀνδρῶν; πόθι τοι πόλις ἠδὲ τοκῆες;
(Od. 19.104–5)
(Stranger, this question will I myself ask you first: Who are you
among men and from where? Where is your city and your parents?)

and he answers, in due course, that he comes from Crete and is
Idomeneus' younger brother:

ἀλλ' ὁ μὲν ἐν νήεσσι κορωνίσιν Ἴλιον εἴσω
οἴχεθ' ἅμ' Ἀτρεΐδῃσιν, ἐμοὶ δ' ὄνομα κλυτὸν Αἴθων,
ὁπλότερος γενεῇ· ὁ δ' ἄρα πρότερος καὶ ἀρείων
(Od. 19.182–4)
(But he went to Ilion on board of the curved ships together with the
sons of Atreus; the name by which I am known myself is Aithon,
younger in age; but he was the elder and braver man).

In modern folksongs, a recognition takes place between two brothers, a
mountain chieftain and pedlar (who has been captured by the former).
The chieftain asks the pedlar:

20b. Ξένε, ποιός εἶν' ὁ τόπος σου καὶ ποιά τὰ γονικά σου;
(Stranger, which is your country and who are your parents?)

The pedlar gives the information he is asked for and supplements it with
a (very functional) reference to his elder brother, which leads to their
recognition:

κι ἔχουν καὶ γιὸν τρανύτερον καὶ πρῶτον ἀπ' τ' ἐμένα,
κλέφτη στοὺς λόγγους, στὰ βουνά, καὶ πρῶτον καπετάνο
(Epirus, Lüd. 29)
(They [my parents] also have another son, a greater man and older
than myself, who is a klepht in the woods, upon the mountains, and
first chieftain).

My last example is a pair of two short formulae invoking the same
image, that of an olive tree. The Homeric formula is τανύφυλλος ἐλαίη:

21a. αὐτὰρ ἐπὶ κρατὸς λιμένος τανύφυλλος ἐλαίη
(Od. 13.102, 346; cf. 23.195).

This pair of epithet and noun is usually translated as 'long-leaved olive
tree', while LSJ offers 'with long-pointed leaves, of olive'. However, the
first translation is evidently wrong, the second one is awkward and
unimaginative. The first part of the compound adjective is the verb τανύω,
which means stretch, and is also found in other Homeric epithets such as
τανυπτέρυξ, τανυσίπτερος, and τανύπεπλος. The last of these words means
long-robed, the other two refer to birds of long-stretching wings. Now in

Cyprus we encounter the formula ἐλιὰν πλατύφυλλην, and again we wonder how an olive tree can this time be called wide-leaved. But in fact neither does Homer call the olive tree long-leaved, nor do the Cypriot singers call it wide-leaved, because they all refer to the tree's *outstretching foliage:*

21b.   τζ' ηὖρεν ἐλιὰν πλατύφυλλην 'πουκάτω τζ' ἐκονέψαν (A 314)
(He found an olive tree with outstretched foliage, and under it they camped).

Proof—if any is needed—that this is the meaning of the Homeric formula is found in *Od.* 23.190, where τανύφυλλος qualifies θάμνος ('an olive bush with outstretched foliage'), and in other poets where τανύφυλλον ([Theoc.] 25.221) or τανίφυλλον (Bacch. 11.55) qualifies ὄρος ('a forest in the hills' is Jebb's translation of the Bacchylides phrase; 'with thick foliage' is D. G. Gerber's rendering of the epithet).[19] I think, then, that our two formulae correspond exactly in what they represent, coincide partly as regards their sound and word forms, and illuminate each other. Also, both phrases are poetic in the sense that they invoke an image tersely and vividly, and are unlikely if not downright incapable of having occurred in casual speech (which is an important test in deciding whether a phrase has been maintained through poetry rather than being recreated anew).[20]

ABBREVIATIONS AND NOTES

A: Academy of Athens anthology of folksongs: Ἑλληνικὰ δημοτικὰ τραγούδια, vol. I, ed. by G. K. Spyridakis, G. A. Megas, and D. A. Petropoulos (1962). B: '*Basike Bibliotheke*' anthology of folksongs: Ἑλληνικὰ δημοτικὰ τραγούδια, ed. by D. A. Petropoulos, 2 vols. (Athens, 1959). Fauriel: C. Fauriel, *Chants populaires de la Grèce moderne*, 2 vols. (Paris, 1824–5). Jean.: A. Jeannaraki, *Kretas Volkslieder* (Leipzig, 1876). Kan.: K. Kanellakis, Χιακὰ ἀνάλεκτα (Athens, 1890). Lüd.: E. Lüdeke, Ἑλληνικὰ δημοτικὰ τραγούδια (Athens, 1943). Laogr.: The journal *Laographia* 1 (1909). Man.: A. Manousos, *Τραγούδια ἐθνικά*, 2 vols. (Kerkyra, 1850). Petr.: D. A. Petropoulos, 'Αἱ παρομοιώσεις εἰς τὰ δημοτικὰ ᾄσματα καὶ παρ' Ὁμήρῳ', *Laographia* 18 (1960), 353–87. Promp.: I. K. Promponas, *Τὰ ὁμηρικὰ ἔπη καὶ τὸ νεοελληνικὸ δημοτικὸ τραγούδι*, 2 vols. (Athens, 1987–9). Sak.: A. Sakellariou, *Τὰ Κυπριακά*, II (Athens, 1891). Zan.: G. Zannetos, Ἡ ὁμηρικὴ φράσις ἐν τῇ καθ' ἡμᾶς δημώδει ποιήσει (Athens, 1889).

1. The problem of the origins of Akritic songs is further complicated by our uncertainty as regards their relationship to the epic romance of Digenis Akritis, the oldest version of which (preserved in a 15th century ms. in the Escorial) was composed, most likely in Cappadocia, in the first half of the 12th century; see S. Alexiou, Βασίλειος Διγενῆς Ἀκρίτης (Athens, 1985), Introducton, 100 (and *ed. minor*, Athens, 1990, 55). It is recognized nowadays that the composition of the Digenis poem was based on a medieval oral-epic tradition that has to be extrapolated from such Akritic songs as *The Song of Armouris* and *The Song of Andronikos' Son* (recorded in 15th-century mss., but also transmitted orally until quite recently), Byzantine narrative poetry in the vernacular, and the Digenis poem itself which, although probably created with the help of writing, displays all kinds of stylistic features—formulae, 'repetition, orderly progression, recurrent details, mirrored scenes', a 'tidy disposition of parts'—showing that like other ancient and medieval epics it was composed 'under the stylistic domination of an oral tradition', B. Fenik, *Digenis: Epic and Popular Style in the Escorial Version* (Herakleion-Rethymnon, 1991), 18. Whether the majority of Akritic songs are remnants of that tradition, as I think, or offshoots of the Digenis

epic, as Alexiou suggests, preserved in either case within and by the mainstream of folksong tradition, seems difficult to decide at the present state of our knowledge. On the relationship of the Digenis poem with folksongs see I. K. Promponas, Ἀκριτικά Α' (Athens, 1985; and Alexiou's review in Ἑλληνικά 39 [1988], 189–95), Sifakis, *Ariadne* 5 (1989 = Festschrift S. Alexiou), 125–39; on the medieval Greek oral poetic tradition see M. J. Jeffreys, 'The Oral Background of Byzantine Popular Poetry', *Oral Tradition* 1/3 (1986), 504–47, and his many other contributions (many with E. M. Jeffreys) in M. J. and E. M. Jeffreys, *Popular Literature in Late Byzantium*, Variorum Reprints (London, 1983); R. Beaton, *The Medieval Greek Romance* (Cambridge, 1989), 32, 40 ff.

2. See now his collected papers on folksong, Τὸ δημοτικὸ τραγούδι, ed. by A. Kyriakidou-Nestoros (Athens, 1978), 169–207.

3. Although we have to admit that the ways a folk tradition uses to construct, deconstruct, and reassemble themes, tales, and stories (some of them real) into an ever-shifting, kaleidoscopic self-adjustment are very imperfectly understood, if at all.

4. On ancient and modern *chelidonismata* (swallow songs) and other ancient children's songs see now the masterful musicological treatment by the late Samuel Baud-Bovy, Δοκίμιο γιά τό ἑλληνικό δημοτικό τραγούδι (Nauplion, 1984), 2–12.

5. See his *Greek Papyri: an Introduction* (Oxford, 1968), 81.

6. This is inevitably too general a statement, and hence impossible to document properly. Conditions must have differed greatly from place to place, in different periods. Widespread literacy has been suggested only for the *citizens* of democratic classical Athens; but even there inhabitants of country districts, women, and slaves were much less literate (F. D. Harvey, 'Literacy in the Athenian Democracy', *REG* 79 [1966], 585 ff.; see also E. G. Turner, *Athenian Books in the Fifth and Fourth Centuries* [²1977], L. Woodbury, *TAPA* 106 [1976], 349 ff.). For the very limited literacy of Sparta see P. Cartledge, *JHS* 98 (1978), 25 ff. However, only the Egyptian papyri allow us to form a reliable picture. Turner, referring to the contents of some of the largest archives of papyri found in Egypt, writes: 'Are we to accept the depressing conclusion that the ordinary man cared little for literature, even if he could read it? These archives are undoubtedly a useful corrective to common optimistic pictures of a widespread literary culture' (n. 5 above, 78). But things are even more 'depressing' than this quotation suggests because the archives in question span a period of six hundred years (the Zenon Archive, 260–240 B.C., the Abinnaeus Archive, A.D. 340–350) and belonged to men of the upper social strata (Zenon was a high ranking government official, Abinnaeus a cavalry officer with the Roman army, Aurelius Isidorus of Karanis was a landowner in the early fourth century who kept an archive of business documents which he could not even read himself). The extent of illiteracy among the middle and lower classes of the population (which however were multi-ethnic) is discussed by H. C. Youtie, 'Ἀγράμματος: an Aspect of Greek Society in Egypt', *HSCP* 75 (1971), 161–76 (=*Scriptiunculae* II, 611–27); see also his other contributions in *GRBS* 12 (1971), 239–61 (=*Scriptiunculae* II, 629–51) and *ZPE* 19 (1975), 101–8 (=*Script. Poster.* I, 255–62). A balanced survey of literacy in ancient Greece (with adequate attention to the concept and degrees of literacy) is offered by R. Thomas, *Oral Tradition and Written Record in Classical Athens* (Cambridge, 1989), 15–34.

7. It should also be mentioned in this connexion that the transition from *aoidos* to *rhapsoidos* was not instantaneous but may have lasted for quite a long time. We lack direct and unequivocal evidence for this but, although what has happened in other traditions proves nothing for Greece, Radlov's extensive field research in central Asia in the previous century is very instructive: it documented the distinction of *shair*, creative singers, as a special category among the *bakshy*, their mostly repetitive colleagues, in Uzbekistan; a similar distinction existed among the Kirghiz *manaschi* (singers of the 'Manas' epic cycle) between the creative *jomokchu* and the repetitive *yrchy*, while the *akyn* of Kazakhstan corresponded with the former (N. K. Chadwick and V. Zhirmunsky, *Oral Epics of Central Asia*, Cambridge, 1969, 327). Creative and repetitive singers, therefore, coexisted in central Asia, and their distinction does not seem to have been so clear-cut as the difference we assume between *aoidoi* and *rhapsoidoi*, who are supposed to have functioned during successive phases of the Greek epic tradition. I submit that long after the establishment of *rhapsoidoi* as the official keepers of Homer's poetic legacy oral singers, more repetitive perhaps than creative, must have kept the tradition of epic singing alive in a minor capacity, away from the pomp of public festivals and their rhapsodic performances.

8. Athen. 14.620b, Ach. Tat. 3.20, Petron. *Sat.* 59.3–7.

9. Neither the Renaissance nor the Scientific Revolution had been felt inside the borders of the Ottoman Empire; the effects of the Enlightenment were limited to a handful of Greeks and other subjects of the Ottomans who had studied or lived abroad; the conservatism of the Eastern Orthodox Church and Ottoman despotism combined to maintain the medieval character of society up to the eve of the Greek Revolution.

10. But this does not mean that all clergymen were literate; on illiterate abbots in Constantinople itself see R. Merkelbach, 'Analphabetische Klostervorsteher in Konstantinopel und Chalkedon', ZPE 39 (1980), 291–4. These clerics must have known by heart the innumerable services of an Orthodox monastery over which they had to preside.

11. See H. Eideneier, 'Leser- oder Hörerkreis? Zur byzantinischen Dichtung in der Volkssprache', Ἑλληνικά 34 (1982–83), 119–50; idem, Krasopateras, Neograeca Medii Aevi III (Köln, 1988); E. M. and M. J. Jeffreys, 'The Style of Byzantine Popular Poetry: Recent Work', Okeanos: Essays presented to Ihor Ševčenko, Harvard Ukrainian Studies 7 (1983), 309–43; N. M. Panagiotakis, 'Μελετήματα περὶ Σαχλίκη', Kretika Chronika 27 (1987), 7–58.

12. It should be added, however, that such oral variants have had no effect on the textual tradition of these works as they originated in the listening to the reading aloud of printed texts. The advent (and spread) of typography eliminated completely the possibility of the contamination of printed works by the parallel oral tradition of the same works or works belonging to the same genre. For oral variants of works of Cretan literature see P. Vlastos, Kretikos Laos 1 (1909), 70 ff.; E. Doulgerakis, Kretika Chronika 10 (1956), 244 ff.; Th. Detorakis, Ἀνέκδοτα δημοτικὰ τραγούδια τῆς Κρήτης (Herakleion, 1976), 98 ff.; Th. Papadopoullos, Kypriakai Spoudai 41 (1977), 211 ff.; W. Puchner, Ariadne. Scientific Yearbook of the Fac. of Philosophy, Univ. of Crete 1 (1983), 173 ff.; S. Alexiou, Erotokritos (Athens, 1980), Introduction, 100, Erophile (Athens, 1988), 77; N. Svoronos, Ariadne 5 (1989 = Festschrift Alexiou), 331–7. The influence of oral tradition on the works in question is examined by D. Holton, Byz. and Mod. Greek Studies 14 (1990), 186 ff. ('Orality' in medieval and modern Greek poetry is the subject of many other papers published in the same BMGS volume.)

13. Alexiou, Erotokritos (Athens, 1980), Introduction, 100.

14. According to the Naval Intelligence Division of the Admiralty, Geographical Handbook on Greece (I 306), quoted (without date) by Harvey (see n. 6), 'at the end of the 19th cent. it was estimated that in most regions of Greece 99% of the women could neither read nor write' (623). It is significant to note in this connexion that women are thought to be more important carriers of traditional culture than men: see S. Kyriakides, Αἱ γυναῖκες εἰς τὴν λαογραφίαν (Athens, 1920).

15. Motifeme, formed by analogy to phoneme, was introduced to folklore studies by A. Dundes (from K. L. Pike, Language in Relation to a Unified Theory of Structure of Human Behaviour, 1954) as an alternative term to V. Propp's function (Morphology of the Folktale, 1958): 'From etic to emic units in the structural study of folktales', American Journal of Folklore 75 (1962), 95–105.

16. See, for instance, I. Th. Kakridis, Homeric Researches (Lund, 1949); Denys Page, The Homeric Odyssey (Oxford, 1955) and Folktales in Homer's Odyssey (Harvard, 1972). On a different (though not unrelated) plane, O. Tsagarakis, in his monograph on Nature and Background of Major Concepts of Divine Powers in Homer (Amsterdam, 1977), has pointed out several parallel expressions in religious usage showing the longevity of certain concepts of popular religion.

17. Interest in this field of research has recently been rekindled by I. K. Promponas's two-volume work on Homer and modern Greek folksong (quoted in Abbreviations). He collects an impressive number of parallels but his method is wanting in that he makes no adequate distinction between vocabulary items and longer or poetic expressions.

18. But if we spell κατάχλια (as the editors of the song do) we will transpose the notion of hotness from the tears to the spring to which they are compared. However, a 'thoroughly warm' (rather than hot) spring is hardly satisfactory as a poetic image (unless it is taken as a case of hypallage).

19. Lexicon in Bacchylidem, s.v.; cf. τανύφυλλον δειράδα at Nonn. Dion. 20.250.

20. I am grateful to Mark Edwards, Odysseus Tsagarakis, and Nasos Vagenas for their valuable comments on this paper, which have improved both its form and its content.

HOMER IN TRANSLATION

By A. G. GEDDES

In the first term of 1985 I had two classes with whom I was reading the *Iliad*. In the Classical Studies class we had to read and discuss the *Iliad* in Richmond Lattimore's English translation,[1] and in the Greek IIA class we read Book I of the *Iliad* in Greek.

The atmosphere in the two classes was strikingly different. The Greek class was interested and energetic, even though their knowledge of Greek was so limited that they had to look up every other word. I think the students felt a sense of achievement and pleasure as they met the language of Homer for the first time.[2] The Classical Studies class on the other hand was bored, apathetic, and irritable. In despair one day I asked them if they liked Homer at all, and they said they did not. They did not think he was any good. I asked them who they *did* think was good, and they hesitantly suggested some names—Scott Fitzgerald, John Steinbeck, and, when I asked for a poet, Bruce Dawe.[3] One girl said that she thought Mary Renault was better than Homer.

This disconcerting experience made me read seriously, I am ashamed to say for the first time ever, Lattimore's translation. I had taught the class for years, but I was confident in my knowledge of *Homer* and had not bothered much with the translation, which was students' only access to the poetry. It was then, when I paid attention to the translation, that I realized how much I was at odds with the students. We were talking about two completely different things. In this article I wish to make a few brief points about the metre, the language, and the style that a Classical Studies teacher might hope to find in an English translation of Homer.

The hexameters of Homer are a relaxing, flowing, comfortable measure. They are capable of great variety because the first four feet may consist of either a spondee or a dactyl, and also because of the caesuras which, by 'breaking against the grain' as A. M. Dale says,[4] and thus creating pauses in the middle of feet rather than at the end of the feet, divide the line into phrases of varying length. The interplay between the metre of the line as a whole and the individual rhythms of the phrases that make up the line prevents the hexameter from falling into the doggerel of a fixed beat, and makes it eminently suitable for the many tones and moods necessary for a long narrative poem—tragic, comic, reflective, descriptive, discursive, and, on occasion, emotionally intense as well.

Rhythm is gratifying in itself, and a poet can give added pleasure by using it expressively, that is, so as to give rise to particular impressions, expectations, and feelings. I shall begin by mentioning a few of the ways that Homer uses the hexameter, with all its permitted variations, expressively. He was, for instance, obviously aware that a series of long slow syllables gives an impression of weight and heaviness, while short, quick syllables give an impression of lightness and quickness. Accordingly Homer uses long sounds for solemn sense and short sounds for disturbance and speed.

> Ὣς ἔφατ' εὐχόμενος, τοῦ δ' ἔκλυε Φοῖβος Ἀπόλλων,
> βῆ δὲ κατ' Οὐλύμποιο καρήνων χωόμενος κῆρ,
> τόξ' ὤμοισιν ἔχων ἀμφηρεφέα τε φαρέτρην·   45
> ἔκλαγξαν δ' ἄρ' ὀϊστοὶ ἐπ' ὤμων χωομένοιο,
> αὐτοῦ κινηθέντος· ὁ δ' ἤϊε νυκτὶ ἐοικώς.
> ἕζετ' ἔπειτ' ἀπάνευθε νεῶν, μετὰ δ' ἰὸν ἕηκε·
> δεινὴ δὲ κλαγγὴ γένετ' ἀργυρέοιο βιοῖο·
> οὐρῆας μὲν πρῶτον ἐπῴχετο καὶ κύνας ἀργούς,   50
> αὐτὰρ ἔπειτ' αὐτοῖσι βέλος ἐχεπευκὲς ἐφιεὶς
> βάλλ'· αἰεὶ δὲ πυραὶ νεκύων καίοντο θαμειαί.⁵

In this passage from *Iliad* 1, the sound of the clang of the arrows on the shoulders of the god as he comes down from Olympus is given emphasis by the spondee at the beginning of line 46 and the two spondees at the beginning of 47; then there is the quick short rhythm of 48, consisting entirely of dactyls as the arrows are shot, and the long slow beginning of 49, five long syllables for the sinister clang of bow. Line 48 is what G. S. Kirk calls a rising threefolder—three phrases of increasing length—'which has a more urgent, progressive or flowing effect'.⁶ The regular hexameter line creates a pause at the end of the sixth foot. On our printed page we pause at the end of the line before moving to the beginning of the next line, because we can see the lines on the page. In oral poetry the fixed rhythm of the fifth and sixth feet, particularly the two syllables of the sixth foot, brings an end to the unit of six feet, before the speaker begins afresh with the first foot of the next unit. That pause gives emphasis to the first word of the following line, particularly if the sense flows on across the break and if it is the rhythm *alone* that forces an otherwise unnatural pause. In 52 the word βάλλε, 'struck and struck again', in the imperfect tense for repeated action, is given emphasis by its placing and then given renewed emphasis by the stop immediately following—a break this time required not by the metre but by the sense.

This passage is an example of Homer's most deceptively simple style, the simplicity of great artifice. It looks like a straightforward description of physical events in the outside world. As E. Auerbach said in *Mimesis*⁷ there is no background. Everything seems to be expressed and fully understood. Homer has used simple words for simple actions and nothing lies hidden underneath the words.

And yet the passage has most sinister content. Homer, I think, achieves the effect of menace by means of simplicity itself. He does not spell out Apollo's intentions; the god does not shout or threaten angrily. There is not a word of pity for the innocent victims of the god's anger. That would decrease the threatening atmosphere, not increase it. He simply describes the exterior events. The style is similar in some respects to that of Thucydides. When Thucydides came to the plague in Athens, he described the symptoms and the results quite clinically. He said that many bodies were left unburied, but that scavenging animals died if they ate the flesh of the dead. And so there were no birds of prey round the bodies, or anywhere else at that time. Dogs, he said, being domestic animals provided the best opportunity for observing this characteristic of the disease.[8] The deadpan manner is not really simple at all, but it is a most powerful technique if fear and threat are the desired effect.

Homer in our passage makes careful use of repetition and variation. The priest prays and Apollo hears. The god himself is silent; it is the arrows and the bow that make the noises, ἔκλαγξαν ('they clanged'), and then the variation δεινὴ δὲ κλαγγὴ γένετο ('there was a frightening noise'). He moves down carrying the bow on his shoulder and the quiver. βῆ δὲ κατ' Οὐλύμποιο καρήνων χωόμενος κῆρ ('he came down from the heights of Olympus, angry in his heart'), is gone over again in . . . χωομένοιο, αὐτοῦ κινηθέντος, but this time the word for moving is κινέω, the passive form, used for starting animals from lairs, setting them on the move. Then he came like the night, another word for moving, εἶμι. He squatted at a distance from the ships.[9] The ships here position us on the beach which we will, in a moment, see lit up with the funeral fires of the dead. ἀπάνευθε νεῶν ('at a distance from the ships') is a reminder of ἀπάνευθε κιών, in line 35, a different grammatical form but presumably something of the same sound. He crouched down at a distance from the ships and sent out an arrow, ἰόν, as a variation on ὀϊστοί. There will be another variation in a minute—βέλος. Βιός, the silver bow which makes a clang, is a variation on the τόξα of 45. And then there follow verbs for attacking, ἐποίχομαι, βέλος ἐφίημι, picking up ἰὸν μεθίημι, and of course βάλλε looking back to βέλος. I would not be surprised if there is consonance and assonance between ἐπῴχετο and ἐχεπευκές. And the frequency of hard sounds is most striking. I have counted 21 κ, χ, ξ, not counting hard γ sounds. All in all this is a most musical passage, the repetitions and variations operating like baroque music, or the psalms, to create an impressive piece of poetry, lifting the events out of the everyday world and giving them importance. What is a translator to do with such a passage?

Here is Pope's translation:[10]

Thus Chryses *pray'd; the fav'ring Power attends,*
And from Olympus' *lofty Tops descends.*
Bent was his Bow, the Grecian Hearts to wound;
Fierce as he moved, his Silver Shafts resound.
Breathing Revenge, a sudden Night he spread,
And gloomy Darkness roll'd around his Head.
The Fleet in View, he twang'd his deadly Bow,
And hissing fly the feather'd Fates below.
On Mules and Dogs th' Infection first began,
And last, the vengeful Arrows fix'd in Man.
For nine long Nights through all the dusky Air,
The Pyres thick-flaming shot a dismal Glare.

Pope uses here the iambic pentameter couplet which was his chosen poetic form and he uses it in the traditional manner of English poets with substitutions giving variety and flexibility to the lines. *Bent was his Bow, Fierce as he moved, Breathing Revenge*—the first two syllables of these phrases are what might be called trochees instead of iambs. They throw the first word of the line into emphasis. *Long Nights* and *thick-flam(ing)* are more like spondees, and they intensify the force of the adjectives by disturbing the pattern and thus calling solemn attention to themselves. Pope uses the sounds of the words imitatively too. The shafts are not silver in Homer; it is the bow there that is silver. But silver has been moved up for the sake of the s and v sounds. *Fierce as he moved, his Silver Shafts resound.* There are seven s sounds in this line, if the sh of shafts is counted as an s sound. The sibilance is revived in *hissing* lower down. The arrows take off with f and v sounds, *Fleet, fly the feather'd Fates, Infection first* and *vengeful Arrows fix'd.*

One thing we can detect in the poetry of Pope, which can only be assumed in the poetry of Homer, is the extent to which his poetry is irradiated by the poetry of the past. *Feather'd Fates*, for instance, was a direct borrowing from Dryden. *And last, the vengeful Arrows fix'd in Man* is to be compared with Dryden's *And last in Humane hearts his arrows fix'd.*[11] Readers appreciated this re-working of the poetry of the past and liked it. It had developed to such an extent that there was a language of epic poetry, removed from the language of everyday life, in some ways, I suppose, similar to the epic language that Homer himself used. So well known was this language that Pope could parody it in poems like *The Rape of the Lock*. But our students in South Australia rarely know any poetry at all when they come into our classes. They have been betrayed by the education system and society at large. There has been a decisive break in a continuous tradition of reading and enjoying English poetry that lasted from Chaucer until the Second World War. So complete has been the loss that a translation of Homer might well be the first encounter with poetry of any kind that our first-year students have ever had. They will almost certainly be unfamiliar with any exclusively poetic vocabulary or expressions.

If, in Homer, there is little or no background, Pope's *Iliad* is heavy with background. There is the landscape for one thing. Apollo spreads light, darkness rolls around his head, the air is dusky, the pyres thick flaming and the glare dismal. What is more this visual background is impregnated with sensibility. There is a moral background conveyed at the same time as the physical background. Apollo breathes revenge, the darkness is gloomy, the arrows hiss with menace like snakes, the arrows are vengeful like Apollo. Arrows are in fact *feather'd Fates*; that is, their killing potential is built into their name and the death that they bring is interpreted as destiny. It is exciting to load nature with all this feeling, but the simplicity of Homer's style is lost.

None the less what Pope has written is poetry. It may not be Homer, but Pope certainly conveyed the idea of a poem. He made Homer mean something to a non-Greek-speaking public. And they made him a rich man by buying his translation, and were pleased by him for over a hundred years, until the day that Keats opened Chapman's translation and threw off the Augustan legacy, when he stood like stout Cortez silent upon a peak in Darien.

But what of our students who have Lattimore to introduce them to Homer? Lattimore claims that his verse is a free six-beat line. I am unable to find any rhythm in his lines at all. It is true that each of his lines may have six stresses, although sometimes you have to impose six stresses, rather than recognize them. *So go now, do not make me angry so you will be safer* is line 32. If I put some pressure on that line I could easily find eleven or twelve stresses. In fact the only word that must not have a stress is *be*. But even granting six stresses to a line, it takes more than six stresses to make a line of poetry. It is possible to take a prose translation, for instance E. V. Rieu's Penguin translation,[12] and divide the lines into lengths of six stresses:

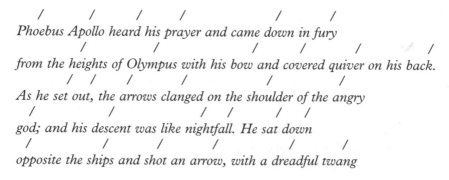

/   /   /   /   /   /
Phoebus Apollo heard his prayer and came down in fury
        /   /   /   /   /   /
from the heights of Olympus with his bow and covered quiver on his back.
        / /   /   /   /   /
As he set out, the arrows clanged on the shoulder of the angry
    /   /   /   /   /   /
god; and his descent was like nightfall. He sat down
    /   /   /   /   /   /
opposite the ships and shot an arrow, with a dreadful twang

/　　　/　　　　/　　　　/　　/　　　　　　/
from his silver bow. He attacked the mules first and the nimble
/　　　　/　　　/　　/　　　　　/　　　　/
dogs; then he aimed his sharp arrows at the men, and struck
/　　　　/　　　/　　　/　　　/　　　/　　　/　　　　　/
again and again. Day and night innumerable fires (consumed the dead).

I would maintain that this is no less poetic than Lattimore's version.

One of the advantages of Lattimore's translation is supposed to be that he is faithful to the phraseology of Homer. Bernard Knox,[13] who admires Lattimore, said that he had preserved the significant enjambments, that is, the runovers from one line to the next. But in this translation of the descent of Apollo, the enjambments are totally insignificant and seem to be nothing more than a convenience in the layout. Why is *angered* separated so emphatically from *in his heart?* Why is *hooded* separated from the quiver? Why is *walking* separated from *angrily?* These enjambments are not in the original. The one significant enjambment in Homer, the βάλλε of 52, he misses altogether. (It is striking that when Rieu's translation is set out, in 6 stress lines, similar insignificant enjambments occur.) Nor can I hear any music in his lines. The students may get some meaning from Lattimore; it is a fair paraphrase. But they get no idea at all that this is a poem. If they are told that it is a poem, no wonder they find they do not like poems. If it were a more honest and unpretentious translation, they might retain some curiosity about what Homer's poetry was really like.

I want now to make a point about the style of Homer, and the style of the translations that we have to use. Book 1 of the *Iliad* is an extraordinarily dramatic book. 373 of the 611 lines are direct speech, well over half. This means that expression becomes very important. Stereotyped fustian is always bad, but in direct speech it is very bad indeed. Homer offers few clues to character other than the words and the actions of his gods and heroes. Just as we are told very little about Apollo apart from his actions, so there is little discussion of the fantasies, feelings, habits, or personality traits that lead the heroes to speak as they do. We ourselves have to deduce their characters from what they say. Early in the first book the dispute between Achilles and Agamemnon is described by recounting the conversation of the men themselves. Upon this quarrel the whole plot of the poem depends. The dispute begins with Agamemnon's insult to the priest of Apollo who had come to ransom his daughter.[14] The speech lets us, the audience, know what Agamemnon is like. *Old man*, he calls the priest, γέρον. Lattimore renders this *Old Sir*, which is so unusual to me that I do not know if it is insulting or respectful.[15] He orders him off. *I will not free her*, he says. Before that old age—he had just referred to her father as already an old man—*will come upon her in my house in Argos far from her fatherland* (πάτρη reminds us, and him, of his fatherhood), *going up and down by the loom and visiting my bed.* Chapman sweetly translates this as *making* the bed,[16] *and see prepared With all fit ornament my bed.* Pope is lovely, *Till Time shall rifle ev'ry youthful Grace And Age dismiss her from my cold Embrace.*[17] Lattimore has *being in my bed as my companion* which is euphemistic and odd. The audience should have the full force of this forecast, so particularly wounding to a father's feelings. As when he translated γέρον with *Old Sir*, Lattimore seems not to have asked himself what Homer's intentions were here. A thoughtful translation would have let the reader know, at this early stage, that Agamemnon is arrogant, cruel, and impulsive.

The plague strikes and Calchas, after a promise of protection from Achilles, is persuaded to lay the blame upon Agamemnon's refusing the ransom. Agamemnon's reaction is immediately very angry. He accuses the priest of always prophesying ill for him. The scholiasts at this point remember the incident at Aulis when Iphigeneia had to be sacrificed, on the advice of Calchas.[18] But Homer does not say anything about that, and I would think we are not to take this accusation of always prophesying ill as a factual statement referring to the past. We are not to wonder whether Calchas *did* always prophecy ill, because this is the kind of thing angry men say and they do not want to be taken literally. Agamemnon goes on to insist that he loves this girl more than he loves his wife Clytemnestra. Again we understand that this need not be literally true. We understand that he is saying it so that he will sound more generous and self-sacrificing when he says he will give back the girl, *so that the people may not perish from the plague.* Finally he calls upon everyone, the whole people, to see that he has compensation. He makes no special mention of Achilles at this stage—he speaks as if compensation is the responsibility of the whole people.

But when the reply comes it is Achilles who answers him. He begins by calling him φιλοκτεανώτατε πάντων, 'most acquisitive'. *Insatiate King,* says Pope, *greediest for gain of all men,* says Lattimore.[19] Kirk points out that the word may not be insulting in the context of the Homeric world where Odysseus asks the Cyclops for a gift, Eumaeus for a cloak, and everyone loves the booty of war.[20] A true translation may be more like *a lover of fine things.* It is, of course, important for the interpretation of the quarrel to know whether it is insulting or not. I think it is not meant to be very much so, for the rest of Achilles' speech is reasonable and conciliating, A new division is not possible now but they will recompense Agamemnon handsomely when they sack Troy. But Agamemnon is angry enough to pretend that Achilles is trying to trick him; he is so angry that the grammar becomes uncertain—there is a co-ordinate clause where the reader expects a subordinate clause.

Why does Agamemnon say that Achilles is trying to trick him? There is no mention of it elsewhere, no idea that such a thing is indeed the case. Agamemnon again is angry at the thought of losing his prize and is speaking as angry men do—wildly. If he does not get compensation, he continues, he will take someone else's prize, the prize of either Achilles or Ajax or Odysseus. *Whomever I visit will be sorry.* At this moment he seems to pull himself together, realizing perhaps the seriousness of where the quarrel is leading him. In a change of tone and subject he says, *But we will talk about this matter another time.* And he suggests that meantime they take the girl home. Achilles can lead the expedition. I take this to be a kind of compliment paid to Achilles, an olive branch, an attempt to give him an opportunity to settle things peacefully, without actually saying so. Kirk on the other hand says that the way Achilles is named and described here 'certainly is malicious'.[21] At any rate Achilles is not placated, nor persuaded to leave the subject for another day and cooler tempers. He abuses Agamemnon (*O wrapped in shamelessness*, says Lattimore[22]), and he goes on to reflect upon warfare and the life of soldiers.[23] He has no quarrel with the Trojans, he says, they have never wronged him. He came to Troy to please Agamemnon and now, after all, Agamemnon plans to take away the prize that he fought for so hard and so thanklessly. Tired after fighting he comes back home with something small but his own . . .; the tone is wonderfully human. Far from being appeased Achilles actually makes things worse by taking Agamemnon's vague threat, *I will take your prize or Odysseus' or Ajax'*, for himself alone. *I will go home to Phthia*, he says, *and not stay here without honour in order to make you rich.* He is not going to go home of course, but he says that he will. And as the quarrel continues to escalate Agamemnon also makes it worse. He puts the worst possible construction upon Achilles' words. *Run away, then*, he says. *Other men will stand by me and so will Zeus.* This is ironic because, by the end of the book, Zeus will have granted the request of Thetis and agreed to bring disaster and suffering to the Achaeans. Agamemnon even turns Achilles' courage and prowess against him, *You take pleasure in battle. Wars and Horrors are your savage Joy*[24] says Pope. And Agamemnon finishes by repeating his threat, directing it now specifically against Achilles. *Since Apollo has taken Chryseis from me, I will take Briseis, going to your tent myself, so that you may know how much stronger I am than you.* He names Briseis specifically, and drops all mention of any alternative to this special insult to Achilles. And it is at this point that Athene intervenes to prevent bloodshed.

I have not done justice to this wonderful quarrel, described so realistically and vividly, so full of life and humanity. What I have tried to bring out is the way it is full of empty threats, rhetoric, exaggeration, provocation, accusation, and touchy feelings. Anger here is not described in such a way that we share the anger of either side. It is not the righteous anger of, say, an Old Testament prophet, nor anger such as King Lear's anger which wins the sympathy and rouses the indignation of the audience. This is more like a fight between two children that gradually gets out of hand.[25] Homer describes it objectively with a great deal of detachment, with what might well be a certain amount of amusement, which we, the audience, are invited to share. It is a heroic quarrel but at the same time, all too human.

The quarrel occurs in the first couple of hundred lines of the book. The audience cannot possibly have forgotten the introduction where Homer says that he will tell of the wrath of Achilles, which will bring countless sorrows to the Achaeans, send many fine heroes to Hades, and feed their bodies to the dogs and birds.[26] The juxtaposition of this bad temper with the seriousness of the consequences that will flow from it, cannot be fortuitous and must be intended by the poet. It is characteristic of Homer, and a characteristic that he shares with other Greek writers, that he is sensitive to the way suffering can begin so light-heartedly and thought-lessly. But in Homer this awareness is accepted casually, without bitter-ness, as if it is in the nature of things. This, in my view, is the sort of effect that a translator should try to capture.

When Pope came to translate this passage he had another theory about what was happening. From his own eighteenth-century world he brought to Homer a concern with the power of the state, the authority of the king, problems of leadership, and the rights of individuals in face of authority.[27] Accordingly Achilles and Agamemnon seem to quarrel about power. Angry with Calchas, Agamemnon in Pope says, *For this are* Phoebus' *Oracles explored, To teach the* Greeks *to murmur at their Lord* (135–6). Achilles says to Agamemnon, *But to resume whate'er thy Avarice craves, (That Trick of Tyrants) may be borne by Slaves* (161–2). *O Tyrant arm'd with Insolence and Pride* (194) he says a bit later when he is getting angrier. *But know proud Monarch I'm thy Slave no more* (221). And Agamemnon finishes his grand speech, the speech which makes Achilles half draw his sword, *And hence to all our Hosts it shall be known, That Kings are subject to the Gods alone* (249–50).[28]

When Pope describes the quarrel then, it is a serious quarrel—the two men do not make fools of themselves because they have (in Pope) a real difference. Pope's interpretation of the difference is not, in my view, true to Homer. In some ways it is simpler and less interesting than what I understand Homer to be intending to convey. But what can truly be said about it is that it is absolutely coherent.

With Lattimore however it is just that coherence that seems to be miss-ing. What Lattimore makes of the quarrel I do not know. I think maybe he has not asked himself why Homer has them quarrel in this way, or what impression Homer wants to make by recounting their words so carefully and with so much acknowledgement of real life. Or, if Lattimore has interpreted the passage, he has not managed to convey his interpretation in the translation, or not at any rate to me. With remarkable fidelity to the words, reproducing some English equivalent for every phrase, he none the less produces a simply incomprehensible quarrel.

Risking (I know) tedium and pedantry, I will elaborate slightly upon a few of the things that are so unfair to Homer. The following passage is from the speech of Agamemnon when he turns in anger upon Calchas:[29]

> *Seer of evil: never yet have you told me a good thing.*
> *Always the evil things are dear to your heart to prophesy,*
> *but nothing excellent have you yet said nor ever accomplished.*
> *Now once more you make divination to the Danaans, argue*
> *forth your reason why he who strikes from afar afflicts them,*
> *because I for the sake of the girl Chryseis would not take*
> *the shining ransom; and indeed I wish greatly to have her*
> *in my own house; since I like her better than Klytaimestra*
> *my own wife, for in truth she is in no way inferior,*
> *neither in build not stature nor wit, not in accomplishment.*
> *Still I am willing to give her back, if such is the best way.*
> *I myself desire that my people be safe, not perish.*
> *Find me then some prize that shall be my own, lest I only*
> *among the Argives go without, since that were unfitting;*
> *you are all witnesses to this thing, that my prize goes elsewhere.*

Seer of evil, he begins. *Seer* is understandable although my first response is the man who sees rather than the seer. For seers (prophets) are either good or evil, but they are not in English *of* evil So this is my first criticism of Lattimore. His expressions are not idiomatic. They are quaint. *Never yet have you told me a good thing.* A good thing is idiomatic but it is very dull. A good thing here is a translation of κρήγυον, a word that is very rare, only occurring this once in Homer. Its meaning is a little obscure but in English it surely deserves something less mundane than *a good thing*. And so my second criticism of Lattimore is that his expressions are prosaic. Then we have, *always the evil things are dear to your heart to prophesy. Evil things are dear to your heart* is all right but *they are dear to your heart to prophesy* is not English. *Now once more you make divination to the Danaans, argue forth your reason why he who strikes from afar afflicts them, because I for the sake of the the girl Chryseis would not take the shining ransom.* In Greek the meaning is quite clear. But an English reader would naturally take *because* with the main verb, *argue forth*. An English reader would not immediately understand it to be an explanation of *your reason why*. It is not idiomatic English. It is a literal translation of what Kirk has called Homer's cumulative style,[30] where every new thought flows straight from the last one, rather than being subordinated to the main verb. And finally, *Find me then some prize that shall be my own lest I only among the Archives go without, since that were unfitting.* I ignore the archaic *lest*, the uncertain subjunctives; what I object to here is *that shall be my own.* Since the line begins *find me some prize, that shall be my own* is unnecessary. And so my final objection to Lattimore is that he is garrulous. One of the reviewers said that his lines were congested.[31] There are several lines in Book 1 where Homer uses as few as four words but where Lattimore needs thirteen or fourteen to translate them. Some of these characteristics are the same ones that Matthew Arnold objected to in Newman the translator who provoked his essay, and Lattimore to me is best described by the word that Arnold invented—he Newmanizes.[32] He is quaint, prosaic, garrulous, low, and unidiomatic as well.

The same sort of criticisms have been made of the modern translation of the Bible called the Good News Bible which can turn this, the King James version:

I returned and saw under the sun, that the race is not to the swift, nor the battle to the strong, neither yet bread to the wise, nor yet riches to men of understanding, nor yet favour to men of skill; but time and chance happeneth to them all[33]

into:

I realized another thing that in this world fast runners do not always win the race and the brave do not always win the battle. Wise men do not always earn a living, intelligent men do not always get rich, and capable men do not always rise to high position. Bad luck happens to everyone.

This is what Arnold would have called low or ignoble. The translators, I imagine, thought that sincerity and fidelity, in the sense of a dictionary equivalent for every word, would amount to style. But sincerity and fidelity are not enough. Fine language (and poetry is language at its finest) needs artifice. Translators should realize that it is careful, calculated, totally unspontaneous poetry that finds its way into the heart. And if the original is poetry, then inarticulate plain-speaking is not more but less true to the original. Pope, as translator, interpreted, reworked, and then made a new act of creation. Our translators have not got such confidence in themselves.

What has happened to us in the twentieth century that translations such as this have appeared, sometimes to critical acclaim, and are used by students in serious academic courses? We have become so anxious to be true to Homer, so reluctant to introduce anything which is not in the original, so suspicious of interpretations, that literalness has become a virtue. Maybe we are forgetting what poetry is and what it can do.

Our greater knowledge of Homeric formulae and the techniques of oral poetry has made us, temporarily, deaf to the individual voice of the poet. If something appears odd or inconsequential in Homer our translators have a ready explanation—it must be the oral technique. And the science of archaeology has given us a dread of reconstruction. Our translators therefore do not, as Pope did, worry over the problem until they find a meaning that satisfies them and their readers. They give us words cleaned (so they think) of extraneous matter like shards in a museum. But poems cannot be treated in this way. A poem is much more than its paraphrasable content. And to offer a paraphrase to our students, as if *that* is Homer, is an insult to them, to the language of Shakespeare, and most of all to Homer himself whose wonderful poetry ought to be given the chance to show up the shoddy of the twentieth century.

NOTES

1. R. Lattimore, *The Iliad of Homer* (Chicago, 1961).

2. The Greek IIA students wrote an up-to-date version of Matthew Arnold's essay, 'On Translating Homer', as part of their assessment. This article is the result of many discussions with these students. I would like to thank Tracey Duller, Claire Flenley, and Louise Prest for their interest and ideas.

3. Bruce Dawe is a poet and an Australian, and by choosing him from among the options on the English matriculation syllabus, students satisfy two compulsory requirements of their course.

4. *The Collected Papers of A. M. Dale* (Cambridge, 1969), 240.

5. Iliad I. 43–52. 'So he spoke in prayer and Phoebus Apollo heard him. He came down from the high places of Olympus with anger in his heart. He carried his bow on his shoulders and his covered quiver. The arrows clanged upon the shoulders of the angry god as he started out. He came down like the night. He crouched at a distance from the ships and shot an arrow. The silver bow made a frightening noise. He struck the mules first and the swift dogs but then, sending the sharp arrow against the men, he struck and struck again. Thousands of fires for the corpses were burning continuously.'

6. *The Iliad: a Commentary* (Cambridge, 1985), I. 21.

7. *Mimesis* (Princeton, 1957), 4 ff.

8. Thucydides 2.50.1–2.

9. He crouched rather than sat; cf. the marble figure from the east pediment of the Temple of Aphaia at Aegina, Munich, 84.

10. The Twickenham Edition of the Poems of Alexander Pope (London, 1967), vii. 89, 61–72.

11. J. Dryden, *The First Book of Homer's Ilias*, 378; from *The Works of J. Dryden* (Edinburgh, 1885), xii.

12. *Homer, The Iliad* (Harmondsworth, 1950), 24.

13. *Hudson Review* 14 (Winter 1961–2), 620.

14. *Iliad* 1.12 ff.

15. The scholiast took it to be insulting: V. H. Erbse, *Scholia Graeca in Homeri Iliadem* (Berlin, 1964), 16.

16. Lines 30–1, Chapman, *The Iliad* (London, 1901), 2.

17. Op. cit., 41–2. This is a good example of the backward-looking tendency of rhymes in English poetry. The word *grace* leads back to *embrace* instead of moving us forward in the progressive Homeric manner. Matthew Arnold points this out in his essay 'On Translating Homer' in *Essays Literary and Critical* (London, 1911), 218–19.

18. Erbse, op. cit., 41.

19. Pope, 155, Lattimore, 122.

20. Kirk, op. cit., 66.

21. Kirk, op. cit., 68.

22. Lattimore, 149.

23. It is characteristic of Achilles to reflect upon the nature of war; cf. J. Griffin, *Homer on Life and Death* (Oxford, 1980), 99–100.

24. Pope, 232.

25. Agamemnon was in a 'filthy temper', as H. A. Mason, *To Homer through Pope* (London, 1972), 23 describes it.

26. They will not yet know, however, how Achilles will be appeased in Book 24 by his ability to understand the grief of Priam.

27. V. D. Knight, 'The Augustan Mode' in *On Translation* in HSCL (Harvard, 1959), 202. He explains that this gives Pope's work an 'overriding interpretative coherence'.

28. The editors of the Twickenham edition say that Pope '. . . made translation a political act' (ccxxi).

29. Lattimore, 106–19.

30. Kirk, op. cit., xxii *et passim*.

31. V. Young in *Hudson Review* 28 (Autumn 1975), 429. Mason in a review of Lattimore's *The Odyssey of Homer* in *The New York Review of Books*, May 9th 1968, reproduced as an epilogue to *To Homer through Pope*, says 'anyone who has conscientiously read without interruption all the twenty-three books to this point might well be pardoned if he likened the experience to that of some poor rat forced to wade up to the whiskers through an endless morass of chewed tram tickets', 201.

32. Arnold, op. cit., 263.

33. Ecclesiastes 9.11. G. Orwell, *Inside the Whale and Other Essays* (Harmondsworth, 1967), 149 has translated this passage into public service jargon as a joke. The translators of the Good News Bible, however, are perfectly serious.

SUBJECT INDEX

Achilles: and Agamemnon 25, 32; and Briseis 87–8, 91, 92, 193; quarrel 65–6, 68, 70, 73–4, 76–7, 86–92, 95, 191–4; reconciliation 43; arming 57–8; death 76, 111; and decision-making 44, 164, 169 n.3; and Hector 44–5, 48–51, 58–9, 62–4, 68, 74, 96, 103–4, 106; and Priam 72–3, 77, 79, 80, 81, 105, 108–9, 111, 114 n.33, 198 n.26; and shame 16; shield 10, 23, 27, 33, 48, 58, 96–112; and Thersites 86, 87–92, 93, 95

Adkins, A. W. H. 167–8, 169 n.7, 170 n.13

Adrados, F. 160

Aeschylus: and decision-making 164; and influence of Homer 10; and myth 6

Aethiopis 46

Agamemnon: and Achilles 25, 32; and Briseis 87–8, 91, 92, 193; quarrel 65–6, 68, 70, 73–4, 76–7, 86–92, 95, 191–4; reconciliation 43; arming 57–8, 61; and Chryses 65–7, 68, 71–3, 75, 78–81, 191–2; and Clytemnestra 126, 140 n.1, 156; cuirass 23; shield 22, 96; and Sparta 20; and Thersites 86–7, 89, 91–5

Agenor, soliloquy 62–3

agriculture, seasonal tasks 102–4

aidōs (shame/respect) 14–18, 77, 79–80

Ajax, and Odysseus 61

'Akritic' cycle of folksongs 171, 183 n.1

Albertus Magnus, *de Mirabilis Mundi* 158

Alcinous: and good life 23, 99, 100, 105; palace 23, 99, 105; and truth and lies 144–5, 153 n.21

Alexiou, S. 174, 183–4 n.1

Amory, Anne 127–8, 130, 142 n.54, 162 n.10

anagnorisis 153

ancestry, importance 85–6

Andreev, Juri V. 123–4

Andromache: and Hector 15, 68, 81, 111, 114 n.25; lament 106; and peacetime Troy 101, 102, 108–9

D'Annunzio, Gabriele 159, 162 n.10

Antinous: and return of Odysseus 146, 150; and succession to Odysseus 116, 118–22, 135, 142 nn.52,53

Apollo 17; and Achilles 16, 48, 70, 79; and Chryses 66–8, 71–2, 73–5, 78–82; and Patroclus 46–7, 50

archetype, and Homeric characters 9, 10–11, 79, 85–6

Arend, W. 56, 57

aretē 139, 146, 149

Argos, in Mycenaean and Dark Age 31

Aristarchus 114 n.27

aristeia 57, 58, 61, 96

aristocracy 4, 32–3, 84, 151–2

Aristotle: and Homer 5, 10; and the self 168, 170 n.16

arming-scenes 39, 54, 55, 56–8, 61, 96

armour, Dark Age 25–7

Armstrong, A. E. 157, 158

Arnold, Matthew 1, 7, 72–3, 196, 197 nn.2, 17

assembly, summoning 8, 71, 117

atē 70, 166, 168–9

Athene 96, 105; and Achilles 74, 90, 193; and Ares 16; and Hector 48–50; and recognition of Odysseus 126–7, 134–6, 139, 140 nn.1, 8, 142 nn.42, 44, 48; as swallow 156, 157–8; and Telemachus 17, 144, 145; and truth and lying 151, 152

Athens, and literacy 173, 184 n.6

Auden, W. H. 97–8, 112

Auerbach, Erich 73–4, 187

Austin, Norman 54, 155, 160

awe, religious 16–18

bard *see* singer

basileus 103; and succession to Odysseus 116, 118–24

Bassett, S. E. 82 n.3

battle-descriptions 38, 43, 44, 46–51, 54; and shield of Achilles 98, 102, 107–12

Beethoven, L. von 160, 163 n.22

Beye, C. R. 83

birds, imagery 155–61

Boeotians 30

Boraston, J. M. 158, 162 n.13

Borthwick, E. K. 8, 155–61

bow: contest of 127–8, 129, 130–1, 136–7; and swallow symbolism 155, 157–61

Bowra, C. M. 83, 95 n.9, 98–9

bronze, and Dark Age 25–7

burials: Dark Age 23–4; heroic 77

Cartledge, P. 35 n.34

Catalogue of Ships 4, 29–32, 149

Cave, T. 153

Chadwick, J. 29–30

Chapman, George 190, 192

characterization 61, 85–6, 139–40, 151–2, 191

chariots 27

INDEX OF PASSAGES